# ANYTHING GOES AT SEA

## A GAY SEAFARER'S MEMOIR

**MICHAEL RUDDER**

First published in Great Britain in 2025 by
The Book Guild Ltd
Unit E2 Airfield Business Park,
Harrison Road, Market Harborough,
Leicestershire. LE16 7UL
Tel: 0116 2792299
www.bookguild.co.uk
Email: info@bookguild.co.uk
X: @bookguild

Copyright © 2025 Michael Rudder

The right of Michael Rudder to be identified as the author of this
work has been asserted by them in accordance with the
Copyright, Design and Patents Act 1988.

All rights reserved. No part of this publication may be
reproduced, transmitted, or stored in a retrieval system, in any form or by any means,
without permission in writing from the publisher, nor be otherwise circulated in
any form of binding or cover other than that in which it is published and without
a similar condition being imposed on the subsequent purchaser.

The manufacturer's authorised representative in the EU
for product safety is Authorised Rep Compliance Ltd,
71 Lower Baggot Street, Dublin D02 P593 Ireland (www.arccompliance.com)

Typeset in 11pt Minion Pro

Printed and bound in Great Britain by CMP UK

ISBN 978 1835742 327

British Library Cataloguing in Publication Data.
A catalogue record for this book is available from the British Library.

To all the wonderful seafarers, past and present, we were honoured to have the privilege and pleasure to sail with.

# Contents

| | |
|---|---|
| Foreword | vii |
| Introduction | xi |
| I Think I'm Going to Like It Here! | 1 |
| Early Daze | 4 |
| Teenager in Lust | 17 |
| Nothing's Queer Once You've Left the Pier | 32 |
| Up in the World and Down (Under) | 41 |
| Too Much of a Good Thing (Is Wonderful!) | 56 |
| Love "Is a Blonde and Slender Thing" | 61 |
| The Joy of Shaw Savill | 69 |
| Canberra Revisited, and the 'Phantom Gobbler' | 79 |
| Maid with Balls | 91 |
| 'The Strange Case of Blondie' – Unforgettable Lee | 107 |
| 'Florence Flightingale' | 121 |
| The Focks Mutiny | 130 |
| 'Queen of the Seas' | 135 |
| A Caribbean Queen's Brush with Death | 152 |
| Northern Star Revisited and 'Viva España' | 166 |
| Dominic Comes into My Life | 174 |
| Shanghaied! | 181 |
| Interesting Time with RFA | 187 |
| Run, Baby, Run | 200 |

| | |
|---|---|
| Far East Fun Run | 210 |
| Return to Oz | 219 |
| Domestic Bliss at Last | 227 |
| Flying Sauce Bottles! | 231 |
| A Skin Boat, and Lee | 240 |
| Sun Princess, and a Strange New Disease | 258 |
| The Falklands Conflict | 271 |
| Two Royal Princesses | 283 |
| Celebrity Maiden Trans-Canal Cruise | 293 |
| Approaching Demise of British Seafarers | 301 |
| Mona's Queen and Others | 320 |
| The Vomit Comet | 324 |
| End of an Era | 332 |
| Moving On | 337 |
| Acknowledgements | 345 |

# Foreword

This is the first frank LGBT+ maritime autobiography in the UK. Michael Rudder took off into 'floating gay heavens' in the most exciting time in non-heterosexual travel history, the 60s and 70s. 'Homosexuality' had ceased to be a hanging offence in 1829, although it was still illegal in the Royal Navy until 2000.

On commercial ships devil-may-care hospitality staff sashayed their way 'free' across the Atlantic to post-Stonewall clubs. London and Southampton swung too; the pink pound entertainment world took off. Lady boys in Singapore bars taught visiting matelots and maître d's that sexual identity was not a fixed matter and that the gender spectrum was huge. HIV-Aids had not yet hit. Fancy merchant vessels such as RMS Andes vied for the title 'the queerest ship afloat'. Tom of Finland's art celebrated butch sailor studs. Authenticity-seekers such as deck-boy-turned-super-model April Ashley transitioned illegally into Casablanca. On the BBC from 1965-68 Julian and Sandy introduced Polari, the 'secret language' gay seafarers used afloat, into every home. Male air cabin crew 'queered the skies.' *Spartacus International Gay Guides* emerged to help tourists round rail routes and bus stations, safe cottages and local customs. US publishers churned out sailor porn. The first waterfront sodomy movie came out:

*Fassbinder's Querelle* (1982). And Michael was there, in that hedonistic and supportive camp subculture. He tells the hidden story of a makeshift posh-dodgy world below decks. Postwar shipping companies marketing cheap cruises welcomed flamboyant 'queens' for their supposed 'feminine touches' and off-beat hilarity: 'We couldn't have done without the poofs', HR bosses and captains boasted. Gays stayed. Passengers learnt acceptance, even homophilia.

Sometimes these revealing pages also tell us the quiet individual story of an ordinary lad with an initially homophobic dad. Michael fell in love with Dominic, an able-bodied seaman from another ship, and thereafter made a life with him. They're Southampton citizens who delight in helping people locally and overseas, not least in sharing memorabilia with those maritime museums bravely embracing diversity, equity and inclusion.

Read between the lite lines about laughter-fuelled shenanigans and exotic ports. You'll pick up traces of the inevitable sadness and anger that gay men had to negotiate in these residential workplaces far from home; the shamed cover-ups by aspirational officers who knew that honesty would bring career suicide; and the hostility of some homophobes. Though upbeat, this story is realistic about the enduring power of bigotry and ignorance.

Michael was daring to live differently in a very early pre-revolutionary situation where his shipmates routed lingering traces of heteronormativity. He and his friends helped make 'the scene' more revolutionary by carrying the news of possibilities between shore and ship, and thereby contributed to ports developing into thriving Proud neighbourhoods. They spread the word, the wisdom and the fun.

In reading this book you'll be reading about a creative, way of life and the irreverent pioneers who carved extrinsic pleasures from an occupation where once 'men like that' were pilloried. You'll be grasping the extent of the broad, larky, offshore challenge to narrow ideas about gender and sexual identity, decades before 'Gay Liberation' emerged on the streets.

You can't understand travel as a potentially transformative situation without this book. Nor can you understand twentieth-century gay life without reading Michael's maritime revelations.

Jo Stanley Ph.D, FRHistS, A RINA
Hon Research Fellow, Blaydes Maritime Centre,
University of Hull
Chair. Rainbow Seas in Maritime Museums

# Introduction

After the book *Hello Sailor! The Hidden History of Homosexuality at Sea*, by Professor Paul Baker and Dr Jo Stanley, was published in 2003, Merseyside Maritime Museum extended the book into a travelling exhibition in 2006. While Jo gathered material for this exhibition and the related Sailing Proud Archive, we met many times. My partner Dominic and I, having spent over twenty years at sea, contributed to the exhibition, with photographs and brief stories of gay sea life, meeting each other, and our subsequent relationship. The exhibition travelled around the UK and abroad. It came to Southampton, where we said a few words at the opening. A friend, Ron Whitworth, who previously worked many years at sea, also contributed. (Nearly all names in this book have been changed to protect the individuals' privacy.)

Ron wrote and self-published his life story, *Sailing Round My Oyster* (Grosvenor House Publishing, Guildford, 2008). While he was writing it, Jo Stanley advised. His book was good, though he omitted almost all references to his homosexuality, on the grounds that people would read between the lines and pick it up anyway. Jo felt they couldn't or wouldn't; they didn't.

His memoir wasted an important opportunity to help the world understand a gay seafarer's story. It also missed a chance to reveal a wonderful, joyous period of history at sea, the like of which will never be seen again.

I agreed with Jo, adding I'd like to write about my, or our, somewhat unusual life. Fundamentally, this is a history book, documenting a unique and sometimes comical period in modern times, although it is also a turbulent love story. She recommended including all parts that were gritty, deeply real and truthful. They may be seen as graphic or risqué, while also amusing and informative. I will include all those aspects, even though it's awkward, embarrassing even, to write explicitly about private, intimate parts of my life – especially sexual details, which some people may find uncomfortable, or distasteful. However, I'll be frank, telling it *how it was*. It's not for the faint-hearted. If you are easily offended, not broad minded, sensitive, or homophobic, I suggest you put this volume back on the shelf immediately. Another reason I wanted to write my story: many of our good friends, like our dear friend Norman, had amazing lives, partially at sea; sadly, his and others' stories died with them.

My book portrays life at sea and ashore in the sixties, seventies, and eighties, an amazing, incredible period, never to be repeated. Some people may not 'get it', understand, or believe it. I'll write as truthfully as my memory serves me. However, much of it happened many years ago; some memories and dates are a little hazy. If I make mistakes, please forgive me. Strangely, my dear mother kept all the letters I wrote to her, early sailing schedules and a diary, which assisted me writing early sea chapters. It's almost as if she reached out from beyond the grave to help me, bless her.

I never planned on or ever imagined working at sea, though it was the best thing that happened in my life, a marvellous time.

While Mediterranean cruising, I met Dominic, the love of my life for the past fifty years. He was an able seaman on P&O ocean liner *Oriana*. I, a cabin steward on the immigrant/ocean liner *Northern Star*, at a time when passenger ships were gay-friendly places in a world still *extremely* homophobic. Both ships' last port was Lisbon, Portugal, berthing near each other on October 28th, 1974. Dominic heard the *Star* was a fun ship (it was) and he visited with some of his *crowd* for a lunchtime pint. I went to the bar as usual, saw this beautiful man; he looked at me. It was love at first sight, although we didn't know it at the time. Buying a pint, I sat at his table, joining in with usual seaman's banter. Dominic didn't return to his ship. We sat drinking and chatting. He asked what I was doing later. We agreed to visit Lisbon city centre for a drink and something to eat. He'd meet me aboard my ship after work.

    I thought he wouldn't show up and delighted when he did. We walked to town for a few drinks, enjoying a local meal. Back on the *Star*, we'd more drinks, climbing into my bunk to get to know each other better. Sharing a four-berth cabin with my gay cabin mates, we'd made full-length bunk curtains for privacy. We both fell into a deep sleep. Little did I know, next morning, Dominic was still on board my ship, locked in the brig (ship's prison) as a stowaway, MY stowaway – a punishable, sackable offence, with the possibility of imprisonment. However, I'm getting ahead of myself. What happened next appears in future chapters.

# 1

# I Think I'm Going to Like It Here!

July 3rd, 1969, I'm travelling in Dad's Vauxhall Viva on my way to join a ship in Southampton docks, feeling a mixture of excitement and terror. To be honest (and rather vulgar), I was shitting myself! Although only seventeen, I knew I was gay, and at that time it wasn't as acceptable as it is today. It made you deeply ashamed of your sexuality, and I was. Great care had to be taken to hide it from people, or face public ridicule, possible physical assault even. For years homosexuality was illegal; men faced heavy fines, persecution, shame, even imprisonment. In 1967 a bill passed through Parliament partially decriminalising homosexuality, but only in private, between two consenting adults over the age of twenty-one. This did not apply to the armed forces or the merchant navy at that time, where it remained illegal.

I could never open up to my parents about my sexuality. They were old-fashioned and would never understand, especially my father. I'd never even seen or met any gay person at school or college, hearing *those* people were queers, poofs, homosexuals, nancy boys, and so on, usually portrayed as disgusting. Eventually, in Guildford, the town near where we lived, I finally met some of *those* people in a pub, the Bulls Head, and in nearby Fullers restaurant, where I worked. At this time I first learnt we referred to each other as *gay*; it was kinder than *queer* and less well known. Most people then were completely unaware what gay meant, unlike now.

Whilst working in Fullers, I'd talk to one of the managers, a charming man, these days what you might call a bit camp. I suspected he was gay, but of course at that time wouldn't dare ask him. He knew I attended a local catering college, asking what I intended to do when I left. I admitted I'd no idea. He told me he'd worked at sea on passenger ships, saying it was a great life; you get paid to see the world. Then, giving me a knowing look, he quietly said, "You'd love it." I thought it sounded interesting, though had no idea how to go about it, nor did anyone else, it seemed. Then fate stepped in.

George, the gentleman who taught waiting table at college, previously worked as restaurant manager of the Silver Grill, a private dining room on the cruise liner *Oriana*. When he asked me what I intended to do when I left college, I admitted I'd no idea. He talked about his job at sea, offering to write me a glowing reference to give to P&O London that might get me a job aboard one of their ships. That's how I came to be in the back of Dad's car en route to Southampton. I was joining the P&O liner *Oriana* as a tourist-class waiter.

I'd never visited Southampton. I was excited to be starting a new life, with maybe good things ahead; however, I felt terrified. I'd no idea what life on a ship was like, having never been near a cruise ship in my life. The fact the ship apparently held over two thousand passengers and a thousand crew intimidated me. Arriving in Southampton, we drove down the lush green Avenue, towards the docks, following signs to 106 berth, Mayflower Terminal, where we saw this massive vessel berthed alongside. I was awestruck. I'd never seen an ocean liner up close. I was feeling excitement and apprehension. Collecting my bags and saying an emotional goodbye to Mum and Dad, I climbed the gangway. Near the top, before entering the ship, I looked up, amazed by the sheer size of the ship towering above me, saying loudly, "Bugger me" (I may have said, "F—k me"), and walked aboard. As I did, a good-looking man I took to be crew gave me a friendly smile, laughingly saying, "Is that an offer?" Returning his smile, I thought to myself, *I think I'm going to like it here.*

# 2

# Early Daze

My upbringing was fairly ordinary. My parents were both born in 1919, a time of Victorian attitudes, especially regarding sex. They dated prior to the Second World War; when war broke out in 1939, Dad enlisted as the medical officers' driver in the Royal Fusiliers and was sent overseas. In June 1940 he was one of the lucky survivors of the Dunkirk evacuation, rescued by a London excursion paddle steamer, the *Crested Eagle*, built on the Isle of Wight. On its next rescue voyage, the ship was attacked by German forces and sunk. All three hundred servicemen and crew on board were killed. At low tide the wreck can still be seen to this day on the beach of Zuydcoote, France. Dad had a lucky escape; if he hadn't, I wouldn't be writing this.

On arrival in the UK he went AWOL (absent without leave) to see Mum. He proposed and they married shortly afterwards. Dad returned to the front line, seeing service in North Africa, Italy and Greece. One warm summer Dad was based briefly in Stockbridge, Hampshire. The weather was hot, and officers requested he drive them to the River Test to bathe, swim and cool off. They graciously allowed him to swim also – *as long as* he was down river *from them*. It shows class attitudes in those days. Officers didn't want their water *polluted* by a lowly private! As a wartime medical officers' driver, he saw some shocking things, picking up wounded and dead soldiers fighting on the front line. Though he was a hard man, he rarely talked about it. He was an atheist, believing when you die, that's it, finito. To my surprise, when he passed, he chose his own religious funeral service, including his favourite hymn, "Abide with Me."

My father, Mick (named Maurice, but always known as Mick), was a working-class lorry driver, part of a large family in Hounslow, London. Both his parents passed away before I was born. Mum's family were upper-working-class business people, running a dairy in Westminster, London. Her mother died young, and her affable father, Joe, remarried Gert. My mother, Peggy, was educated, charming, kind, extremely loving, and a wonderful mum. She was truly dignified, with a great sense of humour. Amused by risqué humour, she forbade swearing and vulgarity. During the war, Mum worked in a factory manufacturing sonar devices for submarines. She'd cycle there with Dad's sister Hilda. They both narrowly escaped death when a doodlebug, a kind of flying bomb, narrowly missed them. In 1942 Mum's house was bombed. They lost all their wedding presents, except a silver tray Hilda gave them. It was rumoured that Mum lost a baby during the war. Like many personal things with my parents, this was never openly discussed.

Mum moved in with Dad's mother, now living on Eel Pie Island, Twickenham. It really *was* an island in those days, until 1957, when a footbridge was constructed. It has a fascinating history, getting its name from actual eel pies baked there, made from River Thames eels. At one point my uncle Fred owned or managed the famous Eel Pie Island Hotel. I have a faded post card of it, bearing the words "Proprietor Fred Rudder," but thus far have been unable to find out exactly when he ran it. In the

1950s, the hotel was a home of jazz, then in the 1960s the island became famous for the birth of the British blues, rock and roll, pop music, and so on. Such names as the Rolling Stones, The Who, David Bowie, Eric Clapton, and Rod Stewart played there, with long queues forming over the footbridge.

Surprisingly, according to my sister Josephine, Dad was educated at grammar school. He was a real cockney, constantly using cockney rhyming slang. As kids we thought his slang was just another word to use, like *Germans* for hands; we didn't realise it rhymed with German bands. Later in life I'd learn a secret language, Polari, that included some cockney. He was a good father in many ways, providing for the family, but extremely hard, rarely showing emotion. He loved Mum dearly. However, he was a terrible misogynist, often referring to women as ugly moos, fat moos, and the like. He was strict too. I was scared of him. He also appeared homophobic. I think this was due to the times, when it was a criminal offence and viewed as disgusting. He rarely showed us any love, or hugs. To him, affection was a woman's job, which was most men's attitude then.

He mellowed over the years and as an adult, I surprised him by giving him a hug. "I've never been hugged by a man before," he said. I told him it was about time he started. After that we hugged often and in later years became close. I forgave him for the unkind ways he treated me, calling me a "useless four-eyed nit" and so on. But I could never forget it. He was even worse towards my sister Josie, which is hard to understand, or forgive.

There were four children: Josie, the eldest, born in 1946, and elder brother Peter in 1948. Then, in 1951 my twin brother John and I were born. We're not identical – far from it. We're fraternal twins. We were born in Enfield, north London, living in Swanley Bar Farm, Swanley Bar Lane, Potters Bar, in what was previously the farm house, but now is no longer a farm. Our uncle Les (on Dad's side) bought the farm, converting it to a secure yard with workshops and so on to operate a fleet of Jensen furniture lorries for Lebus Ltd. Dad helped run things, carrying out lorry maintenance which he'd learnt while driving the medical officers' truck during the war. In return Les paid him a wage and we all lived in the delightful, spacious old farmhouse.

I remember little about being a toddler, though some things stuck in my mind. We inherited a bad-tempered male goat named, not surprisingly, Billy. Us kids loved him but he constantly butted visitors. To deter him, he was tethered to an apple tree in the orchard. We had a Rayburn solid fuel stove for cooking in the kitchen and for heating, with open fires in other rooms. I developed a strange fascination for flames, starting fires around the place. I even remember starting a fire behind the sofa while the family were sat there. I was thoroughly scolded and as a punishment tied to the apple tree with Billy the goat for the whole day. I wept buckets; visitors were horrified. It brought a swift end to my pyromania.

When we were young Mum listened to BBC Light Programme on the radio, or wireless as it was known then. Programmes like *The Archers*, "an everyday story of country folk." She also loved *Mrs Dale's Diary*, a radio programme about a doctor's wife, broadcast from 1948 to 1969. It was the first British mainstream drama to sympathetically feature a leading character known to be homosexual, the husband of Mrs Dale's sister, Sally. It was brave of the BBC, as homosexuality was illegal in the 1950s and 1960s. "The love that dare not speak its name" was a taboo subject. At that time, many gay men married (in so-called lavender marriages) so as to appear straight. They often led rather sad double lives.

In the 1950s we were lucky to own a rare television, probably helped by Uncle Les. It was small, a black and white picture, with only one channel, I believe, the BBC. We thought it was wonderful. With Mum we watched the Liberace show in the afternoons. I was absolutely spellbound seeing this handsome, smart man in beautiful surroundings, playing the piano, singing and winking. We'd never seen a candelabra. I found him truly fascinating, thinking how great it would be to be like him.

There were children's programmes too, though programmes like *Muffin the Mule* and *Flower Pot Men* were bizarre. Especially *Andy Pandy*. I wasn't sure if he/she was a boy/girl, and he/she climbed into a basket with Teddy at the end of every show. Extremely weird. No wonder I became confused! TV was so different in those days. Programmes ran from 9:00a.m. to 11:00p.m. They were allowed no more than two hours before 1:00p.m. and a break between 6:00p.m. and 7:00p.m. to get the kids to bed. At 11:00p.m. BBC programmes finished and the national anthem was played. Then a man or woman in posh clothes with a posh voice said, "Good night. Don't forget to turn off your set!" Sounds like I was obsessed with TV but I only mention this historically, so today's young will know how it was then.

We were lucky to have a magnificent car, again I think with help from Uncle Les. Before the 1939–45 war, Chrysler built a factory in Kew, London. They imported cars into the UK in a kit form to beat import restrictions. Between 1932 and 1939 these cars were assembled and finished in Kew and known as the Chrysler Kew Six. Huge cars, powerful, beautiful and luxurious for the time. Uncle Les was offered one by his dentist. Les only drove Jaguars, so he arranged for Dad to buy it. The car was gold, which we thought wonderful. But it was too ostentatious for Dad. He had it painted black and it ended up looking like a hearse. It was a fine motor car, big enough to accommodate all the family and more. Brother Pete was friendly with the Lobbans, a dark, swarthy-skinned Italian family. The boys would come on days out to the seaside with us. Mum got funny looks in those days, with children of all different colours in the car. During this time we inherited a dog from one of our drivers, a beautiful Alsatian called Judy. Mum loved walking, taking us all on long walks through the fields and woods at the back of the farm. We all loved Judy, especially Josie, who took her alone for walks.

Dad enjoyed going out for a few pints, drinking in a pub at the top of our lane, the Green Man. We were glad to see him go; it seemed to make him happy. Mum liked a drink too, especially while cooking, drinking tiny bottles of Babycham, a sparkling wine, from a champagne coupé, both with "Babycham" and a little Bambi etched on them. One Christmas our grandparents, Joe and Gert, came to stay, and Dad went to the pub before Christmas lunch as usual. Josie owned a large doll, its blonde hair peeling off like a wig. Dad was practically bald and, returning home merry from the pub, for a laugh he put the doll's wig on his head. Poor old Gert nearly had a heart attack, saying, "Oh dear, Mick, I do hope you're not turning funny" (meaning queer). He thought it was hilarious. But Gert's response illustrates what a homophobic world it was then.

With four kids to feed, money was tight for our parents. But we never went hungry. We owned a pet black rabbit, Treacle. One day on arriving home we found the door open and an empty hutch. Dad said Treacle must have escaped and we all searched in vain. Next day's dinner was a very strange chicken; the meat darker than usual, with four legs!

I remember our first day at infants school. My twin and I walked there with sister Josie and friend Angela. We burst into tears, hating the whole idea. One day, on our return from school, Billy the goat had disappeared. Dad explained he was too much of a handful, so he'd taken him to pets' corner in Whipsnade Zoo. We could go visit him any time we liked. He never took us to visit the zoo. Dad was a hard man; Billy was probably fed to the lions. Sister Josie tells me around this time she felt Dad really didn't like her. She said he made her feel she was a nuisance, really upsetting her. Young girls usually look up to their dads, so his behaviour made her feel unwanted, unloved, and affected her for the rest of her life. When Judy aged, having trouble with her back legs, Dad took her to be put to sleep at the vets. Surprisingly, it upset him, which was unusual; he had little compassion for animals. Poor Josie was heartbroken that she couldn't be there for Judy.

In 1958, Uncle Les decided to sell the business and property, including our home. Being a kind man, he helped arrange a loan for Dad to buy a business and home for us. They bought a general store with living accommodation in Hatfield Broad Oak, a small village in the sticks near Stansted Airport, Essex. It was just before Christmas. Mum and Dad went ahead to get it ready, then we followed. Uncle Les drove us in his Jaguar early one evening. He was extremely merry as usual, chain-smoking huge cigars. On arrival, Mum had put up Christmas decorations and we were thrilled. We inherited a lovely large black cat, 'Nigger'. At the time we thought nothing of the name, nor associated it with anything; it was just her name. She was a good mouser and Dad locked her in the shop at night to deal with the mice and rats.

The following morning we explored the village. Next door was a pub, The Cock. That was probably why Dad bought this shop – handy for a beer. It was an old-fashioned boozer, run by landlord Bert and his gossipy wife Mrs Brooks. The village was a typical English village with a couple of shops, couple of pubs and a church. The shop was heaven for us kids – a never-ending supply of free treats. Unbeknown to Dad, we'd help ourselves to all sorts of sweets and chocolate. We hid them in the outdoor toilet, in the yard at the back of the shop. It had an old-fashioned flush system rarely seen these days. The metal cistern was high up and flushed by pulling a long chain. We'd hide sweets on top of the cistern. Using the toilet one day, when Dad pulled the chain he was showered with packs of chocolate and sweets.

Furious, he rounded us up, giving us a good talking too. We thought it funny, suppressing giggles. Afterwards he was more watchful and we more careful.

Us three boys all slept in a massive bedroom above the shop. One night in bed I felt unwell and went downstairs to tell my parents. I was given the usual remedy, milk of magnesia, and sent back to bed with a bucket, as I felt sick. Sure enough, I woke up after a while, crouched on the side of the bed and proceeded to be violently sick in the bucket. Dad, hearing the commotion, ran upstairs to see what was occurring. As I was being sick, I farted. To my horror it was more than wind; a torrent of diarrhoea squirted out my arsehole and up the wallpaper. I was absolutely mortified. Father was not amused; it probably gave him another reason to intensely dislike me. To my further embarrassment, the poo stain on the wallpaper was so bad that no amount of cleaning removed it. It stayed as a reminder until the room was redecorated.

My parents were given a hard time taking over the village shop. Locals liked the previous owners and didn't take kindly to us 'Londoners', as they called us. The countryside outside the village was rural, with no bus service. Dad bought a van to deliver groceries, making Mum obtain a licence too, in case he got sick. There were high dramas teaching our mum to drive; she never liked it, or ever drove. Vehicles were primitive in those days: rough gears, no synchromesh, no power steering and useless heaters that feebly demisted. When Dad started deliveries, he gradually got to know the locals. Some houses were without electricity or main sewers, using candles, paraffin stoves, solid fuel cookers and cess pits. The shop needed to sell everything, including paraffin, and even meths (methylated spirits) unknown to them, requiring a licence.

Dad heard Bert, the husband of one of his lady customers, had died, so on arrival was somewhat surprised when she asked if he wanted to say goodbye to Bert. (Dad didn't believe in 'all that'.) He said, yes, of course, and she showed him to the parlour where Fred was laid out. Taking his hat off, he said out loud, "Goodbye, Fred." This tickled him and, as he burst out laughing, he quickly pulled his hat over his face. He was absolutely convulsed with mirth, shoulders heaving. She thought he was sobbing. "There, there, Mr Rudder, don't go upsetting yourself," she said, as he made a swift exit. Next day it was all round the village: "What a kind, compassionate man that Mr Rudder is." They'd won the respect of the entire village.

We attended a local primary school, getting to know other boys and girls. My friends were predominantly girls living near the shop. I remember most of their names: Gaye, Fanny, and one who became my childhood sweetheart, delightful Susan. We keep in touch now, though she lives in New Zealand. She'd an amazing collection of dolls, a doll's house, even a 'wetting dolly'. This absolutely fascinated me and my twin. You fed it a bottle of water, and then water dribbled from between its legs. When I mentioned I'd been playing with dolls, Dad was horrified. "Boys don't play with dolls," he told me. "Why not?" I asked. "They just don't," he told me.

Dad despised Josie's best friend Jennifer. She had the nerve to call him a miserable old git or worse, to his face. As the shop took up all her time, Mum employed Jenny's granny to clean our living accommodation. She arrived on a creaky old bike. She creaked and smelt, and we were terrified of her. With Mum busy in the shop, Josie cooked our tea. Granny would buy fresh fish from a travelling fish van, storing it in our fridge. One day, by mistake, Josie cooked her fish. When Granny found it gone, she was furious, ranting and raving. Dad said she could help herself to as much fish or whatever she wanted from our newfangled deep freeze but there was no consoling the old dragon.

At the local school, Peter was in a different class from us. The headmaster was extremely strict and, although married, looking back I believe he was a sadistic paedophile. He truly enjoyed punishing us boys. If we were naughty or not paying attention, he would give us 'the cane'. He savagely whipped boys on the palm with a stick, in front of the class. Sometimes he thrashed your bottom with a slipper in his study. One day brother John and I were naughty, and we were ordered to his study. He laid me across his lap, proceeding to thrash my arse with a slipper. Had I been aware of it, I'd have no doubt noticed a large bulge in the crotch of his trousers. Due to the intense pain, I let out a series of truly enormous farts. He quickly switched victim, laying my twin John on his lap, proceeding to thrash him. The same thing occurred. John let off massive farts. 'Dear Sir' couldn't get us out quick enough. Despite the pain, we couldn't help giggling about it.

If you were extremely naughty, he particularly liked to take boys' trousers down, in front the class, viciously caning bare buttocks. Brother Peter badly misbehaved one day, suffering this extremely painful, humiliating punishment. When he got home, noticing he was walking in some discomfort, Dad asked, "What's the matter with you, boy?" When Pete told him, showing him the painful red weals on his bottom, Dad flew into a violent rage. He drove to the school and burst in on the headmaster, telling him if he ever laid a finger on Pete again, "I will give you a punch in the mouth!" (I doubt if he'd have done the same for me.)

Next door to our shop stood an old courthouse, supposedly used by Judge Jeffreys, infamous 'Hanging Judge' of the 1600s. Opposite the shop a fairly steep downhill road led to Cage End. It was reputed that prisoners were held in cages there before going before the judge to be possibly sentenced to hanging. Josie often went out on her bike, telling me about one evening she was heading home as it was getting dark. As she was pushing her bike up the hill from Cage End, towards the shop, a customer approached her, a man known as Boxer Billy, who lived on a nearby rough 'Barn fields' estate. He offered to escort her home. As they walked along, he started touching her, fondling her breasts. She felt most uncomfortable about this. (She was twelve or thirteen, with big tits.) On arrival home, she told Dad. Though shocked, he told her he really couldn't say anything to Boxer, "As him and his family are one of our best customers!"

One customer, Edna, regularly bought dog food for her dog Tommy. This food smelt truly vile, small dark biscuits stored in a large-lidded tin hopper on the shop floor. It was scooped out, weighed, priced, and put in bags. Dogs loved it. One night, as Dad locked our cat Nigger in for rodent duties, the dog food lid was open. To his horror he saw she was using it as a toilet. No wonder it smelt so appalling! Not long after this, Edna visited the shop without the dog, Tommy. Dad enquired where he was. "Poor boy started howling, had a fit and dropped dead," she said. Dad wondered if it was anything to do with the evil-smelling dog food/cat toilet, but kept shtum.

The shop developed into a nightmare for my parents. I remember in winter, poor Mum ran vegetables under the cold tap in the yard to freshen them. They inherited old stock, some from before the war. Many groceries arrived in large pieces: sides of bacon, whole cheeses and so on. They needed slicing. Poor Mum developed a hernia carrying these heavy pieces, finishing up in hospital for an operation. We wept buckets when Mum was taken to hospital, missing her, worrying about her. Operations were a big thing in those days. Thankfully, she recovered. Next Dad became so stressed with worry, he developed painful stomach ulcers. This left us children to clean the shop and scrub the floor. After a year or two, they'd had enough. Dad decided to sell up, then get a job. His brother, Uncle Stan, owned an extremely large house on a pig farm near Camberley, Surrey. He said we could stay there while Dad was looking for work. Thankfully they found a buyer for the shop, and we went to live with Stan and his wife Cis.

It was indeed a large house on the farm. Cis's fearsome mother, like the gran in the *Daily Express* Gambols cartoons, lived there too. Cis and Stan were very kind to us, and it was a novelty living on a pig farm. We soon became accustomed to the smell, helping feed the pigs, and mucking out. I thought pigs were delightful creatures. For some reason, probably that there was not enough room, Josie was sent to live with cousins Jeff and Pat. She didn't mind. By this time Dad and her *really* didn't get on. I remember watching the very first episode of *Coronation Street* there, thinking the way the cast spoke very strange. We'd rarely heard northern accents before, and never on the TV or wireless. There'd only been posh BBC accents till then.

Eventually, in 1961, with Uncle Stan's help, Dad found a job with the Fatstock Marketing Corporation (FMC). Basically a pig buyer, he went visiting farms, viewing livestock, and arranging transport and slaughter. The job included a brand new company car, a Ford Anglia. We moved out of Uncle Stan's. First we went to a house in Binscombe Lane, Farncombe, near Godalming. Mum hated it there, so thankfully we didn't stay long. John and I attended a school in Farncombe. It was appalling; the other pupils were truly ghastly. One girl, Pauline, was a "bit slow," (now called special needs). She was chubby, her clothes had seen better days and other kids were cruel, taunting her and making fun until she cried. Then her nose would start running. I'd feel so sorry for her and give her my clean handkerchief. (Mum always made sure we'd a clean hanky.) I consoled her, saying, "Don't cry."

At weekends the family often went to the coast for the day. Josie and I weren't good passengers. We fidgeted, asking the inevitable, "Are we there yet?" Dad would tell us, "Shut your bleeding cake holes." (Charming.) Eventually he decided to leave us at home; we were delighted. Josie and I'd heard about this new cathedral in Guildford, with a beautiful golden angel atop. One day while they went to the coast, we decided to walk to Guildford to see it. We were walking along Guildford Bypass, with some difficulty, as I don't think there was a footpath, when a police car stopped. The police asked us what we were doing. They were horrified to hear we'd been left 'home alone'. (I was eight or nine and Josie thirteen or fourteen.) And we were walking along a dangerous dual carriageway. So they drove us home. When our parents found out, it was no big deal. I think Mum was a little concerned but didn't show it; she was always loyal to Dad. I have to say that although our father was very strict, threatening violence, I don't remember him actually striking me. Threats were enough.

# 3

# Teenager in Lust

Following a short duration living in dreadful Binscombe Lane, Farncombe, we moved to Jacobs Well village on the outskirts of Guildford, Surrey, to a three-bedroom bungalow, with a loft bedroom big enough for us three boys. Home life for us was like that of many others in those days, extremely basic. We had one small bathroom. I developed a phobia about having to use toilets as quickly as possible. Dad shouted, "Hurry up! You're not the only one who wants to use it." We had no central heating, just an open fire in the lounge which also heated water. There was an immersion heater for summer hot water. I hated baths. They were limited to one a week; the rest of the week we had a wash down with a flannel. Baths were taken on Sunday night. Josie was first, Pete got in her water, then us twins followed. By the time we got in, the bath water was tepid, with thick scum floating on top. It was truly vile. Our bungalow was so cold, especially our loft bedroom, that ice formed inside the window.

    Dad purchased a couple of paraffin stoves. One went in the hall, where some heat drifted upstairs to our bedroom. The other was in the tiny bathroom. Dad wasn't one to waste money or heat. He also cooked on these wretched stoves. I loathed the smell of cooking drifting up to our bedroom. He even cooked in the tiny bathroom! You'd be sat on the toilet, with something like a stew or gammon bubbling away between your legs. It sounds revolting now, though we thought nothing of it at the time. Even now the smell of ham or gammon boiling brings back vivid memories of the tiny, extremely busy toilet.

Mum was a 'mend and re-use' person: holes in socks darned, worn-out shirt collars cut off, turned over and stitched back on. She also knitted. One of the worst things was the use of Dad's worn-out Y-front underwear. His underpants were bleached, dried and used as dusters and kitchen dishcloths. It sounds dreadful, but again we thought nothing of it at the time. Mum worked hard in that little kitchen, with a small fridge, a larder and a little electric cooker. She did so well. Aunts and uncles came to stay, and she fed them all. God knows where we all slept. We always had proper meals too, no such thing as fast foods then. (We still don't eat it.) The table was laid and we had to ask permission to leave the table. It taught us manners and respect. Mum *never* wasted food, always reminding us, "I lived through a war." She taught us not to waste food. Even now Dominic and I *never* waste food.

Mother had a dressing table in their bedroom, with a chair, mirrors, and all sorts of brushes, powders and potions on top. It fascinated me. She also had eyelash curlers. These are popular again now. They supposedly curled your lashes, except they didn't. They made lashes L-shaped, appearing from the front curled. When my parents were out, I'd sit at Mum's dressing table, pat my face with a powder puff and curl my eyelashes. I thought no one knew, though I wouldn't be surprised if Mum suspected all along. She had pet names for us all, calling me Dickerbum. (Did she have an inkling?)

Our parents could afford little pocket money. We tried many ways to make cash, such as chopping firewood to sell round the village; everyone had coal fires in those days. The hardship started my life's passion: I always wanted to work, make my own money. At twelve years old, we were delivering newspapers, in all weathers. Every house had papers delivered in those days. My round was one of the longest, but I was glad of the money. With my first week's pay, fifteen shillings (75p) I felt rich and went to Guildford Market, buying some melon, taking it to a small nearby park, Quakers' Acre, to eat. I thought it was amazing. I'd never tasted melon before. With money coming in, I could now buy my own clothes. Truly wonderful. It was the Swinging Sixties. I went for a mod look, slim-fit trousers, button-down shirts, and the like, all in bright colours and patterns. Previously we only wore shoes to school, or going out. When playing we wore Wellington boots. Now I could afford Chelsea boots. Dad was horrified!

John and I attended George Abbot Comprehensive Boys' School, in Burpham, Guildford. Pete, being older, was in a different year. We didn't see much of him. It was a good half-hour bike ride to school. We cycled every day, even in bitter cold and pouring rain. There was no Mum's taxi in those days. At school I excelled only in English. Eventually, we became teenagers. Puberty reared its ugly head. We were never told the facts of life at home, where the subject was avoided completely, nor at school: sex was a complete mystery to us all. At thirteen I felt sexual urges, but didn't completely understand what they were. I found girls attractive. Although *not* through choice, I found boys more attractive. Looking at men in underwear adverts especially turned me on. In 1965–67 the Sexual Offences Act was going through Parliament, legalising homosexual acts between consenting adult men in private. I'd read about it, yet at home the subject was completely taboo. It was avoided and never openly discussed. Finding men attractive, I wondered – shock, horror – was I a homosexual? My sister Josie suffered from constipation, using large glycerine suppositories to solve the problem. I had occasional constipation too, and tried one of her suppositories. Much to my private embarrassment, I actually liked the feeling as it slid in. Though only fourteen, this confirmed to my deep shame over what I suspected; I must be homosexual.

During this time Josie and Dad *really* didn't get along. She loved Dusty Springfield, backcombing her hair in a Dusty beehive, and wearing dark eye make-up. Dad would say, "You can wash that bleeding muck off your minces (mince pies/eyes) before you go out." She'd visit pubs in town, sometimes coming home a little worse for wear. (Ironically, she rarely drinks now.) Josie was a boy magnet. Dropping her home late, they'd chat through her bedroom window. One night they woke Dad, who was furious that she was talking to a boy so late. Saying she was out of control, he arranged for a female police officer to give her a 'talking to'. After their chat, the officer told Dad it was *him* that had the problem, not Josie. He was furious. Then one night Josie went to a party, and I think someone spiked her drink. When she arrived home she was extremely drunk, and violently sick. It was the last straw. Dad threw her out of the house, even though she was only fifteen. Josie moved in to the YWCA, one of the youngest girls ever to live there. Eventually she moved into a bedsit. I'd cycle over to see her and we'd listen endlessly to our favourite music: Dusty Springfield and anything Tamla Motown, like The Temptations, Four Tops, Marvin Gaye, and Smokey Robinson.

Boys at school reaching puberty talked endlessly about sex. From pleasuring themselves, most knew what a climax was. But like me, they hadn't a clue about what *real* sex was exactly. They started seeing girls. I began dating a lovely girl at the adjacent girls' school, Jane. She was delightful, with a wonderful mum and dad. They seemed so *worldly* going to Italy for holidays. Jane told me Italian boys were gorgeous and sexy; I wondered if she'd had an Italian boyfriend. We dated for some time, kissing, having sexual fumbles and the like. Occasionally we'd get *dolled up* in fancy formal clothes, and go for dinner and cabaret at the famous London theatre restaurant The Talk of the Town. She loved Cliff Richard. She really had the hots for him; I think it was after one of his shows we first had proper sex. I remember well, as it was the first time.

Following the show, I stayed at Jane's house, waited until her parents went to bed, and crept into her room. She was wearing a sexy baby-doll nightie, showing off her large breasts. I slipped into bed beside her. I began playing with her tits and sucking her nipples, though I really didn't have a clue what to do. After a while she gently guided my penis into her. Feeling myself enter was sensational. As my cock slid in and out, it was unbelievably pleasurable. After a while I felt the delicious tingling of a climax building up. She was really enjoying it too, groaning, shaking, her nipples large and hard. For contraception we used coitus interruptus (withdrawal method). I was too young and embarrassed to buy condoms. Both of us hugely liked sex, enjoying it many more times, though I still secretly lusted after men and boys. In fact, I was gagging to *commit an act of Gross Indecency* (as it was known). I never thought this would be possible; I'd still never encountered a homosexual, or someone who also liked men.

Sister Josie meanwhile found a job as waitress in an old-fashioned restaurant, Fullers in Guildford High Street. She served coffees, their own famous cakes, luncheons, and afternoon teas. Teas were silver service; silver pots were delivered on a silver tray. Fullers sold toasted tea cakes, Welsh rarebit, poached eggs on toast, and so on. In later years Josie got me a job there too, as assistant kitchen porter/general dogsbody under the watchful eye of a grizzled old kitchen porter, Fred. My work involved preparing vegetables, salads, etc., plus plenty of pearl diving. The sinks were huge and deep. I practically dived in to get the utensils out and wash up huge greasy pots and pans. I also prepared potatoes. I poured them into a drum-like machine with a rough lining, turning on the water and pressing a button so the machine revolved, peeling the potatoes. Peel gushed out of a pipe, a revolting brown slurry. When ready, a side trapdoor allowed the potatoes to slide into the sink.

Fred smoked disgusting roll-ups, balancing them, alight, on top of the wobbling spud machine. To my horror some fell in with the spuds and he just shrugged it off. I prepared chips with a chip machine. Placing a peeled potato on a grid, I pulled down a lever and the potatoes were pushed through, coming out as chips. They were blanched in cool fat and, when soft, tipped into a large colander to drain. Now they were ready to dip into hot fat when ordered, taking only minutes to fry. Fred showed me how to drain, clean and refill fat fryers, a mucky job. It was all hard work, but I was glad of a job, especially the money.

Mum encouraged my interest in cooking. She was always patient. We'd watch TV cook Fanny Cradock on television, a tall, imposing lady, eccentric, truly camp, with heavy make-up and huge eyelashes. She looked like a bloke in drag. Her posh husband Johnnie wore a monocle, and always looked a bit squiffy. She bullied him mercilessly on the show. Together they wrote cookbooks, such as *Bon Viveur*. Mum bought me one. While I was working in Fullers, cooks, mostly ladies, taught me how to prepare and cook a range of food – Welsh rarebits, bacon, omelettes, gammons, vegetables, pies, and so on. I learnt restaurant-style cooking. My twin John worked there too, earning a few bob helping the old girls Mrs Warne and dotty old Lil, who washed up by hand.

I was sat at home with Mum and Dad one day when Josie came home in tears, wearing her waitress' uniform. Her lunch orders were still on her pad. She'd been working an extremely busy, hectic lunch shift, and food service was slow. Customers were getting irate and extremely rude. It was unbearable, so she walked out, taking a bus home. Needless to say, she was sacked. However, I happily carried on working there. Finishing work in the evening, I often walked home, hoping a guy like me would stop, offer me a lift, and I'd go home with him. It never happened. Josie meanwhile found a job as barmaid in the Carpenters Arms. I'd visit her for a beer. Although only fifteen, I looked older so I got away with it. I bought a little second-hand motor scooter, more convenient than the bus, and easier to visit Josie.

Around this time brother Peter was a mod. He drove a Lambretta scooter, with mirrors along the handle bar, and wore a parka with a fur-lined hood. In those days engines were 'two stroke' fuel, a mixture of oil and petrol, giving exhaust fumes a distinctive smell. Mods would get together driving to the seaside. There were also rockers at this time, driving motorbikes. They'd meet on rallies to Brighton and there'd be clashes, which made headlines the next day. (Fifty years later they have scooter rallies on the Isle of Wight. If an old scooter passes, those exhaust fumes bring back many memories.)

Time came to sit for GCE exams. After helping Mum and cooking at Fullers, I wanted to take cookery O-level: Domestic Science. However, it wasn't taught at my boys' school. (Why not?) They arranged for just me to study at the nearby girls' school. Being one boy out of hundreds to learn cookery, I was a something of a novelty. Even the headmaster summoned me to his study to sample my fairy cakes (how embarrassing). The boys thought it funny, nicknaming me Mary Baker after the cake-mix manufacturer. I enjoyed my time at the girls' school, passing my GCE O-level Domestic Science.

Being good with their hands, my brothers went into the building trade, to Dad's delight. He was fond of them, especially Pete, who he adored and could do no wrong. If his car broke down, Dad would say, "Boys! Pete's broke down. We've got to go and help him." If John or I broke down and asked for help, he'd say, "Better call the AA, boy." When young he hated my sister Josie and I, and he showed it frequently. Probably he was bitterly disappointed that first-born Josie didn't have a penis and all that goes with that. Maybe he also hated the way Mum adored Josie, lavishing attention on her, instead of on him. When Peter was born next, Dad was thrilled to get a son, absolutely adoring him. I came along next, with a penis, but unlike my brothers, useless with my hands, not good at anything much. I wore glasses as a child, so Dad called me a *useless four-eyed nit*. Josie had a weight problem and he called her *a fat, ugly moo*. It was extremely unkind, terrible for our confidence and self-esteem, especially for Josie. I tried to ignore it, but it really damaged her.

I had no idea of a career or job. I enjoyed school plays and would have loved to be an actor. But I had no idea how to go about it. Dad thought all actors and actresses were poofs or tarts anyway. He rarely went to shows. Mum loved the theatre. As a girl in London she'd seen shows starring Jessie Mathews and French actress Yvonne Arnaud. When *Lady Windermere's Fan* opened at the Yvonne Arnaud Theatre Guildford, starring Jessie Mathews, I just had to take Mum to see it.

I enjoyed cooking at home and Fullers, and was thinking about a career in the catering industry. Before leaving school I applied for a full-time Hotel Management and Cookery course at Guildford Technical College. It covered every aspect of running hotels and restaurants – training to be a chef, waiting tables, housekeeping, hygiene and nutrition. I'd always been interested in nutrition. As expected, Dad wasn't happy. "Cooking! That's women's work. No son of mine is going to be a cook," he said. Of course it made me even MORE determined.

I was given a place on a two-year, full-time course at Guildford Technical College, Stoke Park. I loved it. We'd go to a nearby pub, the Stoke Park Inn, for lunch, even though I was only fifteen or sixteen, two years under age. For the course we had to buy chef's clothes, including a tall chef's hat and a set of chef's knives, which was quite expensive. Luckily I was earning money evenings and weekends. Mum helped out as usual. I really enjoyed college, learning so much. Mr Luck, the head chef, was brilliant. He really knew his stuff. His hero was the famous French chef Auguste Escoffier. Learning about cookery and nutrition taught me to eat a healthy, balanced diet. Consequently I've stayed more or less the same weight my whole life. If the government made schools teach cookery and nutrition now, I'm sure the nation would eat healthier. There'd be less obesity and diabetes, which is bankrupting the NHS. After starting college, Jane and I slowly drifted apart. I can't remember why exactly. We never actually fell out.

While working at Fullers I became friendly with a waitress, Katie. We got on extremely well. Most days Fullers closed early evening and Katie would ask me to go for a drink in a pub behind the restaurant – the Royal Oak, Sydenham Road. She didn't want to be on her own waiting for her friend Chris. Chris had short, manly blonde hair and wore trousers. One day on our own, Katie said she wanted to ask me something. Whatever my answer was, it wouldn't make any difference to our friendship, she said. She asked if I was gay. I said yes. It felt a relief to actually open up to someone about my sexuality. She told me she was gay, too. But like me, she kept it to herself. Chris was her lover. It all made sense now. We became good friends.

They regularly visited a lesbian bar at 239 Kings Road, London, the Gateways Club. Founded in 1931, it closed 1985. Gay celebrities like Dusty Springfield visited. Even straight celebs like Diana Dors went. In 1967 the Gateways was made women-only, so although the girls would love to take me, they couldn't. Katie had a brilliant idea. I was about the same size as her, and she owned a couple of wigs. So why didn't I get dragged up? Next time they went to the club, she made me up and dressed me in her clothes. I looked amazing, she said. I had to agree, though it was strange seeing myself as a girl. I was only sixteen at the time. Little did I know I'd be doing this years later, entertaining on ships. We piled into Chris's little old car, a Standard 8, setting off for London. Music blasting on the radio, we bombed along, listening to 'I Heard It Through the Grapevine' by Marvin Gaye.

The club was behind a green door, down steep stairs in a cellar. There was a bar at one end, loos at the other. Small, around thirty-six feet by eighteen feet (twelve metres by six metres) the place was thick with smoke and absolutely *heaving*. We joined some of their pals, letting them in on our secret, which they went along with. It was a brilliant evening. I went again with them, and visited Brighton with them one weekend with some of their gay girlfriends. One truly manly one was known as Boot Lace, which tickled me. She was so butch that they called her a bull dyke or diesel dyke. Probably you wouldn't be allowed to say that these days. We stayed good friends until I went to sea, sadly losing contact.

Life at home was still extremely closeted. If something slightly gay came on the TV it was hastily turned over. A BBC radio comedy, *Round the Horne*, featured two camp characters, Julian and Sandy (Kenneth Williams and Hugh Paddick). They got up to all sorts of mischief, including talking in a camp manner, and using gay words (Polari). They'd meet a terribly straight front man, Kenneth Horne, saying, "Ooh, hello Mr Horne. How bona to varda your dolly old eke!" (Hello Mr Horne. Good to see your pretty face.) The audience roared with laughter; even Mum and

Dad laughed. (Amazingly, we were allowed to listen to it.) Most people really didn't understand what they were saying. It just sounded amusing, in fact, hilarious.

Later, in 1968, a book called *The Naked Civil Servant* was published. The true life story of Quentin Crisp, an openly gay man, it caused a sensation. Yet at home and college, it was never mentioned. People refrained from discussing anything *so distasteful*. I only heard about it in later years, when it was aired on TV. I was still deeply ashamed of my secret sexuality. I could never reveal it to my family. It was seen by most people as disgusting, though I never could understand what was so bad about it.

Seeing that Josie had freedom, I rented a little flat in Sydenham Road, the centre of town, near to college. I was hoping to meet a guy like myself, maybe have some *consenting fun in private*. One evening after a few drinks in Josie's pub, I got the courage to go to the Bull's Head, notorious for being frequented by *queers*. Only sixteen, I was extremely nervous. But I went in, buying a pint of Watney's Red Barrel and sitting down in this lovely old traditional corner pub, with a grill room upstairs, all cosy, with a buzz of conversation. It was easy to work out who the gays were, small groups of mostly good-looking smart men. It wasn't long before I got talking with one of them, eventually getting to know quite a few. I was so pleased and excited. It was the first time I'd heard the word *gay* used. Straights didn't use it/ understand it at that time. I became friendly with Barry, who lived in Guildford and worked in Putney, London. He owned a Ford Cortina; I was impressed. He asked if I'd like a lift home. Thrilled, I said, "Yes, please," guessing what might happen.

I asked him in for a coffee and, as guessed, no coffee. We went straight to bed. I was excited but nervous, not having a clue what to do, again needing guidance. Stripping off, we laid on the bed kissing and caressing, which felt rather strange. Then he went down on me, taking my cock in his mouth. I enjoyed oral sex for the first time, or a blow job as it's known colloquially. It felt so good. I could see he was enjoying it too. After a while I thought I'd try it on him. He wouldn't let me. Instead, he casually lubricated my dick, guiding me in to him. It felt extremely pleasurable, though to be honest, like sex with a woman. Maybe it was a bit tighter, or was that just him? Whether because I was so inexperienced and nervous, it wasn't quite as thrilling as I'd imagined it would be.

I enjoyed it and we saw each other many times. I couldn't help thinking gay sex is so incredibly different. With girls, you date, maybe get a phone number, get to know them, then have sex. With guys you have sex immediately, then get to know them and maybe get a phone number! I also thought now I've had sex with another man, I *must* be homosexual, although I enjoyed sex with Jane, so maybe I'm bisexual? (As it turns out, I am slightly.)

Occasional weekends Barry drove us to the numerous gay clubs in Soho, London. Most clubs required membership or to be with a member. Luckily, they never asked my age. Clubs I recall were the Apollo in Wardour Street, A&B, Arts & Battledress Club in Rupert Street, and nearby LeFoyer Club. They were seedy, dark places, full of mainly gay men and *dilly boys* – rent boys. One night Barry pointed out a guy, saying, "That's Ronnie Knight over there. He runs a nightclub." I'd never heard of him at that time. The Kray Twins frequented the same Soho gay clubs. Thankfully, I never bumped into them, later hearing about their reputation, especially Ronnie. I don't remember hooking up with anyone sexually at this time, probably because I looked underage at sixteen. I saw Barry many times. He was a good man, very kind and I was fond of him, but he didn't really 'do it' for me. We weren't lovers as such, remaining 'friends with benefits'.

I often went to London on my own by train, Guildford to London Waterloo. London was really swinging in those days.

I just had to go and see it for myself. I soon mastered the underground, visiting the places I'd heard about, especially Carnaby Street. Fashions were casual and quite shocking at the time: bright flamboyant floral shirts, different bright colours and patterns, some with frills, satin and nylon even. Slim-fit trousers, velvet outfits, boots, and so on. I actually wore one of my most colourful shirts home. Dad nearly had a heart attack, saying, "You look like a big poof." I told him he was old-fashioned, though I was secretly pleased. I didn't wear it home again.

In May 1969 I passed my City and Guilds Certificates in Cookery for Hotels and Restaurants, including Waiting, Nutrition and Hygiene. I now just needed to decide my future. During college holidays, catering students went for work experience in hotels and restaurants. You can't imagine how awful it was. Fullers' kitchen was noisy. However these were like Hell's kitchens. Not for the faint-hearted. Long, late hours, extremely hot and loud working conditions. Chefs screaming, shouting and waving knives around. The pressures were intense. These experiences completely put me off the idea of working in the kitchen of a hotel or restaurant. I still had no idea what path to take. Meanwhile, I'd given up my flat and Josie took it over. Then fate stepped in.

The gentleman who taught waiting at college, George, had worked at sea as head waiter of the Silver Grill, a private dining room aboard the passenger ship *Oriana*. Saying he'd write me a reference for P&O, to get me a waiter's job aboard, he told me, "You'll see the world for free, boy, while saving a few bob." Returning home, I told the family. Mum said, "You must be joining the Merchant Navy, dear." So innocent, I said, "No, Mum. It's like working as a waiter in a floating hotel."

George gave me the promised reference, arranging an interview with P&O on July 3rd, 1969. Catching an early London train to Waterloo, I took an underground train to

Aldgate East tube station. My interview was in what I imagined to be the grand, oak-panelled P&O headquarters, Beaufort House, St Botolph Street EC3. It was easy to find. Uniformed doormen directed arrivals but it wasn't as grand as I'd imagined. (It mainly dealt with crew.) Elevators were suicide lifts (now banned) with no doors, and cars continuously travelling up and down. I got into one going up, stepped out at my floor, found the room where the interview was to take place, knocked, and heard, "Enter." Introducing myself, I handed them George's reference. After reading it and having a chat, they offered me a job as a tourist-class waiter on the liner *Oriana*. The thought of running away to sea was scary, but getting away from home and having freedom was very appealing. Feeling excited, I said yes, remembering what the camp Fullers' manager said about life at sea: *You'd love it.* I was thinking maybe it'll be a whole new life.

Following my interview, I had a medical in the same building, and was handed a letter with instructions to go to the nearby Mercantile Marine Office in Dock Street. Arriving at this grim building, I showed them P&O's letter. My mugshots were taken. An official completed a Seaman's Discharge Book (a kind of passport-size record of all your trips, with discharges saying whether you were a good or bad worker). Plus I completed a Seafarer's Identity Card. Sure enough, I *had* joined the British Merchant Navy! Also I joined the National Union of Seaman (seafaring was a closed shop in those days). A Union representative issued me with a Union book containing membership number, payment records, and so on.

Back at P&O, I showed them my papers, and was surprised when they asked if it was possible for me to join *Oriana* in Southampton the following afternoon. They told me the ship was in overnight (they were in those days) and that I'd have time to settle in. It was going on a ten-day Mediterranean cruise. I was shocked, but excited. "Yes," I said, thinking, *I may as well jump in at the deep end*. They advised that I'd need black trousers, shoes and socks (which I had). The rest they'd order for me. Did I know my sizes? Luckily, buying my own clothes, I did, except my hat size. This they guessed, and I thought, *Will I need to wear a hat?* Uniform was to be delivered to the ship from a local naval tailors. It was all to be paid for by me, to ensure I took care of it. I was given joining instructions: *Oriana* would be berthed at 106 berth, Southampton Docks (now Mayflower Terminal).

Taking the train home, I arrived in the afternoon to break the surprise news. Dad kindly offered to drive me to Southampton next day. That evening I partly packed my bags. Next morning Mum ironed things, helping me finish. As I was to collect my uniform on the ship, I left room in my bags.

Only seventeen, I felt extremely nervous about joining an ocean liner. I'd never been anywhere near the sea or a cruise liner in my life, apart from a seaside paddle. Mum and Dad dropped me off, saying an emotional farewell. Feeling exhilarated but nervous, I climbed the gangway. A good-looking man on the gangway smiled, joked and laughed with me; all my fears dissolved immediately.

# 4

# Nothing's Queer Once You've Left the Pier

My first day aboard was a blur. I was shown to crew office, given my uniform parcel, assigned a cabin, and handed my emergency/boat stations card and so on. Told where/when I needed to *turn to* (start work) next day. I was lastly directed to my cabin: a two-berth room with a washbasin. The showers and toilets were situated nearby. After dreadful baths at home I was delighted that here we could shower as often as we liked, and took full advantage of it. My cabin mate was friendly and helpful, telling me when and where I could get food, in the crew mess. In fact everyone was kind. I unpacked, including the uniform: white jackets, with silver buttons, and blue epaulettes. I had two casual jackets for cleaning, plus the peaked hat, which I later learnt was for embarkation/boat drill. Then I visited the crew mess, where people seemed to know I was new, and were helpful as I collected a meal.

That evening we were free to do whatever we wanted, and I decided to go ashore for a beer. As I walked off the ship, a guy was waiting for a taxi. Not knowing how far town was, I asked could I share a taxi with him, telling him I was going for a pint, in the High Street I supposed. He was friendly, good-looking, with black hair, and charming. I wondered if he was gay, and later discovered he was. We keep in touch still.

He dropped me at the bottom of High Street, not far from the docks. I went to a corner pub, The Queens. It was a large pub, with huge pictures of Queen Mary and Queen Elizabeth. I sat with a pint. It was fairly quiet and after a couple of beers I made my way back. Along Simnel Street, I saw a pub on the corner called The Queen. (Strange! Both pubs had Queen in their names.) I went in for a beer. Then I headed back to the ship. It was quite a walk. If I had turned right, I'd have ended up in the notorious Juniper Berry. I went left, down Bugle Street, then right, through Dock Gate 8, walking back to *Oriana* shining in the distance.

My first night in Southampton I found rather dull, although I later discovered Southampton was awash with fantastic gay and mixed pubs, clubs and dives. The Juniper Berry pub on Bugle Street, right near the docks, featured drag entertainment and a mixed crowd (meaning straights, gays, lesbian and tarts). The infamous Horse and Groom pub in East Street, with a famous stuffed bear in a bar, was also mixed and rough: a haven for seaman. This pub became notorious when a US sailor was stabbed to death there in 1959. The Lord Roberts, a gay pub in Canal Walk, was heaving with gays. I was amazed at the openness when I visited. Another mixed pub on South Front was the Robbie Burns.

Next morning we'd an early call with a cup of tea from a 'peak boy'. The tea wasn't good. My cabin mate explained the lad was Goanese, and they didn't drink tea as we do. Apart from his main job, he gave us a morning call, and serviced our cabins for extra money. I was happy paying him; he made sure the cabin was ready for weekly captain's inspection. I took a long shower, thrilled to feel really clean, especially my privates. I was clean inside and out and rather enjoying the feeling.

After breakfast my cabin mate confirmed what to wear: the casual jacket. Then we started work, or turned to as they called it, doing odd jobs, mainly cleaning. At some point during the day we *signed on*, signing the ship's articles of agreement, plus a few other formalities. Again, it was a blur. In the afternoon, in uniform – black shoes, socks, trousers, white starched jacket buttoned up with silver buttons, blue epaulettes and peaked hat – I assisted with embarkation, greeting boarding passengers, helping them with hand luggage, showing them to their cabins. I worried at first but cabin numbers and decks were easy to understand, a piece of cake.

My next turn to was at 6:00p.m., to serve dinner. This was my first time in the dining room, which was accessed via the galley through revolving doors. Rather disappointing – pleasant, but not as grand as I imagined it would be; however, I thought, *This is tourist*. Everyone had their own stations. I was assigned a long table with eight or ten seats. These were known as 'aircraft carriers', because of their length. The restaurant staff then were all male and mixed ethnicity: British, Indians, Goanese and a few other places. I befriended a boy working near me, Alan, nicknamed Donks, short for donkey. I naively thought he was called Donks due to his large nose and ears! He was kind and helpful, telling me what I needed to do: check table, collect bread rolls, butter, milk, water and so on from the galley. We had a brief meeting with the head waiter at 18:25. He explained items on the menu, then told us to stand by. At 18:30, loud music played over the tannoy (public address system). Large green doors opened. Crowds of passengers swarmed in.

Once my passengers were seated I introduced myself, taking orders. I wrote the orders down (some guys remembered them) and then went to the galley (kitchen) collecting various courses. It was fairly straightforward but extremely hectic. I was slow and nervous. When my table finished their meal and departed, I slowly tidied up. Donks shouted, "Hurry up, mate. Get ready for the second sitting." What a shock! I was so green I didn't realise there *was* a second sitting. Luckily Alan and the nearest guys rallied round to help. By the time the music played, and the next crowd of passengers poured in at 8:00p.m., I was ready.

I returned to our cabin around 10:00p.m. I'd heard there was a crew bar, the Pig & Whistle, on board. (Passenger ship crew bars are always known as this.) I changed, venturing up there for a drink. Life at home made me think I'd better be extremely careful on board not to reveal I'm gay, in case they're intolerant and hostile like ashore. Buying a beer, Tennent's or Allsopp's, for less than two shillings a pint (about 8p), I found it was a busy bar and almost completely male. (There were a few stewardesses and other females on the ship. However, at that time they used their own mess room.) It was smoky too. Indoor smoking allowed in those days and crew cigarettes were extremely cheap. I was a nonsmoker. Despite cheap fags, I never did smoke. I noticed there were a few guys who appeared gay. Some were sitting with what were possibly other gay guys. Everyone seemed to be friendly and enjoying themselves.

Next day the peak boy, who cleaned cabins for extra cash, called us early with another cup of dodgy tea, for a 6:30a.m. start. We were to serve breakfast from 7:00a.m. to 10:00a.m. Following that, there was a morning job, polishing, etc. Later we served lunch from 11:30 to 2:30p.m. In the evening, dinner was 6:00p.m. to 9:30p.m. Our emergency drill occurred during passenger drill. P&O took drills very seriously indeed. Guys were reprimanded for wearing sandals; you had to wear proper shoes. We also wore our peaked hats, making us instantly recognisable as crew to passengers. Hats were also for protection from the sun if we abandoned ship.

I soon settled in to the routine. The boys in the restaurant enjoyed a laugh; the Scouse lads in particular were most amusing. One lad asked me, "How old are you, La?" When I said seventeen, they asked how I got a waiter's job, an adult rating's position, when seventeen-year-olds were classed as 'boy ratings'. It just happened, I told them. I had no explanation. They made lewd comments like, "It's not what you know, it's who you blow." I blushed to my roots. However, it was all good-natured fun. They talked and joked about the ship's gay men too, in an amusing way. Hearing them referred to as queens, and by their camp names, surprised me. They were talking about a queen in first class, Nicky, known as the Black Widow. I asked why they called him Black Widow. "Does he eat his husbands?" "No," they said, roaring with laughter. "He only swallows a bit of them." I knew exactly what they meant, and laughed along.

I began to realise these guys were very accepting of homosexuality. That was a pleasant surprise after my experiences ashore. That they laughed and joked about the possibility of me doing sexual favours to get the job made it seem it was quite acceptable to them. I began to discover working aboard ship had finally brought me freedom from homophobia and bigotry ashore. I was now in a place where you were completely accepted as one of the crew: a shipmate, regardless of your sexuality, race, gender or sex.

*Oriana* was on a ten-day Mediterranean cruise, departing the Solent, sailing the English Channel and going through the Bay of Biscay. The weather turned beautiful, warm and sunny. One of my good weather morning jobs was to collect a tray of ice cream tubs from the galley, hang it round my neck and hand out ices to passengers on the sun deck. I was like an ice cream girl in a cinema, camp or what? I also saw more of the ship. Under the aft sun deck was the stern gallery bar, a massive room with floor-to-ceiling windows and wonderful views out the stern (back) of the ship. At the bow (front) of the ship was a crew deck with a swimming pool, for crew to sunbathe and relax. It was a good place to eye up guys in their swimming trunks. So many fit young men! I'd always loved looking at partially clothed men, especially if they were muscular. I was fit too, with cycling I'd strong legs, and in my teens bought a 'bull-worker', building my muscles. Alan would be on deck too. I couldn't help notice he had a beautiful body, well-built, with gorgeous smooth olive skin and a large bulge in his swim trunks. Sometimes he'd ask me to rub oil on his back. I think he enjoyed it as much as I did. It was a right turn-on, looking at him lying there glistening with sun oil.

After two sea days our first port was Lisbon. I asked Donks what it was like. He laughed and joked as usual: "Full of lisbions." We walked ashore for a beer. He was good company and I was enjoying myself. Next port was Athens, Greece. We docked at Piraeus. After breakfast service I asked Alan what Greece was like. He made his usual jokes. "How do you separate the men from the boys in the Greek Navy?" "By their uniform?" I asked. "No, with a crowbar," he said. Everyone laughed and I thought it a really broad-minded joke for a straight guy. Alan and I walked ashore, noticing various souvenirs on sale. I bought a small statue of the naked David, who'd only a fig leaf for modesty. I thought it looked beautiful and sexy. Donks gave me a knowing smile. I felt sure he'd guessed I was gay, and wondered if he was interested. (I still have the statue to this day.)

Evenings in the crew bar were interestingly entertaining, sitting with various crew, stewards, including gay guys, deckhands and greasers who worked in the engine room. They were from all over the country. Scousers, Geordies, Yorkshire, Belfast, Irish and Scots. I heard accents I'd never heard before. Gays sometimes used words I didn't understand and I didn't like to ask for fear of appearing stupid. No one seemed to judge each other, and no one appeared homophobic. I soon realised that being at sea was a whole new way of life. I'd found true freedom. Everyone got on with their job, helped each other, and partied together after work. Most referred to each other as 'shipmates', a name that seemed to be earned, not given. It required team work, duty, courage, honour, love, a bond formed in adversity, storms and comradeship.

Some language was very colourful – swearing, rude jokes, comments like, "Nothing's queer once you've left the pier." Mum never allowed swearing, bad language and such, so initially I was a bit shocked; I soon got used to it. Lads talked about other shipping lines and ships they'd sailed on. As this was my first ship, I loved these stories. They talked about Cunard: hard work, great for passengers and good money. Shaw Savill Line: immigrant ships, *Northern Star* and *Southern Cross* (known as the Suffering Cross), which they said were very rough. They sounded dreadful to me. Little did I know that two years later I'd join Shaw Savill, and enjoy an amazing time.

Crew used seaman's terms. I soon picked them up: port = left; starboard = right; deck = floor; deck head = ceiling; bulkhead = wall; dhobi = laundry; dhobidust = soap powder; soogee = washing or scrubbing down with soapy water. Also there was a kind of unspoken code on board: everyone looked out for each other. If someone was late for work you'd nip below to give them a shake. If they were late often, you'd give them a shout on your way to work. I'd give Alan a shake, having an ulterior motive: I enjoyed seeing him naked, even if only his sexy top half. We'd become so friendly. He was amusing, great company and easy-going. The way he looked at me, I wondered if he was interested in me. He must have noticed the way I looked at him too, but I was too nervous to make the first move. I was thinking maybe one day of 'accidentally' slipping my hand beneath his bed covers, touching his dick, to see if he liked it. But I was worried in case I was wrong. Fate stepped in again.

One day giving Donks (Alan) a shake, he pulled *my* hand under the bed covers, placing it on his cock, now growing hard.

I began fondling it – what a beautiful big dick. No wonder he was called Donks! (Donkeys are famously well hung.) It was huge! He murmured quietly, "You like it?" I nodded. He obviously enjoyed it. So did I and was eager for more. Later we talked about getting together. It was difficult sharing a cabin with straight guys, but we found a solution.

Most crew used communal bathrooms. On *Oriana* there were also individual shower cubicles accessed by doors in cross-alleyways. A shower, with a folding seat, a clothes hook, then you stepped into the shower. They were quite spacious, and doors locked from inside, a perfect place to get up to mischief! We arranged to meet here, sneaking in the shower and locking the door. I was so excited, trembling with anticipation. It was such a thrill undressing, caressing his strong body, and silkily smooth skin. I felt in heaven, kissing his lovely muscly tits, sucking his nipples (men love that too) and licking further down. He gently guided my face level with his crotch, where I let his beautiful cock slip between my lips. It was so massive that I had a struggle to get it in. He groaned with pleasure, loving it. After a while his legs trembled, and he moaned with excitement. I felt something deliciously warm and sweet in my mouth: he was happy.

We later indulged in anal sex. As he was so well-endowed, I was rather concerned. I needn't have worried. With relaxation, plenty of lubricant and much excitement, his cock worked in easy, feeling extremely erotic, sensuous, and sexually enjoyable. He was loving it too, moaning and groaning with pleasure. It's no secret every year thousands of people, mainly men, visit A&E with objects stuck in their rectum. It's all down to erotic stimulation and sexual curiosity; penetration actually feels truly enjoyable for many guys.

I got such a kick out of our sessions; sex with guys can be thrilling, especially a man who appears straight. Oral sex I really liked and was evidently good at it too. (The secret is breathing through your nose; you can deep throat.) Later I learnt that most men absolutely love what is colloquially known as a blow job. (Apparently skin lining the mouth is similar to skin lining a vagina.) We continued with our clandestine sex sessions. I loved it, and he did too. It wasn't a love thing. As far as I knew he was straight, though ship's lads would call him AC/DC. I assumed he just liked some hot fun, especially a BJ with a discreet gay guy.

As a former Orient Line ship, *Oriana* crew were almost entirely British, unlike P&O who employed many more Indians and Pakistanis. When P&O acquired Orient Line in 1960, they allowed former Orient Line ships to keep British deck and engine room crew, plus most of the catering staff and, of course, officers and leading hands. Consequently, crew were almost entirely British on *Oriana*. While there were many gay men working on the ship, the majority of the crew were straight. I went on to discover guys the gays on board called *trade*. They were bisexual ashore, and some were married or had girlfriends. It wasn't a big deal to have fun with a discreet gay guy, or queen, especially a blow job.

Please note:
1. In future chapters, for clarity, I'll refer to ship's gay men as *queens*, unless they are *gay homies* (gay men who are not effeminate). I'll mainly refer to queens by their camp names, unless they didn't have one. I'll also refer to queens as *he*, and females as *she*, to avoid misunderstanding where females are concerned. Many more female crew worked on ships as time went on.
2. When referring to 'the boys' I usually mean shipmates/lads/other crew and so on. At sea there were slang names for crew, referring to their job. The captain or the master was always 'the Old Man'; the carpenter 'the chippy'.

# 5

# Up in the World and Down (Under)

Summer 1969. I'm enjoying working with a great bunch of lads in *Oriana*'s tourist restaurant, especially my mate Alan (Donks). A year of wonderful chart music, 'Get Back', The Beatles, and 'Break Away', the Beach Boys. At the movies, *Midnight Cowboy*. As first class appeared sedate compared to the tourist restaurant, I wrote to the chief steward, mentioning I was silver service–trained. It did the trick. Next cruise, July 25th, 1969, I transferred to the first-class restaurant, moving into a first-class crew cabin. I'd miss my tourist workmates but would still see them in the bar and ashore. My new cabin mate, Tom, was friendly and good-looking. I had trouble understanding him at first. He was Scottish with a heavy accent. Next morning, we got a call from the peak boy, then another from an outrageous man camping his tits off in the alleyway. Knocking on doors, shrieking, "Hands off cocks, on with socks."

"Who the hell is that?" I asked Tom.

"Just Momma Cass," he said. "One of the waiters."

Compared to tourist, the first-class restaurant was attractive and well-appointed. The deck (floor) was a highly polished, tough type of linoleum with an attractive multi-red pattern. Silk drapes adorned portholes, with clever lighting. The whole effect was very elegant. Tables were a mix of sizes, with comfortable dining chairs. Meals were calm. Waiters served six passengers each. To my surprise, I found that in first class an early and a late seating were offered. Food was served silver service, whereas in tourist class, meals were plated. I felt I'd gone up in the world.

To start, I had a family-six table. The first time through the Bay of Biscay, the weather was rough. My passengers didn't seem affected by the ship's movement, until a man rushed past, vomiting a large blob of sick nearby. A quick-thinking bellboy covered the offending mess with a napkin and scooped it up, loudly saying, "Ooh, it's still warm!" Nearby passengers, including mine, turned green, fleeing the restaurant.

Head Waiter Mr Kendall was terribly dapper, with a dazzling smile. With that surname, his waiters naturally nicknamed him Kay, after the musical actress Kay Kendall. I thought he was gay. We all did, although actually he loved women. He was assisted by section waiters, who also served wine. One of them, Peter, a handsome and friendly Geordie, took a shine to me, much to my delight. Another, Ron, was an elegant old queen known as the 'cultured vulture'. He'd had an amazing life, during the war serving in the Royal Navy. Afterwards he'd worked on airliners as a steward. He'd even survived a plane crash, bravely dragging the radio officer to safety. Rumours were that they were a couple.

The routine in first class was similar to tourist and included serving afternoon tea from 3:00p.m. to 4:00p.m. I collected cake trolleys from the galley and took them to the public rooms, where teas were served. Lounges, especially the Princess Room, were furnished in elegant pale colours, with soft curves and deep carpets. There was a restrained, classy and sophisticated feel. I went to look for the Silver Grill, George Miles' elegant private dining room. Sadly, it was closed down. The space had been converted into more cabins. Orient Line ships, like *Oriana*, *Oronsay* and such, all had Silver Grills, as a delightful alternative place to eat and spend an evening. P&O decided the space would make more money as cabins, closing all the grills and converting the spaces. It was a sad, bad move. Ships were not sailing full by this time, as the airlines took a large chunk of the business, although in later years they were busy when cruising really took off.

Next door lived Nicky, the Black Widow. We hit it off right away. Before going to sea, he'd worked in the theatre and was theatrically camp, calling everyone Doll, or Darling. Half-Greek, he had jet-black hair, with a fringe draped over one eye (a la Veronica Lake). He usually wore black casually; I guess that's how he got the name. His dark beard showed even after shaving, so he covered it with a bit of slap (make-up). His cabin mate was Pussy, a down-to-earth gay guy, who quickly became a friend too. I asked Nicky if they were a couple: "Oh no dear, we're not *tootsie*. She's a lady like me." I got the meaning. They were both after the same thing: men.

Their cabin was cosy. It had full-length bunk curtains, a table lamp, music, an ice bucket and other touches. I guessed they'd made these improvements. Many seamen, even butch deck and engine ratings, did similar things to make their cabins cosier, a home from home. Some, like me, did it with a Woolworths table lamp adapter, pushing it into the neck of a bottle, like a Mateus Rosé bottle. It only required a shade and bulb to make a table lamp. Some queens went over the top, making their cabins extremely elegant: posh bedspreads, cushions, rugs and so on. On Royal Mail's *Andes*, reputed to be the campest ship afloat, well-established queens in a six-berth cabin even wallpapered the bulkheads. Their cabin was so beautifully decorated it was known as Clarence House, after the Queen Mother's residence. They even had a posh telephone for show, not even connected! Entry was by invitation only. Visitors were ushered in by one of them acting as a butler.

Nicky asked, "How are you getting on with that bona homie in your latty, dear?" He had to translate the meaning: "How are you getting on with that attractive man in your cabin?" Nicky explained. "It's camp Polari, darling. You'll soon get the hang of it, dear." I did, though there was a lot to learn. Nicky helped, telling me the meanings: trade = sex; cartes = cock; fake on = get hard/stiff; orderly = come; starters = lube; jaree = eat or suck; harver = shag; homie = man; palone = woman; HP/homie palone = queen; palone homie = lesbian; cottage = toilet; varder = look; naf/cod = not pleasant; lallies = legs; aunt nell = listen; dish/gash = bum; ogles = eyes; nantie = don't or small (as in nantie cartes); shoosh = tease, tidy or improve; screech = mouth or throat; eke = face (back to front, i.e., ecaf); schloof/pit = sleep/bunk. Bona has many meanings: attractive, sexy, plenty, or big (as in bona cartes, or big cock) and so on. There was no such thing as a Polari dictionary then, as there is now. You just picked it up, like cockney rhyming slang.

Thelma was an eccentric queen living in a nearby cabin. She held regular tea parties. When passenger teas finished, Thelma took a tray of leftover cakes to his cabin. Invited guests arrived, and he served camp afternoon teas. These parties were a hotbed of gossip and scandal, great fun. Broadcast systems were fitted in crew cabins, with volume and on/off controls (overridden by emergency broadcasts). Before dinner, Radio *Oriana* aired; a DJ chatted and played requests. Some of these had hidden scandalous meanings. The DJ was usually in on the true meanings. "I'd like to play a request for one of the deckhands, from a first-class waiter: The Shirelles, 'Will You Still Love Me Tomorrow?'

P&O occasionally sailed with well-known guest radio disc jockeys, who DJ'd in the bars and discos for the passengers' dancing pleasure. They even guested on the crew radio show. Among these was the notorious Jimmy Savile, who in later years also sailed on *Oriana*. He was unpopular with some of the crew, being so full of his own self-importance and rather brusque. He refused to dress for dinner, instead wearing his multicoloured casual shell suits. He'd sit on an afterdeck early mornings, smoking his cigar and signing autographs. Deckhands scrubbed and hosed down the wooden decks with a salt water fire hose in early mornings. One morning a leading hand politely asked him to kindly vacate the deck to allow them to finish washing down before breakfast. He refused; they carried on regardless, hosing him down too!

In 1978, Jimmy Savile was actually thrown off the *Canberra* in Gibraltar. He was travelling as a first-class VIP guest en route to the Mediterranean, when two tourist passengers complained to a ship's officer about his inappropriate behaviour towards their fourteen-year-old daughter. After listening to the distraught couple, the captain (not named) sent for Mr Savile to question him. The more they talked the more the captain was convinced Savile was lying. He was "a very shifty chap, his eyes darting all over the place." The captain told Savile, "You disgust me. I want you off this ship by Gibraltar." He instructed a ship's officer to accompany Savile to his stateroom. He was to eat all his meals there and not leave the room under any circumstances except shipwreck (sinking). This is what ensued and he was put off when they reached the Rock.[1]

Even though I'd left tourist, I still saw Donks in the bar. We got together occasionally. I got to know many more queens:

---

1 'I kicked sleazy Jimmy Savile off cruise ship', *Daily Mirror*, 13 Oct 2012. https://www.mirror.co.uk/news/uk-news/jimmy-savile-thrown-cruise-ship-1376532

John, from the first day; and a likeable guy, Trish, a dairyman and baker. We became firm friends, also meeting on leave. We're still friends today, though he lives in Torrevieja, Spain. Maurice, Rose, was from Tralee; we keep in touch. Mattie was a tall, tough Belfast queen, with a wicked tongue. He must have been hilarious compèring crew shows (also known as Sods Operas) on ships. I asked him why *Oriana* didn't have them anymore. He said they'd fallen out of favour with the company. However, on some lines they still took place: on *Andes*, some Cunard ships, and Shaw Savill. Little did I know a few years later I'd be helping to arrange (and star) in Shaw Savill shows. (See later chapters.)

Peter, the handsome Geordie section waiter, invited me to his cabin for a drink. I guessed what was coming and looked forward to it. While having drinks, he pressed his leg against mine, running his hand over my thigh, giving me thrills of anticipation up and down my spine. He smiled; I smiled. With hardly a word spoken we undressed and lay on his bunk. He was rather hairy, though still sexy. He fondled me, positioning me on the bed, and was up me like a rat up a drainpipe. When we'd finished, after small talk, I departed. Next day he was extremely cool towards me, and I realised it was a one-off. I felt a little miffed, though being hairy, he wasn't really my type. Peter was a gay homie. Gay, although nothing about his demeanour suggested he was. He liked young men 'feelies/chickens' like me. He thought he had *droit de seigneur* (feudal right of a man of rank to have sexual intercourse) over young men. Strangely, I met him years later and he'd settled down with a charming young Geordie lad.

Nicky's men had to be *all man*; he definitely wasn't interested in other gay men. Most queens and gay men on board were the same: extremely rarely getting together sexually with another gay man. Nick told me an amusing story about when he picked up a beautiful big hunk in San Francisco, going home with him for the night. Everything went wonderfully, until breakfast, when the hunk offered him toast with marmalade he'd "made himself." Nicky couldn't get out the door fast enough, thinking Real Men don't make marmalade!

UK summer cruises were coming to an end, and *Oriana* was due to make a round trip to Australia. I went home August 3rd for a week, returning August 10th. John, my twin, drove me back. On my return I'd a nasty sore throat. As usual the lads joked about it: "You know what's meant to be good for a sore throat?" (I didn't.) "Get your tonsils whitewashed." They laughed, meaning have oral sex. Next day at turn to I was sweating, feeling truly unwell, and was sent to the ship's hospital. The crew doctor diagnosed acute tonsillitis, admitting me. I worried they'd send me home. However, I languished in the hospital for five days and, when fit, went back to work. We were sailing August 12, my birthday, so Mum and Dad drove down with my birthday cards. They were allowed to visit me in the ship's hospital and were much impressed. It was well-equipped, and the medical staff were wonderful.

*Oriana* was a fast ship, crossing the Atlantic in five days. Clocks went back an hour each night, meaning plenty of cabin parties. Nicky's parties were wonderful. He always invited a mixed crowd: witty, camp, entertaining people. Many crew owned tape or record players. With the ship's rolling and pitching movements, record players were a problem. Records would play slow or fast and sometimes the arm slid right across the disc. To overcome this, a coin such as a shilling would be taped to the arm, the extra weight holding the needle down. Some queens owned Della Reese LPs like *The Classic Della*, songs based on the classics. Later I bought a cassette player, and also some of her tapes. There was not much music at our home, and going to sea introduced me to all kinds of wonderful music, especially later music from shows and musicals.

After five sea days, *Oriana* anchored off Bermuda, then continued to Sydney via Panama, returning the same way. I was excited about new places and ports to come. I won't go into details of every one; that could be tiresome. All were interesting, some more than others. I felt excited about our next stop: Port Everglades, Florida. I'd never been to America and noticed the retired Cunard liner *Queen Elizabeth* berthed nearby. All crew that morning attended a US Immigration inspection.

Border officials checked our passports and seaman's books, issuing paper C-1/D seaman's visas. Later I walked over to look at the massive *Queen Elizabeth*. Showing my seaman's ID, I was delighted to be allowed on board. *Queen Elizabeth*'s art deco style was magnificent: large corridors, high ceilings and vast lounges. Decorative panels, painted and carved wood, all in warm restful autumn shades. Huge bronze grille doors opened into the first-class restaurant. Beautiful. It was everything I'd imagined a grand ocean liner to be.

After Nassau in the Bahamas, *Oriana* arrived at Cristobal to await the transit. It is the port for Colón, on the Caribbean and Atlantic Ocean side of the Panama Canal. When cleared, we began the slow journey through the canal, which was absolutely amazing. *Oriana* passed though giant locks, guided by electric 'mules' (trains) with inches to spare each side. Then we sailed on through lush jungles and lakes. There was plenty of wildlife to see, including primates, fish and tropical birds. The transit lasted all day. A buffet passenger lunch was laid on and served on the top deck. I assisted, affording me a wonderful view of the transit, an absolutely incredible experience. Later that day we arrived at Balboa, the port for Panama City on the Pacific Ocean side. *Oriana* then sailed on towards Acapulco. Completed in 1914, the Panama Canal is one of the Wonders of the World, an incredible feat of engineering. It connects the two mighty oceans, Atlantic and Pacific, saving ships a 15,000-kilometre voyage around Cape Horn.

Most passengers were delightful, but occasionally we'd get vile ones. If they thought a dish wasn't right, they'd be extremely rude to the waiter, sending it back. Some waiters retaliated. They'd 'accidentally' drop replacement food unseen on the galley floor, 'accidentally' step on it, pick it up, dust it off and put back on the serving dish. The unsuspecting passenger then tucked into it, saying it was utterly delicious! I heard of steaks being wiped round lavatory bowls. Bad passengers were punished by being given the shits with Goddard's silver polish. But I never actually saw it. One lady on my tables made a big fuss that the plates weren't hot enough, placing her hands flat on the plate. I asked the galley if they would make sure my plates were extremely hot. So they placed them under the Salamander (grill) and then I used a waiter's cloth as usual to lay them on the table. Madam immediately slapped her hands flat on the plate. She let out a loud yelp. I could almost hear the red-hot plate sear the flesh, much to my amusement. She never complained about cold plates again.

Acapulco sounded exotic, marketed as a glamorous playground and casino resort for A-list jet-setters. Sadly I didn't have enough time off to go and see it. Though there was an amusing incident one visit. On board was a very eccentric crew member known as Roman John. Although from London, he always maintained he was Roman. When not working, even ashore, he always wore Roman-style clothing, like togas, that sort of thing. He went ashore in Acapulco where some local villains thought he was a rich Arab sheik. They kidnapped him, thinking they'd be able to demand a huge ransom. As no commotion occurred, and nothing was mentioned in the news, they realised their mistake and released the hapless John. He was eventually returned to the ship.

Next port was a day in San Pedro, Los Angeles, then an overnight stop in San Francisco. I visited Fisherman's Wharf and the city. However, the legal age to drink was twenty-one, which spoilt evening enjoyment there for me. In the next port, Vancouver, I was the first UK visitor for my cousin Angela and husband Dick, who'd emigrated there six months earlier. After work, I telephoned Angela from a pier phone (there were no mobiles then) and she arranged to pick me up later. We saw the sights of beautiful Vancouver. Then we went to her apartment for drinks and supper. I stayed the night. Next day *Oriana* sailed, and we made an emotional farewell, not knowing when we'd see each other again. Next stop, Honolulu, Hawaii, for a day. Locals welcomed disembarking passengers by handing them a lei, a colourful garland of tropical flowers. On departure it was customary to throw leis overboard, as a farewell and a promise to return. Honolulu was a beautiful, clean city – wonderful beaches, with plenty of eye candy.

Following Hawaii, we crossed the International Date Line, gaining a day: two Wednesdays. A Crossing the Line ceremony was organised. King Neptune and motley gang (dressed-up crew) boarded the ship. Novices who were crossing for the first time were blindfolded and led to the ship's pool. Smothered in shaving foam, plus all sorts of vile mixtures, they were then pushed into the water. It was all good fun; everyone enjoyed seeing others being humiliated. I heard stories of swill and such being used, but I never saw this. Crew ceremonies were much messier than passenger ceremonies. Blood, offal, and even paint were used on victims. Working, I missed it. Next time we crossed, I'd already crossed, and so I never endured the indignity. Our next port was Suva, the capital of the Fiji Islands. As we docked, I noticed men, even the policemen, wearing skirts. I thought, *That's a bit camp*. Later I discovered the skirts were *sulus*, traditional wear for men, Fiji's national dress.

Most evenings I'd visit the Pig (crew bar). In the nearby crew recreation room the company screened movies previously shown in the passenger cinema. There were also occasional band nights, great evenings. Nicky sometimes screened blue movies in his cabin. They really fascinated me; I'd never seen one before. *The Prime of Miss Jean Brodie* was the latest passenger/crew movie. One evening a mixed crowd in Nicky's were watching a blue movie. As a young 'lady' was going down on a well-endowed man, one queen in a Maggie Smith voice said loudly, "You've gone too far this time, Mary McGregor." Everyone roared with laughter.

Nicky had a box of Leichner stage make-up. One night he talked me into letting him make me up. Later that trip a band night was staged in the Pig. A passenger band came down and Lou Purdy performed numbers by Elvis, his hero. Nick and the lads talked me into doing a drag number. Nick did my eke with his Leichner make-up. I appeared in a borrowed dress, tights, heels, a bra (stuffed with socks), wig, and false eyelashes. I can't recall what I did. Probably wasn't very good, but it went down a storm. Afterwards I was truly out the closet and extremely popular. I was even invited to spend nights with a handsome young officer, whose accommodation was strictly out of bounds for common ratings like me.

After a quick stop in Auckland, New Zealand, I was extremely excited regarding our next port: Sydney, Australia. We passed the famous harbour bridge and the nearly completed iconic Opera House. Berthing in the heart of the city, we were alongside for two nights. Finally I was what is known as *down under*. I wandered ashore and really fell in love with Sydney, the people, the shops, the everything. Stopping for a beer in a couple of pubs and lounges, I was surprised the décor in many was like tiled public lavatories in those days. They served extremely cold beer in middys, half pints, and schooners (a pint). Glasses were also chilled, which Aussies loved.

Evenings most crew headed to the notorious Kings Cross area. The Cross boasted many pubs, bars, lounges, restaurants, clubs, and even a red-light area. Everyone had a good time there.

Back on board one night, I heard loud noises from a nearby cabin. Feet and legs were banging against the bulkhead and deck heads. There was much loud groaning, grunting and moaning, then it went quiet. Next, a loud female Aussie voice said, "Have you slimed yit, mate?" One of the lads must have got lucky up the Cross.

Next evening I went to the Cross with a few queens, visiting bars straight and gay. Some went *cottaging* (visiting public lavatories for sexual encounters), loving the excitement. Interestingly, most local cottaging men were straight, or bisexual. I wasn't a cottage queen. I felt uncomfortable in public toilets; that scene didn't appeal to me at all. Some queens would go cruising round the docks, looking for bits of rough trade, loving the excitement. That didn't appeal to me either. I liked to do that sort of thing in comfort. Our departure from Sydney was quite amazing. Crowds packed the pier, music played, and thousands of paper streamers were thrown. It was quite emotional and it's not allowed now.

The voyage home via the Panama Canal duplicated the trip out, except there was no Vancouver stopover and I had an overnight call in Auckland. That night I visited a bar the lads talked about, the Snake Pit, in the basement of the South Pacific Hotel, Lower Queen Street. It was sleazy, packed and heaving with all types: locals, bar girls, hookers, Maori, gays, drag queens, crew, all drinking and having a good time. Some of the girls brazenly got their tits out. I'd never seen anything like it before. Great fun. Next morning as we sailed in the opposite direction to outbound, clocks went on an hour at night and the ship got quieter. Crossing the dateline, we lost a day, going from a Wednesday to Friday. I don't remember any Crossing the Line ceremony, though I recall it on later trips. We docked in Southampton October 19th, 1969.

*Oriana* was due to sail November 3rd for a world voyage, with three cruises from Vancouver. I signed off, signed back on, and went home for a short break. I was good at making formal cakes and I made a wedding cake for sister Josie, who married her boyfriend Ian on November 8th. Dad's attitude had changed when I went to sea. He seemed somewhat proud of me, especially in later years when I became restaurant manager (a leading hand) and finally purser (catering officer). He still didn't *get it* that I was gay. He refused to discuss or accept it, even when others in the family told him to his face. If he'd ever asked me, I'd have told him the truth. Sadly he refused point-blank to ever discuss it, or accept it.

I rejoined *Oriana* October 31st. Brother Peter and his girlfriend Linda drove me to Southampton. They married shortly afterwards, emigrating to Vancouver in 1971, and now have children, grandchildren, and a beautiful home. *Oriana* sailed November 3, this time out via the Cape: South Africa. First port was Lisbon overnight. The lads said they were going to a street of seedy bars and clubs, the Rua Nova do Carvalho. I went with a few of them, including Donks. We finished up in the notorious Texas Bar, another sleazy joint, full of locals, sailors, ships' crews, pimps, bar girls and other dubious characters. In a sort of half-dinghy attached high on the wall (to keep them safe from fights?) a small band played. It was obviously a knocking shop. Young bar girls asked, "You buy me drink?" and you'd go off with them. They were quite annoying, so I persuaded Donks to let on we were a couple, keeping them at bay. I heard an amusing story from a previous visit; an innocent stewardess from the ship said, "These girls look so young, you think they'd be in bed by now." "Some of them will be soon!" the boys joked.

Life on board was much the same as before: great nights in the crew bar, occasional movie and band nights. I often sat talking to Pussy, a sensible queen, and very down-to-earth, who said exactly what he thought. I'd heard *BMQs* mentioned, and didn't understand. I asked Pussy. He explained, "A BMQ is a black market queen, a gay or bisexual man, dear. He's either ashamed of his sexuality, or lacks courage to admit it." They could be trouble, he said. They resented men like us who'd got the balls to be open about it. They often disliked us. Strangely, BMQs were usually the only guys we had problems with at sea. Genuine straight guys were usually fine with gay people, queens and such.

John, a bellboy, observing I was gay, made a sly comment about me I can't recall. Suspecting a *hint of lavender* in him, I mentioned he too may end up like me. He was most indignant. "Definitely not, never," he said. I thought, *He's young and frightened to admit it. He's in denial.* A few years later, I bumped into him on the *QE2*. "Hello, dear, remember me? I'm now Janis Joplin." (He wore the same type of granny glasses.) In later years he was on the *Atlantic Conveyor*, which was sunk during the Falklands war and rescued by Prince Andrew. That's another story. He lives nearby in Southampton. We talk and meet regularly.

After a stop at Las Palmas for bunkers (fuel) we sailed to Cape Town, with its impressive Table Mountain. The racial discrimination ashore truly shocked me, as I'd never seen anything like it before. Separate post office counters and train platforms for whites and blacks. Taxis with signs, "net Blancs – Whites only." There were even segregated public toilets. After Durban we stopped in Fremantle, the port for Perth, where I had a few beers in the famous First and Last pub. And then we continued to Melbourne, then finally to Sydney for two days. We had a great run ashore. This visit I discovered Les Girls, a wonderful theatre/restaurant/cocktail lounge, "where every night is New Year's Eve." You drank and ate a meal while watching a show: an all-male revue of female impersonators, wearing fabulous frocks. A great show and a marvellous experience. I thought it'd be good one day to try to do something a little similar on board.

We left Sydney December 2nd, 1969, trans-Pacific to Vancouver. I visited the bar most nights, enjoying beers with the boys and sitting with the queens, camping it up, gossiping, so funny. They were talking about someone who wasn't there. "Yes, dear, she's a TOJ queen." I wasn't sure what this meant, later asking Pussy. Telling me in his own inimitable way, he said, "Well, dear, TOJ means turn over job. TOJ queens turn homies over on their fronts and give 'em one." TOJ homies are men who like to turn over and let queens give 'em one. Now I knew. Ship's crew often gave other crew nicknames: A guy whose surname was White was nicknamed Chalky, for example, as in the armed forces. But our ships were far more camp. Queens usually gave other queens camp names, based on their names, what they were like, where from and so on. Hence Les from New Zealand became *Kiwi Liz*. They tried to name me Michele; I thought it unimaginative. I'd have liked something more exotic. But Michele kind of stuck. I quite liked it shortened to Miche or Mish.

# 6

# Too Much of a Good Thing (Is Wonderful!)

December 17th, 1969, *Oriana* docked in Vancouver. I caught up with Angie and Dick, sailing next day for a Christmas Caribbean cruise. The ship was beautifully decorated, the atmosphere incredibly Christmassy and jolly. The cruise must have cost a few bob. Passengers were all well-heeled, polite, no trouble and generous. Mine were delightful. It was a good omen. The ship sailed down the US West Coast, through the Panama Canal to the Caribbean, with calls at Aruba, St Thomas, Barbados, Trinidad and Curaçao. The Caribbean islands are truly beautiful. However, I won't bore you with too many details; I don't wish longueurs to creep in the story. At first the islands all seem different: some Dutch, some American, English and French. But when you visit them repeatedly, they're much the same. They have three things in common: wonderful weather, duty-free shops, and beautiful beaches.

Christmas was celebrated sailing between Los Angeles and Panama. The atmosphere was wonderful. Everyone was full of Christmas spirit, plus plenty of beer. It was a perfect excuse to have more than usual. Everyone was extremely jolly, the bar heaving with plenty of laughs. At closing time one evening I was sitting with a deckhand, Alex, a fearless big hunk of a man. I'd a few drinks and he looked like he'd a few too. He quietly asked me if I'd like to go to his cabin for a night cap. I agreed. As soon as we got to his cabin, he started stripping off. Realising it's not just a nightcap I'm getting, I undressed squeezing onto his bunk. He was uninhibited and enthusiastic, wanting to try everything. After giving me a good rogering, he turned over, pressing his rump against my cock. I guessed he wanted much the same thing and I obliged. Next day, prior to lunch, I sat with a few queens having a beer, when in walked big Alex. He stopped at our table, looked us over, saying, "Some c—t shagged my arse last night," and glaring at us. I was positively mortified. Thankfully one of the queens said, "None of us, dear. We're all *ladies*."

Jim, a 'donkey man' or leading fireman, another hot guy, had a single cabin. Always clean, like all engine room/deckhands, he had beautiful smooth skin, and was extremely muscular: a right turn-on for me. One night after drinks in the bar, it closed. He smiled asking if I wanted to go to his cabin. As it was Christmas, I asked, "Why, have you got me a present?"

"Yes," he said. "Just not sure how to wrap it!"

He was one of those rare men, so sexy and such a turn-on. He made you climax while he made love to you, without doing a thing. I had the time of my life that cruise; one of my best Christmases ever. I'm embarrassed to admit, us young queens even *greased the dish* before going out, just in case of some unexpected trade!

But there was to be a fly in the ointment with all this fun I was enjoying. One day I developed an itch around my pubic area, which seemed to get worse at night. On close inspection I found dark spots in my pubic hair. When I scratched, I dislodged one. To my horror it appeared to be a tiny insect. It quickly dawned what the problem was: pubic lice, or in vulgar slang, *crabs!* I'd heard crew joke about them, calling them undie bugs, minge mice, mobile dandruff and such. Now I had them. At the earliest opportunity, I visited the crew surgery. The crew doctor confirmed my diagnosis. I can't remember if he shaved my pubic hair, but I do remember he brushed some thick white lotion around my genitals. It was pungent, and stung quite badly initially. I was instructed to change bedding and send all used clothes to the laundry. After a few days the vile matter was resolved.

Later in the cruise a delightful lady at one of my tables, Marie, asked if I'd like to meet her in Vancouver. She'd show me the sights, and we'd have lunch. It sounded great. I graciously accepted. While in Vancouver for two nights, I caught up with Angela again, and Marie, who took me for the drive and lunch. We saw each other many times; it was just a friendship, nothing sexual, and I was fond of her. When I mentioned her in a letter to home, they assumed she was a girlfriend. I let them think she was, knowing it'd make them happy. They were always asking, "When are you going to find a nice girl?" If only they knew!

*Oriana*'s next 1970 New Year cruise was a ten-day trip to the Hawaiian Islands. Then we had another month's cruise to the Caribbean, same as the first one, returning to Vancouver February 25th. I saw Angie, Dick and Marie again while there. Next day, after emotional farewells, we sailed to Southampton via the Panama Canal. It was a usual run home, except this time overnight in San Francisco. I borrowed an ID from a lad over twenty-one who wasn't going ashore. Luckily it wasn't a picture ID. If I memorised the name, and bartenders didn't ask for photo ID, I could get drinks.

I went ashore with some lads, stopping in various bars for drinks, ending up in Finocchio's nightclub. *Finocchio*, Italian for fennel, is a negative word for homosexual, like fag. It was a notorious place, starting life as a speakeasy on Stockton Street, North Beach. Then it became a world-famous nightclub, with female impersonators, plus other gay and straight acts. It moved to 506 Broadway, and was advertised as a place for "entertainment and fun," not specifically gay. It was very mixed. Many famous Hollywood stars visited, including Bette Davis, Marilyn Monroe, Judy Garland, Barbra Streisand and Cher. After a great night, we staggered back to the ship.

The ship sailed east, losing an hour some nights. Being a teenager, my love life was extremely busy, though I still dreamt of finding a special person, *the one*, who'd want to spend time with me, settle down. *Love, even?* After a great night with one or two of the boys, I felt a bit loose down below, wondering if perhaps people thought I was a bit of a tart sleeping with different crew. Maybe thinking I was *slack as a yak*. (Word got around on ships.) It wasn't entirely my fault. Only eighteen, was I maybe seen as fresh young flesh. I thought, *Perhaps I'm having "too much of a good thing"?* (As Liberace said, "Too much of a good thing – is wonderful.") Time for a change of scenery? When *Oriana* returned in Southampton, I decided to sign off, go home and ponder my future. Arriving in Southampton on March 22nd, 1970, I paid off, said farewell to friends like Nicky, and proceeded on leave.

It was good to be home. I enjoyed the rest, though it seemed strange. I felt I'd changed. I was now a different person and out of place. After a while, I became restless, thinking I'd look for a job. The Withies Inn in Compton, near Godalming, were advertising for waiters. Mum and Dad dined there with Uncle Fred and Aunt Doris, saying it was delightful. I applied, was interviewed, and offered the job. We wore smart waiter's jackets and the Withies was brilliant. Superb food and excellent wine, run by a French chef-manager, Tony Magnin. He'd learnt English in London kitchens, so his language was very colourful. I bought a little motor scooter to get to work. Things started well: delightful customers, charming people with money, including a few celebrities.

Then the April showers began. The heavens opened, pouring with rain every day. I'd arrive at work and back home soaked to the skin, wetter than a mermaid's minge. I got so fed up with it. Nights off I went to the Bull's Head Hotel. But I was no longer attracted to gay guys there; I was spoilt by macho shipmates and sailors maybe? I also usually got soaked again. Deciding I'd had enough, I telephoned P&O, who offered me a first-class waiter's job aboard *Canberra*. I accepted, giving notice at the Withies. Soon after, I took the train to P&O London for joining instructions, visiting the Shipping Federation and the Seaman's Union and so on for clearance. On May 17th, 1970, I joined the *Canberra* in Southampton.

# 7

# Love "Is a Blonde and Slender Thing"

If I thought *Oriana* had good lines, *Canberra* was a more beautiful-looking ship, and about the same size, 45,000 gross register tonnage (grt). Collecting my boat card, cabin number, and so on from the crew office, I went to my allotted F deck cabin. Finding the door ajar, I met my new cabin mate, Ray. We had a two-berth cabin, similar to *Oriana*, cosy, with full-length bunk curtains, table lamp and so on. Music came from the opposite cabin. Ray saw me looking and introduced me, saying, "This is Michael. He's just joined." The guy in the adjacent cabin said, "I see you've met Fifi. I'm a Michael too, dear. But you can call me Candy." Johnny Mathis played from the large speakers of an amazing sound system. I came love his songs like 'Chances Are' and '*The Twelfth of* Never'. Candy was a great character. He'd worked for airlines, BOAC, now BA. He was ultra-smart, confident and extremely camp, calling everyone darling or dear. My cabin mate, Fifi, was great fun too. It was great to be sharing with another queen. It would make it easier to *drag back* (entertain). *Canberra* was Mediterranean cruising next day, so that evening we went ashore in Southampton. Candy drove a flash rental car, a beautiful Triumph Stag. I was impressed; I couldn't even drive. We visited the Lord Roberts, the Juniper Berry, and the usual places, ending up in George's Diner in Castle Way. Candy ordered: "Champagne, darling!" We had a wonderful evening.

Next day, given cleaning jobs, we checked our tables were ready. The first-class restaurant was attractive, deep carpeted, with a wide balcony along each side. There were no portholes. They were replaced by blinds, brightly lit from behind, giving a daylight effect. It was clever, almost like the light from *Oriana*'s portholes. Evenings, the lights were dimmed and special tablecloths with holes in the centre were laid. We inserted electric lamps in these holes: they looked like shaded candle lights. It was really effective, giving the effect of intimate ambient lighting for candlelit dinners.

We served a maximum of six passengers each, all silver service and very sedate. Mr Eaton (named Shirley after a Bond Girl, Shirley Eaton), was our head waiter. One of the section waiters was again Ron (Cultured Vulture), who'd changed ships. Ron could be bold when upset. One cruise he ordered an old-fashioned cereal for a passenger. The next day it didn't arrive. He spoke to Shirley, who told him he'd cancelled the order as "no one eats those cereals anymore." Ron was furious. He was overheard saying loudly to Shirley, "Well, mine do. Order some more tomorrow, you incompetent old poof!"

First night I went up the Pig with Fifi and Candy, who drank from 'regal' glasses, usually crystal, silver, or a brightly coloured goblet. I was surprised the bar sold gin. (Spirits weren't sold on *Oriana*.) We sat chatting and having a laugh. Candy was highly amusing, with a wicked sense of humour. The bar, smaller than *Oriana*'s, was busy with waiters, cooks, and bedroom stewards

(BRS), plus a few public room stewards (PRS bar waiters) visiting the bar in uniform for a break. There didn't appear to be any UK deck or engine room ratings. Seemingly, they were all Asians, Indian deckhands and Pakistani engine room crew. They had their own recreation rooms, not mixing socially with each other, or us. The catering department employed many Asians too, mainly from Goa, an island two hundred fifty miles off the coast of India. A former Portuguese territory, consequently the Goan culture and religion reflected five hundred years of Portuguese influence. It was still a surprise to learn most of them were Catholic. They had the use of their own large combined bar and mess room, which we nicknamed the Goanese Hilton. We were welcome to use it and often did.

I became friends with more queens. Natasha (Nevyn) was madly in love with a barman, Peter, the love of his life. Sadly Peter was later killed in a motorcycle accident. The hospital attendant (Connie Elastoplast) loved scandal and salacious gossip. He could give you a heads up on who had the clap. He also had the key to a 'drag locker', a large cupboard full of frocks and wigs from past shows: extremely useful. Unusually, one of the boy ratings, Simone, was as camp as a row of tents. He had buckles on a pair of his shoes. Amusingly, you could hear him coming, mincing down the alleys, buckles tinkling.

I couldn't help noticing there was a distinct lack of available men, with no deck or engine room ratings aboard. When I mentioned this to Candy, he giggled, telling me to try the *ship's bike*, Two Tins Tom, pointing to a good-looking young guy, Tom, at a nearby table. He looked straight. However, Candy told me, "Get chatting with him, buy a couple of cans of beer and invite him down your cabin." I did, and it worked a treat. He was a good-looking boy, with the face of a cherub, but his behaviour far from angelic. After a beer or two, he stripped off and laid front down on my bunk. An obvious, welcome invitation, so I obliged. He was a most marvellous shag, him enjoying it too, pushing against me. Later he dressed, returning to his cabin. Not many words were spoken, the whole experience rather bizarre.

Two lovely old queens worked in the restaurant, Lottie and Dora (Ken). Both were very camp and funny, especially Dora, who called everyone "my dear." If passengers asked for something, it was, "Yes, my dear." They adored him. Repeat passengers requested to sit at his tables. He was much older than me. (I thought he was ancient.) And he had interesting stories, especially about World War II. He told me that, although illegal, gay sex was rampant. Any day could be your last, so inhibitions went out the window. He also told a scary, hair-raising story of when he survived his ship being torpedoed. Dora explained that WWII Merchant Navy crews were volunteers and many of his friends died during this time. They'd suffered dreadful deaths in freezing, sometimes burning, seas.

Nowadays when you mention the Merchant Navy, people have no idea what you mean. What it was. What it is. They don't realise that during the war these brave volunteer men and women, and the ships they worked on, were a lifeline for Great Britain. They supplied us with food, fuel, raw materials, even ammunition. This kept the country going, helping win the war. Over thirty thousand merchant seamen died during WWII, proportionately the highest losses of all the armed forces. This fact is practically unknown to most of the population, especially youngsters.

By contrast, we had great nights in the Pig, sometimes putting on a bit of slap or wearing something outrageous. There were occasional band nights, and horse race meetings. Some people did numbers. A barman, Oscar, sang songs like the Flanders and Swann comedy, 'The Hippopotamus Song'. He's been another good friend over the years. Some of us got tarted up, in a wig or even drag. We'd join in a little and do the odd camp number. One evening I was dragged up, joining in the fun, when a lad standing behind me pulled off my wig for a joke. He, or the people who put him up to it, should remember queens in frocks are still blokes! I completely lost it, went crazy, punched him on the chin and battered him. Everyone thought it highly amusing. I ended up with the unenviable nickname Knuckles Rudder. I felt dreadful afterwards, as I rather liked the lad.

Lennie, one of the wine waiters, was friends with a gay millionaire, Jimmy, who occasionally cruised on *Canberra*. After one cruise he drove us to London in his Rolls Royce for an evening out, ending up in a nightclub, the Astor Club. I ordered a gin and tonic. The waiter arrived with a bottle of gin, tonics, plus ice bucket, doing the same for the rest of us. (How the other half live!) After a fantastic night, we were driven back to the ship in the Roller. You should have seen some of the crew faces!

One evening a PRS visited the bar for a drink, sitting at our table. He was a dreamboat, absolutely gorgeous. Tall, blonde and slender, with beautiful eyes and a mischievous smile. I had trouble keeping my eyes off him. He smiled at me and we began chatting. His name was John. He was handsome, good fun, and I was smitten. Could he possibly be 'the one'? It was mutual and we embarked on a very passionate sexual relationship. He had a beautiful physique and was extremely sexy. I was in heaven. His passionate kisses were so good. Not all men like to kiss and I admit it did feel strange the first time I kissed another bloke. I soon got used to it, thoroughly enjoying it.

Summer 1970 was fabulous, cruising round the Mediterranean. The weather was glorious, we went to interesting ports, and had great meals ashore. 'In the Summertime' by Mungo Jerry was in the charts. It brings back so many happy memories to me when I hear it now. John was so handsome and funny, with a wicked sense of humour. Everyone loved him. He was friends with Peter who, as barman, drank in the leading hands' bar, and allowed guests. He would invite Nevyn, myself and John. In Southampton we'd all go for a meal. Berni Inns and Angus Steakhouses were popular then. Very cringeworthy 1970s food and drink, like sherry schooners, prawn cocktails, steaks, spaghetti bolognese, Mateus Rosé, Blue Nun, and Black Forest gateau.

When Medi cruising came to an end, *Canberra* was scheduled for a world voyage. There was to be a cruise from Sydney to Japan and Hong Kong. John and I paid off August 1970, signed back on for the next voyage, and proceeded on leave. John had a super-fast car, a Ford Lotus Cortina. We drove home to my parents. They liked him on sight, especially Dad. John was a man's man, into sport and football (unlike me). Later, travelling to Brixton, I met John's mum, an adorable lady. I couldn't believe how open he was to her about our relationship. She was fine about it. I guess she was a loving parent who accepted her son's sexuality, as long we cared for each other and were happy. Much to my embarrassment, she christened me Petal. Wanting tea, she'd holler, "Petal, put the kettle on." We drove to Devon, visiting my uncle Les and aunt Edie, and, after a truly memorable leave, rejoined the ship September 4th, 1970.

*Canberra* sailed on September 6th, 1970, via Panama, arriving Sydney October 14th for three days. As usual everyone had a great time. John and I went for meals, visiting Les Girls and such. John was kind, funny and romantic. My life was a dream. After Sydney, we sailed to Yokohama, Kobe, Nagasaki and Hong Kong. John was a hard worker and good at his job, making plenty of tips. He wanted to treat me to something special. I half-jokingly said, "How about a gold watch?" Sure enough, in Hong Kong, he bought me a beautiful, 18ct solid-gold Omega. I was absolutely over the moon, wore it constantly and treasured it for many, many years. We had a great time in Hong Kong. Pubs and hotel restaurants on Hong Kong Island itself were amazing, with superb food. *Canberra* docked back in Sydney November 14th, sailing November 17th to Southampton, via the Cape.

Life aboard was grand. I was so happy. Everyone loved John. He was a bit of a flirt and bisexual, though I took no notice. I couldn't see the storm brewing. We arrived Southampton December 14th, 1970, alongside for two days before a Christmas/New Year cruise. The night before sailing we went for drinks and a meal with friends. On our return, a social hostess invited us to her cabin for a night cap. After more drinks and feeling tired I went to bed, leaving John to finish his drink. When he didn't appear, I returned to that cabin to see where he was. Erotic noises and moaning from her cabin made it obvious they were noisily enjoying sex. Heartbroken, I rushed back to my cabin in floods of tears.

When he arrived back, we had a furious row. Next morning, in a dreadful state, I arose early, packed my bags, and walked off the ship. (If it happened now, I'd probably have seen reason and forgiven him!) I called my parents, made some excuse about going home for Christmas. Later I got a call from John. He'd walked off too. We agreed to talk when I'd calmed down.

Over Christmas and New Year we had endless discussions. I did love him. He was remorseful, and didn't he also walk off the ship? We decided to give it another go. *Canberra* docked in January, with our discharge books still onboard. We drove to Southampton to collect them. I didn't realise I'd get a VNC (voyage not completed) instead of VG (very good). A bad discharge made it harder to get a ship. Your book was no longer "clean." Sure enough, we both were given VNCs! While in Southampton, we visited the Pool (Shipping Federation) for work. Nothing. It was a bad time of year. Most ships had already sailed to Australia, leaving little in the UK. Not having clean books made things worse. John suggested we try the London Pools and we drove to his mum's in Brixton, staying the night.

Next day we visited the KGV (King George V Docks) Pool.

The only jobs for two were as A/S (assistant stewards) on Shaw Savill's *Arawa*. The Pool man said the ship wanted 'clean' books, though we could ask Shaw Savill. Although we'd heard they were rough ships, we'd no choice. We visited their nearby office. The man on the desk confirmed they only accepted clean books, saying he'd have a word with his manager. We heard him talk to his boss in the back room, saying he'd two boys off P&O with VNCs.

The boss asked, "Are they poofs?"

"I think so," he said.

He answered, "Let them *work by*. If they behave, we'll let them sail."

This was relayed to us. The man added they couldn't promise any further employment, as this was the ship's last voyage.

"Really," I said. "The last voyage. That'll be romantic."

Looking me straight in the eye, he smilingly replied, "It might be for some of you." I felt myself blush.

# 8

# The Joy of Shaw Savill

January 1971: Tony Orlando and Dawn were topping the charts with 'Knock three times'. *Fiddler on the Roof* was the big hit movie. John and I joined Shaw Savill's *Arawa*, in KGV (King George V Dock) bound for the Antipodes. We were given single cabins, as only a handful of crew *worked by* (working while the ship was tied up between voyages) for the month, while its cargo of frozen lamb was discharged. She was a fine-looking ship, 15,000 gross tonnage (gt), built 1960 as the Royal Mail *Arlanza*, one of three sister ships designed for the South America run. They were known as the Three Graces. Interiors and lounges were beautiful, especially the first-class restaurant. However, as a Shaw Savill ship, she was now one class: tourist.

Assistant stewards working by looked after officers' cabins, serving them and office staff meals in the ship's dining room. Working by was boring and John went a little stir crazy. He wanted off. I didn't. I loved sea life and thought if we walked off again, we'd never get another ship. He said we'd find a ship easy, or even find work ashore. We argued and argued, both adamant. In the end, I stayed; he walked off. I was devastated, heartbroken, a weeping mess, but I'd made my choice.

The crew working by were a lovely crowd, which helped. Rita the Hackney Man-Eater (Billy), Pollyanna, Scots Jessie and a Scouser, Terry. Near KGV Dock was a notorious docks pub, the Roundhouse. We'd walk there for a drink; it was great fun and always busy.

After World War II, London docks were one of the busiest in the world, importing and exporting goods to and from every corner of the globe. Numerous pubs by the docks were heaving with ships' crews, dockers, and locals. Even posh people like actor Noël Coward visited these pubs. They enjoyed slumming it, as the local mainly cockney types were so friendly and such a laugh. The people you see in the soap *EastEnders* are nothing like real East Enders. Many Seamen's Missions, like the Flying Angel, were near the docks, for crew use. Most had accommodation and a bar. Anchor House in Canning Town was a large popular mission, with a spacious bar and entertainment. Heaving with seaman, and locals, some queens went to stay there just for a good night and a bit of trade. I did too. Sadly, these pubs and missions all disappeared when the docks closed in 1980.

Among my friends at that time was Jesse, a camp, funny Scottish queen. He always wore a hint of slap, including mascara, and talked endlessly. He usually only worked by, preferring cargo ships. He told me they were wonderful, with single-berth cabins. Often being the only queen onboard, he'd be the 'star', having a ball and "gutless [lots of] trade, dear" (his words). As a *feely* or *filet* (boy rating) on cargo ships, he'd slept with nearly all the crew! Wages were the same as on passenger ships. There were no tips, though less pressure. Days were shorter. He knew absolutely everyone who worked in the docks. On our way to the pub he'd pass dockers, saying, "Hello, dearrr," with his Scots drawl. They all knew him too. "Hi, Jess."

Terry the Scouser was friendly, good-looking and well-built. He'd previously been a boxer. He was a good laugh, always joking and making humorous remarks. He was the first person I heard referring to pants as *kecks* and *skiddys*. I understood where the latter amusing term came from. I assumed he was straight, no signs of effeminacy, though he seemed interested in me. Feeling heartbroken, I wasn't interested in him. However during work by we saw a lot of each other. He'd walk with me to the Roundhouse for a beer, was good company, amusing and kind.

He soon showed his true feelings, becoming persistent, bold even in the end. In that Scouse accent he'd say, "Come on, gurl. You know you want to." I *was* feeling lonely, and he had lovely eyes and all the right ingredients. I crumbled. We ended up in bed. I did enjoy it. He was passionate and uninhibited, although I still missed John like crazy. I kept playing tear-jerking music like Della Reese, music to 'weep your tits off to'. To make matters worse, there was a lengthy total postal strike. I was a prolific letter writer, but due to the strike received no mail or replies from my beloved John, nor my dear mum.

A few days prior to sailing in February 1971, the rest of the sailing crew joined. I've never seen *so* many queens troop up a gangway again in my life. There were some right royal characters amongst them too: The Duchess, Kiwi Liz, Lena, Elaine, Barbra, Eartha, Nellie, Morag, Terry, Twinkle, Michele, Denise, and many more. Evenings in the Roundhouse were jumping and it was good getting to know crew and other queens that'd be sailing with me. One night a bold queen walked in the pub. I was only nineteen and she took an instant dislike to me. Looking directly at me, she screamed loudly across the bar, "How long have you been sucking cock, dear?" I was mortified. Some people laughed. Most took absolutely no notice. I'd met Mad Marilyn, an infamous London queen. There were many more like her, such as the legendary Stella Minge, Gilda Gash, and lovely Bluebell. There were also many other mixed docks pubs nearby too, like the Kent and the Steps. Great fun, always busy.

Prior to sailing, work by crew were given their voyage jobs, Terry as waiter, and myself as officers' steward. That suited me. Tourist-class table service was far too much hassle. The only drawback was having to share a four-berth cabin. Luckily my cabin mates were OK. One, Vic, was boxed off with Michele, ex-*Andes*, where drag queens took 'tit pills' (Stilbestrol hormone tablets), which made men's breasts and nipples grow considerably. Michele had a lovely pair of tits, so Vic was a happy boy.

Terry shared with a straight lad too, leaving us nowhere to go for trade. Consequently we didn't see much of each other. I seem to remember our trade took place mainly on the dark open foredeck, plus in drying rooms and ironing rooms. There was also a washroom which actually contained a bath; the bath cubicle locked on the inside. I remember going there with Terry one evening after a beer drinking session in the Pig. With all that liquid in us, I also seem to remember indulging in what is known in vulgar slang as PIYB or a south side lemonade ('water sports').

As officers' steward, up top I worked with a sweet old queen, Dolly, the captain's tiger. (I never knew his real name!) In the past, captains' stewards/waiters wore a sash, like a tiger's stripe, so the galley staff knew who he was, giving him the best food for the captain and his guests. Our Old Man, as the crew called captains, was a delightful man. I sailed with him again quite a few times and served as his tiger. (He was Old Man on *Northern Star* that fateful October 1974.)

The crew mess man was a large imposing queen, Billy, The Duchess. He was extremely cultured, educated, and beautifully well-spoken. Apparently, Billy had trained as a priest in Rome. He wrote a sign in the mess room: "Unless you are crippled, kindly take your plates etc. to the wash area." That amused me. Why indeed should he pick up after everyone?

February 4th, 1971, *Arawa* finally sailed to the Antipodes, via Panama. The crew bar served only beer. I joined the queens, some of whom I knew, and I got to know the others. Early next morning, when I was mopping the officers' alleyway, a young bridge deckhand appeared. I'd seen him in the Roundhouse, a good-looking cockney boy. He said, "Hello, darling."

I warned him to be careful on the wet deck.

"Don't get your knickers in a twist, love. Give us a kiss," he said.

"Certainly not," I said.

He laughed, going on his way. It amused me and cheered me up.

Later Captain Morrison appeared at the pantry door, asking, "Have you seen Dolly?"

I lied, saying, "He's here somewhere, Captain. Can I help?"

He wanted tea, so I made up his silver tray, taking it to his cabin. I flew down to call Dolly, still flaked out on his bunk, full eke (slap) still on from the previous night. I said, "Wake up, Doll," giving him a good shake, thinking to myself, *Is this ship camp or what?* During the voyage the Old Man hosted passenger cocktail parties in his cabin. I'd help Dolly, pouring drinks and handing out canapés. When the captain went to dinner, Dolly and I got the chance to pour a few large gins down our screeches! It was Dolly's job to order the booze for the parties. Some of it found its way to his cabin. No wonder he got so trashed.

We were at sea for over a week. The hours went back on the clocks, so the Pig was jumping. Even though it only served beer, it was swinging. A real character was a big tough queen, Lena. His surname was Horn, hence Lena (Horne, the singer). He really was a singer. The boys would ask him, "Give us a song, Leen."

"Oh no. Oh don't. I can't, I haven't had my black currant juice!" What?

They would persist and eventually Lena would give in and say, "Oh alwight, boys," then stand up and sing. Boy, could he sing! So loud, it was hard to order beer over the noise. Some lads called him Lena Foghorn (behind his back, as he was a big boy). Lena also sang in East End pubs on leave, telling me, "I'm a star, you know. I'm known the world over. They *cry* when they hear me sing."

Les was the engineers' stewards' supervisor. Being from New Zealand, he was known as Kiwi Liz. Being a leading hand, he had a single cabin and was able to drag back plenty of trade. He certainly did. Behind his back I called him Cucumber Liz: I'd seen him in the showers! A delightful man, charismatic and great fun. After a few drinks he'd start dancing, performing amazing high kicks. He was famous all over the coast for his high kicks; the boys loved it. Les now lives in Canning Town, near Anchor House. We're good friends, talk and meet up regularly. There were many queens on the ship. A great deal of them were Londoners who were great fun, and quite a few were a bit rough. I first heard the expression 'baked dinner' on *Arawa*. (If easily offended, please skip the next paragraph.)

I'd overheard a queen talking about another queen, saying, "Dirty cow gave him a baked dinner." I'd never heard this expression before, and asked what it meant. It's rather rude, indelicate, Polari. It means that during sex, the active partner's sexual apparatus becomes rather unclean. I'd never heard this from anyone on P&O. Aboard here they must have thought me very naive. (Before getting to know me, some queens aboard referred to me as "*that* P&O poof.")

Terry, being a Scouser, had a wicked sense of humour. He loved playing practical jokes. He said he'd been talking about me to his second-sitting passengers, who told him they'd like to meet me.

"Really?" I said.

"Oh yes," he said, "I've told them so much about you."

I should have known better, but innocently visited the table one evening.

"Here she is," he said, "me tart, Michele." I nearly died. Some of them laughed, others looked rather puzzled. I fled. For a joke, he'd told his passengers about his 'tart' Michele. Would they like to meet her? *He* thought it was absolutely hilarious. God knows what they thought. I could have strangled him. Thank God I didn't work in the restaurant.

After ten days at sea we docked in Barbados. Ashore, the crew enjoyed rather too much local rum and so dinner that night was chaotic. Escalators carried waiters from the restaurants to the galley to collect food – not a good idea at the best of times. With drunken waiters, it was a disaster. We sailed on through the Panama Canal, towards New Zealand. Preparations began for a drag show, *Cocks in Frocks*. I can't recall who named it, maybe me, as I did on later shows. I can't even remember who arranged it. Elaine, being a ladies' hairdresser ashore, was in charge of the *shyckles* (wigs). When finished, they were amazing. He'd previously sailed on the *Andes*, and had Stilbestrol tits, which made him look fabulous in drag. For the show, most queens brought their own drag, borrowed, or made do.

I was still seeing Terry. It was a strange relationship, like mates shagging. He was fun and good company, I was extremely fond of him, and I sort of loved him. But he'd a most vile temper, flying into terrible rages. I wondered if he'd a hang up about being gay, or suffered from mental health problems. He drifted in and out of my life for two years. Some queens on board were *boxed off* (had a lover, or a regular on board/ashore). For others, there was gutless trade (plenty of sex). Nearly everyone on the ship was at it!

After sailing from London, I realised Shaw Savill Line was *so* different from P&O, with a totally UK crew, many of them from London. The atmosphere was *so* different, so laid back, much more free and easy. Everyone was so matey. One night on my way home along the Burma Road (crew alley) I bumped into the handsome, cheeky cockney bridge lad. We started chatting. The way he was looking at me, I could tell was *dying for it*. He was gorgeous, but I'd nowhere to take him. We went to a communal ironing room. I unzipped his flies, swallowed his dick and gave him a knee-trembling blow job. He loved it. I sometimes wonder why I didn't just stay with Shaw Savill Line. Fate had other plans for me.

The crew show took place on the afterdeck; a temporary stage was erected. A passenger band was brought down. I learnt later this was usual on ships for concerts. Rita sang a Judy Garland number; Barbra did Streisand, of course; Elaine did Shirley Bassey. A deckhand, Kim the Stripper, with an amazing smooth body, performed a striptease. He stripped down to three strategically placed tassels, which he waggled in front of the audience and in the face of a senior officer, who wasn't happy. The officer looked mortified. The audience howled with laughter. After other acts, Lena belted out numbers like 'Ma! (He's Making Eyes at Me)', with a rousing finale. The captain joined in. I can't even recall what I did. Being 'otherwise occupied', I also missed the finale.

Morag was a tough, funny, kind, though rough and not terribly attractive Scots queen. I sailed with him a few times over the years. I heard apparently in the past he too tried the Stilbestrol tit pills. To his horror, only one breast grew! He worked as bathroom steward (cottage queen) cleaning communal ex-tourist passenger bathrooms. Next to these bathrooms were large cleaning lockers, some with spyholes in the bulkheads (walls) where you could see into the bathrooms. Whether the holes were already there, or whether crew members drilled holes in the bulkheads, I don't know. However, they provided endless entertainment for some of the lads and gay boys!

Barbra/John, a cabin steward, and I became firm friends. He was born and lived in Hatfield, near where I was from. An amusing man, great company, he lived and breathed his heroine, singing star of *Funny Girl* (1963), Barbra Streisand. Life on the ship continued to be fun, taking my mind off John, helping me get over him. I eventually heard he'd joined the police force, married with children. We are still in touch. He now has grandchildren and is extremely happy. I am pleased for him; he's a good man.

En route to Kiwi, the ship docked in Tahiti. The crew talked about the infamous Quinn's Bar on Quai du Commerce, reputed to be the "worst bar in the world." The pursers' office warned passengers not to go there. I couldn't wait to see it! Not far from the ship, it was a large shack with swing front doors, like a Western cowboy saloon. Inside was gloomy and smelly, with a horseshoe-shaped bar. Behind this, as protection from fights, a band. Along the sides of the room were booths with curtains. In the middle was a small dance floor. It was sleazy and heaving with locals, sailors, ships' crews, matelots, bar girls and what looked like big drag queens in flowery frocks. These were apparently *fa'afafine*, third-gender Samoans. Born male, due to a shortage of women they were raised as girls to help out at home. The beer on sale was a type of onion ale, which tasted like eunuchs' piss. The music was loud and the place was jumping. Curtains were drawn on some booths; no doubt blow jobs and shagging was going on. After a few beers I needed the cottage (toilet) and found it by walking through a tatty curtain. It was absolutely appalling Unisex and extremely dirty, with palones squatting on the floor peeing. Worse was the unbearable smell. I couldn't get out fast enough. Although Quinn's had a reputation for fights, that evening I saw only minor skirmishes. In 1973 it was closed and demolished.

Next, Sydney for a day, another great run ashore, then we arrived on the Kiwi coast, as it was known. We spent three weeks in New Zealand ports, unloading and loading cargo. We were about a week in Auckland. Everyone was enjoying the pubs, such as the notorious Snake Pit. Ships' lads brought local girls, known as ships' molls, back on board. Some of these girls, or *ringbolters* as they were known on cargo vessels, lived on the ship as we sailed round North Island.

Next port was (windy) Wellington, another great run, where many of us partied at the fabulous home of Aussie Cathy. He was chief steward on the vessel salvaging the wreck of TSS *Wahine*. This inter-island ferry infamously sunk in 1968 at the entrance to Wellington harbour, with the loss of fifty-three lives.

Lyttelton, the port for Christchurch, was our next stop. Crew made their way to the British Hotel, another rough seafarers' pub, notorious for fights. People wondered how rough seamen's pubs were allowed to continue. The police view was that at least they knew where to find all the troublemakers! Strangely, this pub has recently been refurbished and reopened.

Last Kiwi stop was the beautiful Bay of Islands, an amazing place with stunning scenery. When finally loaded, the ship sailed back to London docks via the Cape. Although the bar was busy, queens didn't bother with trade. Most crew slept with ships' molls on the coast, and queens were frightened of catching the clap that way (though with Terry I was safe). Consequently, most nights we held hen parties in our cabins. We had rich mad camp; it was great fun. Barbra and I became very close friends during the trip. Before the end of the voyage, some crew, including us two, received a letter offering further employment aboard Shaw Savill's *Southern Cross*. As mates, Barbra and I wanted a ship together. However, the *Cross* had a notoriously rough reputation. We needed to make a decision soon after arrival. I told Barbra I'd call P&O from home, see if they had any jobs, then we'd decide. *Arawa* docked 23rd of May 1971, in King George V Docks. We signed off, paid off, and went home on leave. Terry returned to Liverpool. He didn't seem interested in shipping out with me.

# 9

# Canberra Revisited, and the 'Phantom Gobbler'

My parents collected me from King George V Dock in the Royal Docks. Being a cockney, Dad wanted to visit London for old time's sake, plus I had duty-free gin and brandy for them. They boarded to find me. Dad took a look at the engine room, then drove me home to Guildford. After a couple of days, I telephoned Barbra (John), as we thought we'd try and ship out together. We agreed to meet in London. I can't recall if from the Pool or P&O, however Barbra got an assistant bedroom steward's job, and me a first-class waiter's job aboard *Canberra*. After formalities with the Shipping Federation, Seamen's Union, and so on, our instructions were to join in Southampton on May 27th, 1971. She was due to sail May 28th, for a summer season of Medi cruises. Australia trade, especially immigration, had declined; P&O liners now cruised during the summer, with line voyages in the winter.

May 27th we reported to the D deck crew office, which was far below the passenger accommodation. Barbra received his work and cabin details. To my surprise, they asked if I'd like a PRS (public room steward) job, serving drinks in bars and lounges. I thought, why not. I was issued a PRS set of epaulettes, with a blue lanyard down one side. My cabin was on D deck PRS alleyway. My cabin mate, Paul, was friendly, and Barbra's cabin was nearby.

I *turned to* in the Meridian Room, the first-class lounge. A large, attractive room, tastefully decorated, it had modern furniture and floor-to-ceiling windows all round. At the top end of the room, a beautiful marble spiral staircase descended down through four decks from the crow's nest bar to the Meridian Room. At one side of the staircase was a grand piano. Beyond the spiral staircase to the front of the ship, the Century Bar was a cosy little room with bar stools. I introduced myself to the barman, Bill, known as Fruity, and assistant barman Fred, who looked like an old queen by the way he spoke and his demeanour. My work mates were all gay: Nevyn (Natasha again), Dennis, who only drank Double Diamond beer (hence Dee Dee) and Ronnie (Martha, so called because of his huge mouth, like US comedienne Martha Raye).

Day one we cleaned, preparing the room for sailing. That evening was free. I went ashore in Southampton with Barbra and a couple of queens I'd known previously on *Canberra*. It was great catching up with some old mates and visiting our usual haunts, the Juniper Berry, the Lord Roberts and such. Barbra and I developed a taste for gin and It (gin and Italian vermouth), which made us incredibly merry. Barbra eventually disappeared to go cottaging, which he loved. I wasn't a cottage queen. The thought of lurking in public toilets for sex is embarrassing, not to mention dangerous.

However, he eventually talked me into going with him one night, visiting the IB Cottage by the city's tourist information bureau, at Above Bar. I lurked in there for a few minutes, but it just *wasn't me*. I fled. He stayed, later telling me what an exciting time he'd had, lots of *cartes* to enjoy. Cottaging was extremely popular in those days, despite being illegal, toilets being public places. Queens loved it. As most other men in cottages were usually straight or bi, the danger enhanced queens' excitement. However, if another obvious queen appeared, queens *flew*.

Next day we turned to, getting ready for the forthcoming voyage. As a new boy, I found everyone was so helpful. We all looked very smart in our starched white jackets, with gold buttons and a blue lanyard. Barman also wore smart waistcoats. Behind the Century Bar on port side of the lounge was a dispense bar, with an open door in and a door out. The starboard side of the lounge had a pantry, for the hot drinks service. We weren't supposed to drink booze on duty but barmen turned a blind eye, allowing us to buy drinks to guzzle in the pantry. We prepared for service by placing a folded napkin on trays with coins inside, and bank notes in our pockets. No debit cards then. Taking drink orders on pads, we placed orders in the 'order glass' at the bar, then went out to take more orders. By the time we placed the next order, the previous one was ready. In February 1971 decimalisation took place. There were new pounds and new pence, not pounds, shillings and old pennies. It actually made adding up easier. After a while it was a breeze. Wandering around with our silver trays, drinks one side, cash the other side in a folded white napkin, I quickly learnt about popular cocktails in those days. They had quirky names like white lady, old fashioned, sidecar, brandy crusta, pink lady, and horse's neck. Also I learnt about garnishes, such as cocktail cherries, olives, lime or lemon twists, swizzle sticks and cocktail parasols.

First day in the Meridian Room was fine, my work mates were helpful and amusing. They nicknamed it "God's waiting room." Business was slow, the room quiet and the clientele mostly elderly. We served coffee mid-morning, then had a little rush at midday, for pre-lunch drinks. Passengers liked to listen to the captain's midday announcement from the bridge:

the weather, speed, miles travelled and so on. We'd have a break in the afternoon and the bar reopened about 5:00p.m. for pre-dinner drinks, with a pianist playing cocktail melodies such as 'Smoke Gets in Your Eyes'. After dinner the lounge was quiet again, its bar closing fairly early, leaving the Century Bar open. This gave us a chance to visit the Pig for drinks before that closed. Time for me to catch up with Barbra and the gossip. He finished work a lot earlier, about 9:00p.m. By the time we met he'd usually be extremely merry.

Days passed happily, cruising around the Mediterranean every fortnight. Work was fun. My workmates were outrageous and we got up to all sorts of mischief. Placing orders at the bar, we chatted and camped it up; Fred the barman would shout, "Pick 'em up! Pick 'em up! And keep the noise down." They'd answer, "Keep your hair on, Freda." He'd scream, "Don't call me Freda.." They'd reply, "Yes, Freda dear." It was hilarious.

Quiet times we parked our trays on the grand piano, removing them when the pianist arrived. One miserable pianist would walk to the grand piano, bow to the audience, then quietly and very rudely tell us, "Take your f—ing trays off my piano." Crew, entertainers and concessionaires usually got along fine, though there could be hostility if anyone looked down on others. We thought this man was possibly homophobic; he couldn't help noticing us lot camping it up and having fun. We plotted our revenge. One morning we taped some of the keys together underneath the piano with strong electrical tape. Later, he came in and bowed. Then he started playing. It sounded hideous and we struggled to keep straight faces. Scratching his head, he pressed keys, looking inside the piano, trying to figure out why more than one note rose when pressing one key. He eventually realised what the problem was, glaring at us. But he had no proof who did it. "Probably *feelies*, dear," Martha commented.

Martha was a larger-than-life character: tall, outrageous, and great fun. He was about forty, had been at sea for a long time, and was outrageous, with a camp voice too. He couldn't remember names, calling *everyone* 'Vision' (of loveliness). No one batted an eyelid. On entertainment nights in the crew bar, Martha made enormous picture hats from cardboard, crepe paper and ostrich feathers; they caused a sensation. I asked him why Barman Bill was nicknamed Fruity. Was he gay? Martha told me at one time barmen paid the galley for fruit to garnish drinks. To save money Bill fished lemon and orange slices out of used glasses, washed them, and reused them. I was horrified at the lack of hygiene, though never sure if it was the truth, or a bit of poetic camp from Martha.

In 1971 parts of the new James Bond Movie *Diamonds Are Forever* were filmed aboard *Canberra*. Crew were advised what to expect. Nevertheless, it was exciting to see the film crew and stars board to shoot the movie. We even caught glimpses of Sean Connery, which really was a thrill. In the film the ship appears to sail, with streamers and such. Actually we were tied up alongside; the movement was clever camera trickery. Towards the end of the movie, James Bond orders dinner in his suite. Of course it's served by the two baddies who intend to kill him with a real bombe Alaska, not just the ice cream variety. I'm sure this part wasn't actually filmed in a suite, as I worked them in later years. However, it was wonderful publicity for P&O. One of their brochures billed *Canberra* as "The James Bond Ship!"

Crew came and went during the cruises. Many ships were finishing because of their age and the diminishing trade due to air travel. A number of interesting queens came from other lines. Cindy and Tanya (Ken and Tony) were off the camp Royal Mail liner *Andes*. Both were delightful queens and great fun. They joined *Canberra* as waiters. Sadly the head waiter, Shirley Eaton, gave them a hard time, probably because they were younger than him and he didn't want too many other queens in the restaurant. They only stayed for a couple of cruises, and paid off, despite the fact jobs were not as plentiful those days.

When I went to sea, from 1969 onwards, it was a time of massive changes. Many passenger ships were being scrapped or sold for various reasons: too old, too thirsty, unsuitable, not making enough money. This included *Andes*, *Queen Elizabeth*, *Queen Mary*, *Franconia*, *Carmania*, *Empress of Canada/ England*, *Southern Cross*, *Arawa*, *Aranda* and *Akaroa*. Jumbo jets were now offering cheap long-haul flights for the masses; the writing was on the wall. P&O still had a huge fleet, *Arcadia*, *Iberia*, *Himalaya*, *Chusan*, *Orcades*, *Oronsay*, *Orsova*, *Cathay* and *Chitral*. The public still travelled by sea, but this was soon to change. They started to travel by air: faster and cheaper. Containerisation of cargo was introduced too, reducing the number of traditional cargo ships.

Plus there was a lot of mismanagement at this time. Companies failed to adapt to these changes, partly because they were run by older gents who thought conventionally. Partly because they couldn't see what was happening. In 1973 the UK joined the European Common Market. People were outraged, as it meant the UK was forced to reduce its imports of meat and dairy produce from Australia and New Zealand. This new step was a slap in the face for these countries that we loved. It was a final nail in the coffin for all the refrigerated cargo ships, which for decades had brought our Anchor butter, lamb and apples from the Antipodes. Things would never be the same again. There'd be no more days and weeks moored alongside in Aussie and Kiwi, enjoying ourselves while cargo slowly came aboard in boxes and crates, instead of in huge containers.

I'd written to my *Oriana* good friend Trish (Trevor), telling him what a great time I was having, and he decided to transfer to *Canberra*. However, he didn't like the ship. There were no

British deckhands, like there'd been on *Oriana*, which kept its UK seaman when P&O took over Orient Line. P&O employed Indian deckhands; they did not socialise with other crew, and you rarely heard of any being gay or trade. Eventually Trish transferred to P&O container ships.

Scouse Terry followed me to *Canberra* too, continuing our strange relationship. He still suffered from terrible rages. We went ashore one night with Trish for a few drinks, stopping at a Chinese restaurant to eat. After ordering, Terry got in a frightful rage about something. I was furious, and returned to the ship. Terry stormed out too, leaving poor Trish with a mountain of food and to foot the bill! Trish was such an agreeable guy. He saw the funny side and forgave me.

During the summer we had a short leave. I actually took Terry home to meet my parents, instead of him going to Liverpool. They took to him immediately, especially Dad. Terry could be extremely amusing. Terry was also a man's man, unlike me. He would wake up earlier than me and sometimes go out with Dad in the car on his farm calls. They'd stop for a lunchtime pint and a snack, one of Dad's favourite pastimes.

I even managed to take a trip with Terry to visit Liverpool, enjoying it immensely. I loved the place. We stayed in a small guest house; he was always rather mysterious about his parents. I never did find out anything about them. After thoroughly exploring the city, we visited the famous Yate's Wine Lodge, which was a new experience for me. We got horribly shitfaced. At that time you only found them up north, in Lancashire and Liverpool. They are now everywhere and are just called just Yates.

When the ship docked in Southampton overnight, crew often ate supper ashore, especially me. I loved going for a meal to places like the Old Oriental, a Berni Inn, or one of the steak houses, like the London, or Angus Steakhouse, or even to a Chinese.

As a PRS (drinks waiter), working every evening until 10:30 or 11:00p.m. was a real drawback. I was unable to spend time in the Pig socialising. If Barbra was still about I'd see him, and sometimes other PRSs before the Pig closed around 11:00p.m. After that we'd have cabin parties, inviting neighbours. I befriended a down-to-earth Yorkshire guy, Barry. Initially I thought he was straight, though we later ended up in bed, where we had a good time. He *took it like a toast rack*. He's a delightful man; I still see him occasionally.

Cabin parties were great fun, though rather loud, ending in the wee small hours. Sometimes the electricity sockets would cut out, and all music stopped. Eventually my new friend Barry laughingly admitted it was down to him. He had to start work early in the morning, so if our parties were going on too late, he'd put silver foil in a plug, push it in, and bang, all the music stopped! I found this rather amusing, using the trick myself later on *QE2*, utilising a coin.

My cabin mate Paul worked in a nightclub disco down aft (the back end of the ship) on the promenade deck. He came home in the early hours. Sometimes, if he got lucky with a passenger, he wouldn't come back until morning. Sex with passengers, male or female, was strictly forbidden, which probably made it more exciting. One PRS, Phillip, liked bringing his guitar to my cabin. We'd drink and he'd play music for me. A charming, attractive young man, about my age, he was gentle and sweet. One night, after a few drinks, I could tell by the way he was looking at me that he was extremely horny. I sat close to him, undid his trousers, swallowed his cock, jarring the *cartes*; he loved it. Nevertheless, he was straight, and later happily married.[2]

Barbra seemed to enjoy the ship. He had a great, funny personality, making friends easily. Unfortunately, if my bar was

---

[2] But Phillip still sends me his regards through a mutual friend.

busy, I finished late and we didn't get to see much of each other. I didn't see much of Terry either, which annoyed him; it didn't take much. Later in the trip word got round that a 'Phantom Gobbler' was prowling on board – someone randomly entering crew cabins at night, trying to give blow jobs (or more) anonymously, not caring if victims were gay or straight. Some guys laid back and enjoyed it. Others, quite rightly, were furious and indignant. People suspected the Phantom Gobbler was one of the new queens on board. Suspicion fell on Barbra. I asked him outright and he denied it. The Phantom's Reign of Terror (or Delight?) continued.

One night after a few drinks Barbra confessed he was indeed the Phantom Gobbler. When the Pig shut at night, he'd try crew members' doors (few were locked) and interfere with them, to see if they were good for a blow job, or more. Most of them were half asleep. Some let him carry on. A few wanted more. Others started shouting. Then he'd flee. However, things came to a head one night. He went in a leading hand's single cabin, interfering with him, and himself, climaxing on the carpet. The guy awoke, jumped out of bed and slipped on the wet carpet. Barbra made his escape, but it had been a close shave. He did it for the excitement, like cottaging, but now decided to stop. I'd heard stories of ships' Phantom Gobblers, though this was the first time it was for real. I was pleased it was over; it wasn't right. Being caught would have meant shame, and probable dismissal.

In July 1971, after a couple of months of Mediterranean cruising, *Canberra* sailed a line voyage to Australia; there must have been sufficient travellers and immigrants to make it worthwhile. (The Assisted Passage Migration Scheme, called 'Ten Pound Pommies', ended in 1981.) We had a few days' break before we sailed. I was summoned to the main bar office of head barman, Frankie, an outrageously camp middle-aged queen. (The company had no problem employing out gay men like him, providing they were good at their job.) He loved gossip. Bumping into him around the ship he'd say, "Anything to tell me, child?" I'd have to repeat any scandal. Ship's bars were cash then, not cashless like today. Barmen, especially head barmen, made really good fiddles on board. When Frankie went on holiday, he'd arrange his smart Daimler to be taken aboard *Canberra*, which had special car-loading facilities. He'd get off in Lisbon with the car, visiting a friend, an English lord resident in Portugal.

This day he'd good news for me, offering me a transfer to the Crow's Nest bar, at the top of the marble spiral staircase. A beautiful observation lounge, it had floor-to-ceiling windows and stunning views over the ship's bow (the front). It was a great bar to work, with just two crew running the room: myself and barman John. He was my sort of build, around thirty years old. A gay man, he was great fun and good to work for. He loved his drinks. Gins before lunch. Whiskys before dinner. Bacardi and Cokes later in the evening. The Crow's Nest bar didn't get too busy. That was a blessing, as I worked the floor solo. With about thirty tables and lounger seats in front of the windows, it could hold around 120 passengers. That was a lot to serve on my own. I enjoyed working there. It was relaxed and John was camp, amusing company. One job I really disliked was pulling down window blinds at dusk so that light wouldn't affect navigation. With forty-one windows, it was hard work, though a profitable location. John would 'bash' (dilute) the spirits in the afternoon and I'd help him. We'd take some spirit out a bottle – about a juice glass full – and replace it with tap water. This addition really didn't affect the taste. In fact it seemed to make gin taste smoother. Barmen also bought duty-free bottles from leading hands who didn't drink spirits, and I believe they bought cheap bottles ashore, making a good profit, as Frankie's Daimler proved. The average wage then was £30 to £40 a week for a barman or head barman. Daimlers cost around £3,500 to £4,000 then.

The Crow's Nest bar closed fairly early, around 10:30 or 11:00p.m. Entertainment, such as it was in those days, was held in bigger lounges and bars. I'd usually manage to visit the crew bar for a couple of drinks when finished. Sometimes barman John would take me to the leading hands' bar. One night I was chatting and laughing with one of the bakers, a handsome young man. I ended up having far too much to drink and must have invited him down my cabin. All I can remember was his enormous cock coming through the bunk curtains, and giving him a blow job. He must have liked it; he came back for more. Towards the end of 1971, Scouse Terry hadn't seen a lot of me, because of my hours, and he wasn't happy. Later he went into another of his rages at work and was dismissed, leaving in December when we docked in Southampton. I was still extremely fond of him, and sort of loved him. Sex was exciting and I felt sad to see him go. It was also somewhat of a relief. I never knew when he was going to get into a rage over something stupid, or even attack me.

I started to intensely dislike working alone in the Crow's Nest. I missed the fun with queens in the Meridian Room, the amusing Polari regarding passengers, like, "Varda the palone with cod naf riah, dear." I was also fed up with my hours of work, from 5:00p.m. to 11:00p.m. every night, with only a short break. I was unable to spend an evening in the Pig, go to crew entertainments and so on. I talked about it with Barbra. He was getting bored, with itchy feet. I think he'd had sex with about a quarter of the UK crew and wanted to try something new (fresh meat on a new ship). We decided we'd sign off *Canberra* and try the Pool for jobs. I'd also telephone Shaw Savill, our old employer on the *Arawa* Antipodes run, to see what was available. Maybe the *Northern Star*, a cut-price migrant ship that went the slow way round the Cape to Australia, with nearly exclusive British crew, which offered even more chance for trade. We'd heard it was a rough ship. Rumour was you didn't sign on, you 'weighed in', like boxers! However, if we didn't like it we could leave. After the Christmas cruise, we paid off January 2nd, 1972, both going home for leave, hoping to get a ship together.

# 10

# Maid with Balls

After a few days home, I telephoned Shaw Savill, enquiring if any jobs were available. I explained my friend John (Barbra) and I recently paid off the *Canberra*, having previously worked on *Arawa*. I spoke with Mr Ayling, a brilliant gay-friendly man in the personnel office. He said *Northern Star* was back soon from Australia, due January 12th, 1972, with jobs available. I gave Barbra the good news and we arranged to meet in London. We both secured bedroom stewards (BRS) jobs on the *Star*. I'd not worked in cabins before; Barbra did on *Arawa*, saying, "It was a piece of cake. You'd love it."

    I imagine we obtained clearance from the Shipping Federation (Pool) in Prescott Street, near London's Tower Bridge. When I went to sea, there were 'established seafarers' who signed a contract with the Pool, and were assigned their work from the Pool. If there was no work, they were paid by the Pool. Other seafarers were 'non-established', obtaining work from the Pool or from the company directly. If there was no work, there was no pay. All seafarers required clearance from the Shipping Federation and the National Union of Seamen. In later years, 1975 I believe, all seafarers became established when the Shipping Federation merged with the Chamber of Shipping, to form the General Council of British Shipping. I have tried to find what date most Pools, as we called them, finally closed, without success. (However, I know the Southampton Federation closed in 1991.)

Following clearance, we were given our joining instructions to join the ship on January 12th, giving us a short leave after a five-month voyage. Nevertheless, we were young, excited, and glad for a job, as things were quiet in January. We decided to have a jolly day in London, a drink near the Pool in the gay-friendly Princess of Prussia pub in Prescott Street. Later a drink in a little-known mixed (gay and straight) West End pub in Piccadilly underground station, the White Bear, then a drink in the Golden Lion in Dean Street, Soho. Finally drinks and lunch in the mixed Salisbury, a pub in St Martin's Lane.

On joining day, Barbra travelled south from Hatfield to Southampton. As I travelled from Guildford, we decided to use our rail warrants to travel from our local stations to meet on board. I joined early afternoon. *Northern Star* was unusual-looking: grey hull, green superstructure, a funnel aft, though with pleasing lines. I visited the crew office to collect boat card, cabin key, and so on, then went to my cabin. I found a large four-berth which, amazingly (being on A deck) had a porthole! Dumping my bags there, I visited the crew mess for a cup of tea, seeing familiar friendly faces. Elaine (Jimmy), Kiwi Liz (Les) and Terry from the *Arawa*. I sat with them chatting. They were pleased to hear Barbra (John) was joining too.

I told them we were both cabin stewards (BRSs) and I wasn't sure what the job entailed. One queen, Fannie, told me, "Basically you're a chambermaid, dear, except you're a *maid with balls*." That tickled me. Fannie was a good-looking, delightful man and extremely amusing. His surname was Brice, hence his camp name, Fannie, from Fannie Brice, the US comedienne who Barbra Streisand portrayed in *Funny Girl*, the film and stage show we all loved.³

I later met up with my cabin mates: Katie, captain's tiger; Alvin, his boyfriend; and Albert, a Scouse waiter. When Barbra finally arrived, he felt rather unwell. Turn to wasn't until the next morning, so we went to town that evening, to sample the delights. We'd quite a few gin and Its on board. Then we had a few drinks in the pubs, the Juniper Berry and the Lord Roberts, ending the evening with supper in George's restaurant, before tottering back to the ship. Next morning Barbra felt extremely poorly, with a nasty rash. He was sent to the ship's hospital, diagnosed with chicken pox, paid off and sent home. I was devastated. My best mate wouldn't be sailing with me after all.

Turning to, a catering officer issued our work sections and pass keys. Mine was B deck aft (the lowest), down by the water level. It actually had watertight doors in the alleyway! I checked my section. Four four-berth cabins and a further four six-berth cabins made a total of forty bunks. None had portholes, so it was obviously an immigrant section. A nearby friendly BRS, Phil, had worked the next section the previous trip, and he knew the score. He took me to get linen, upstairs to the promenade deck, along aft, downstairs to the laundry. UK laundry staff issued sheets for our sections in huge laundry bags. I could hardly lift mine. Phil showed me how to swing it on to your back, as we tottered back to our sections. Just as well we were strong young men.

Making beds was hard work. I was so slow. Phil showed me how to make it easier and quicker. Hold the sheet one end, shake it into position, straighten it out and tuck in. I soon became fast

---

3  Paul was another lifelong friend, now sadly passed away. We worked together later at sea on Princess Cruises, and I kept in touch, even visiting his Spanish holiday flat, until his untimely death from motor neurone disease.

and I still do it that way today. Each section had a cleaning locker for spare linen, towels and, oddly, a large metal teapot. We used this locker as a base, and for storage. Some of them, like on the *Arawa*, had interesting peepholes looking in to the communal bathrooms! Finishing the beds and cleaning the cabins, we made another trip to the laundry for towels. Each cabin had a wash hand basin, and a short curtain on each bunk, with a small folding shelf. Toilets and showers were nearby, thankfully cleaned by bathroom stewards. It took all day preparing the cabins, and we finished late afternoon.

After evening meal, I went ashore with a couple of queens for a few drinks, especially to the gay pubs. When I first sailed from Southampton it was all new to me, after my closeted life in Guildford. Others showed *me* the best pubs. Once I knew where everything was, I too showed new queens the best places, getting a kick out of it. Next day we gave our cabins finishing touches, a polish, and did passenger paperwork, such as the itinerary and details of ship's activities. Later we laid cups and saucers on trays in the pantry for morning teas. (That's what the large tea pot was for!) Embarkation began after lunch. We greeted passengers at the gangway and took them to their cabins. I noticed more queens among the bedroom stewards, having a quiet bit of camp and talking with each other in Polari. Sailing late afternoon January 12th, 1972, we went off to Australia and New Zealand with many immigrants on board. The ship could take 1,437.

In the early evenings, cabin stewards helped in the galley, serving food to the waiters. This was repeated for second seating dinner. We finished about 9:30p.m. After work I visited the crew Pig, a huge room forward on main deck, split in two, stretching the width of the ship The only booze was beer. It was cheap, only 10–15p a pint (about £1.50 in 2024 terms). I got myself a brew and, seeing friendly faces, joined a table. It was busy in the bar and we enjoyed a lively, fun night, almost making up for Barbra's absence. I noticed plenty of good-looking men in the bar too: a promising start to any voyage.

Next morning Phil and I collected a milk jug for our sections. Filling the large tea pot, then cups, we took a tray of tea to each cabin, with a pack of sugar and a Rich Tea biscuit in each saucer. Knocking doors with the pass key, then entering, we placed a cup of tea on each bunk shelf. Easy. But tricky on a rolling ship, or if you had a touch of the shakes after a night out. About 7:00 to 7:30a.m. a loud announcement came from the bridge: 'Watertight doors about to be tested. Stand clear." Clanging watertight door bells were enough to waken the dead; not many slept through that! As they went for breakfast, we flew in the cabins, making them up. Late risers we tackled later, finishing about noon. Then we went straight up to the Pig for a beer or two before lunch. Afternoons were free, time to get a bronzy, or get your head down until about 5:00p.m. Weekly linen change was hard work, even though we only 'topped and tailed'. The top sheet became the bottom sheet. A clean sheet became the top sheet. Only one of the two pillow slips were changed. This half-and-half arrangement was normal practice then. Ships on long voyages needed to conserve water and to carry a minimal supply of linen. (The shortage was made worse by queens nicking sheets to make frocks.)

Nights in the bar were great fun and always busy. I was befriending more queens, such as Welsh Alice/Alan, a tiny queen, feisty, great fun and a heavy drinker of gin. Pretty, with a high-pitched voice and long hair, at first people though he was a girl. He loved being boxed off; his taste in men was for enormous butch bear types. Aussie Flo, from Tasmania, was another fun queen. He'd long curly hair, also with Stilbestrol tits, and looked fabulous in drag. Queens often wore drag if there was a show or entertainment. Most of us, including me, always wore discreet slap in the Pig.

It was good to catch up with Elaine. When *Arawa* finished he had transferred to *Southern Cross*. Then, when that finished, he went to the *Northern Star*. He shared a cabin with Gracie, whose surname was Allen; he was named after the US comedienne, Gracie Allen. Sailing on previous trips, Elaine was firmly established aboard. They arranged a four-berth cabin for themselves, removing the two top bunks. They decorated it beautifully. Wallpapered, stylish bunk curtains, luxury bedspreads, carpet with subdued lighting: a palace. Brighton Gracie was big, tough and great fun. He told me that on the previous trip there were many queens on board, including the notorious Rosie and Patsy. I met these two absolute legends later, adoring them both. Apparently there was a great deal of trouble during the trip: too much outrageous camp behaviour, including fighting. So the ship had a clear out, sacking all trouble makers, including at least twenty of the thirty queens on board. However, another twenty to thirty took their places!

Our January voyage out was a straightforward trip to Australia via the Cape. Only one memorable stop came our way, for all the wrong reasons. Overnight in Cape Town, I went on a night out – drinks in the Coral Lounge, a bar in Strand Street's Grand Hotel, then ending up in Delmonico's, another sleazy dump, where I bumped into Katie and Alvin. Cape brandy is cheap and extremely potent; I don't remember returning to the ship. I think Katie helped me. Next thing I remember, I was awoken by a ship's mate, finding a deckhand also in my bunk. The officer asked which one of us lived in this cabin, and asked the guy to leave. He made Katie and Alvin get in their own bunks, and departed with Albert to find him another cabin.

We realised Albert obviously hadn't taken kindly to us sleeping together and making noise. Or could he have been a little homophobic? Most guys didn't mind sharing with gay men; their cabin was usually taken care of, with a good supply of booze. Nevertheless, if I hadn't been so drunk, it would *never* have happened. Mercifully, next day while we were working, Albert collected his things. Seeing him in the bar later he was friendly enough, not seeming to bear a grudge. I gloomily thought we'd be disciplined and possibly sacked. To my surprise, we heard absolutely nothing more about it. I'm not sure if it was because Katie, being captain's tiger, was protected by the man in complete charge of the vessel, or because they found it so difficult to recruit enough labour.

Shaw Savill ships had rough reputations and difficulty getting crew, especially catering crew. Emigrants' tips were poor compared to other passenger ships, where holidaymakers and well-heeled travellers had more spare cash. That's the reason Belgians worked on board. I believe the company made a special agreement with the Union and Belgian government. Belgian lads were friendly, some of them *dolls* (gorgeous) too, especially Chico, a tall blonde boy. There were a few queens among them as well, including Tilo, who the queens inexplicably christened Tilly Tampax. He even received letters on board addressed to Tilly Tampax. Another with a heavy French accent we christened Fifi; I never actually knew his real name.

When Elaine joined *Southern Cross*, he was apprehensive because of its rough reputation. Happily, everyone had an absolute ball. Crew were extremely friendly, with many bona homies among them. The Pig was ginormous; it had plenty of room to set up a stage, with space for fabulous shows. One HP, Bernie, formerly a *red coat* (an entertainer and dancer at Butlins holiday camps ashore) choreographed crew shows. His dance routines were so spectacular that they nicknamed him Flo, after great Broadway impresario and founder of the famous Ziegfeld Follies, Florenz Ziegfeld. Elaine thought the world of Flo, telling me I'd love him too and he'd probably be joining the *Star* when we returned to the UK. I did.

Later on our way to Aussie, it was decided to hold a crew show. A ship's passenger band usually kindly supplied the accompaniment. Preparations would be fun; I wanted to get involved. Elaine was in charge of the hair again. He travelled with an assortment of wigs, plus polystyrene styling head blocks. To see him backcombing, styling and spraying the wigs was awesome; finished styles were beautiful. Alice, Flo and I wanted to do a number, but didn't have frocks. Elaine suggested we buy crepe paper from ship's shop and make flapper dresses, doing a number like 'Thoroughly Modern Millie', from the musical of the same name. He recommended bright red and white paper: "You'll stand out on stage, dear." He helped us cut, sew and staple the dresses together. My contribution was to help organise a show programme, finished by the ship's printer. I tried to make it amusing. We couldn't call it Cocks in Frocks again; queens would know I'd copied it. It being February, we billed the show February Frock-a-Long.

The Crew Club of s.s. *Northern Star*
Unashamedly (and at great expense) present:
"February Frock-a-Long."
By kind permission of Captain D T Beverage
(listing the acts in order; with comments underneath)
Alice, Flo, Michele and Ensemble "Thoroughly Modern Millie"
(Or up to date misses)
"Fifi" – "La Vie En Rose"
(Direct from mad Gay Paris – where only the river is sane)
Sean – "Sweet Caroline"
(Good God – it's a man!)
And so on.
On back of the programme: "We would like to thank:"
The Ships Band (blowing and sucking so beautifully)

Gordons Distillery (the Artistes' encouragement)
Yul Bruner (for the Wigs)
The Captain's Mum (for letting him attend)
And such like.

The crew bar's deckhead (ceiling) was so low that people's heads almost touched it. Tall backcombed wigs actually did! One night Gracie's wig snagged on something and it got pulled off. It was so lacquered that it bounced. She whipped it back on, carrying on as if nothing had happened! We had no stage or curtains, making do with sheets, tinsel and glitter dust. Prior to the show, we were getting ready in Alice's cabin, guzzling gin (we'd smuggle bottles onboard). I noticed he'd forgotten to shave his legs. He flew to the bathroom with a razor, returning with nasty cuts. When he pulled on his tights, blood oozed through them, but the show must go on! We lined up behind the curtain, where three lads in straw boaters were dance partners. Opening music played, curtains parted, the show began with us Modern Millies dancing around, singing and flapping our hands. Sadly, after much gin, nerves, plus the heat in the bar, we began sweating buckets. What happens to crepe paper when it gets wet? It goes soggy, dye runs and paper melts; we looked like we'd been in a traffic accident. Crew thought it was hilarious, and all part of the act. They loved it.

Shows weren't all drag numbers. Other acts joined in. One lad, George, played his guitar and sang. Archie Andrews, a catering officer, delivered an extremely clever and amusing monologue. Another boy, Sean, sang a song accompanied by the ship's band, who also performed their own numbers. Fifi, dressed as a Parisian tart, complete with fox furs, sang in French 'La Vie en Rose'. Then George went on to play his guitar and sing again. Gracie performed as Shirley Bassey. Elaine couldn't do Bassey, as he'd joined after Gracie, so he chose Dusty Springfield instead. He was good, and looked fabulous, with naturally amazing hair. Gracie closed the show of course, with another dramatic Bassey number. After the show we mingled with the crew in the bar, which was always extremely entertaining.

Gracie liked to organise darts matches and could be extremely amusing. He'd say, "Fancy a game of darts, boys? Winners f—k the losers; we'll try to lose." They'd just laugh, playing a game of darts with us. He loved relating amusing stories, telling me about a time the *Star* was overnight in Barbados with a Royal Navy ship. Crowds of matelots came aboard, drinking in the crew bar, which was heaving. Gracie said that night he'd a queue of sailors outside his cabin; he ended up in the ship's hospital.

"Oh dear," I said. "I hope it wasn't anything serious."

"No, dear," he said. "Just to wipe the smile off my face!"

Belgian Chief Catering Officer (CCO) Mr Masselhoff was in charge of catering. He'd red hair, so was nicknamed the Red Baron. He was quite a character, and enjoyed a drink. I looked after him on later trips. His steward was another colourful character, Lady Gambol, Denise Gambol. He'd previously worked as butler to the Duke of Buccleuch, at Roxburgh Castle. Cultured and educated, he had a beautiful speaking voice. He'd Scottish roots, so he often wore a kilt with all the trimmings, and expensive jewellery. Lady Gambol was extremely smart, always causing a sensation.

Among the deckhands was an infamous rough Belfast character known as Mad Dog. In Northern Ireland he was reputedly attacked by a mad dog, and killed the poor brute with his bare hands. He and Dennis were complete opposites but always exchanged friendly risqué banter in the crew bar, becoming unlikely friends. To me Dennis seemed so old (I was only twenty). I clearly remember his fiftieth birthday party, a grand affair in the two-berth cabin he shared with a queen, Graham. Only those, like me, who received a gold embossed invitation card were allowed to attend. I think Mad Dog came too. Dennis had a soft spot for him, despite his bad manners and even worse language.

Like most ships, *Northern Star* crew didn't make a big deal about the large number of gays on board: about twenty per cent of the crew were gay. Instead they were friendly, accepting and tolerant. Many queens were boxed off, with a regular homie on board or ashore. Others had a good time with the bona men on board. I became friendly with John, a good-looking blonde deckhand. We'd have trade occasionally. Despite appearing straight, essentially he must have been bi or gay. It was another strange relationship. Not much open affection was shown, but it was sort of unspoken. He didn't seem to mind if others showed interest, or chatted me up; he was another one who drifted in and out of my life.

During the Aussie trip, I received a letter from my mate John, Barbra. He'd got a job on a Tate & Lyle sugar boat: Caribbean voyages to collect cane sugar. He seemed happy. We kept in touch for a while, then lost contact. However, years later we'd meet again, in surprising circumstances.

February 26th, *Northern Star* docked in Sydney for a few days, readying for two-week cruises round the Pacific Islands, Fiji, Tonga, Papua New Guinea and New Caledonia. During evenings in Sydney a good time was had by all up Kings Cross, at Les Girls. February 29th we sailed, the ship tarted up for cruising. Menus improved, more choice was offered, and some four-berth cabins were let as two-berths. Fresh fruit was placed daily in every cabin. Even morning teas were upgraded: each tray given a *pot* of tea, plus a choice of coffee or fruit juice. Aussies certainly knew how to party and were extremely hot-blooded too. When we turned to in the afternoon, we'd replenish cabin fruit bowls. We'd knock on the door, and if there was no reply after a couple of knocks, we'd use our pass key to enter. When you knocked they'd freeze, instead of saying they were busy or whatever. Not hearing a response, we'd enter, often catching them *in flagrante delicto*: having a shag!

Aussies loved the *Star*, especially the Tavern. This ship's pub was huge, with one of the world's longest bars on a ship, their all-time favourite bar. In the evenings cabin stewards still helped serve food in the galley and there were delicacies on the menu, such as oysters and smoked salmon. Theme nights such as Island Night were put on for passengers. To create an illusion that lounges were a desert island, bundles of palm leaves had been loaded in port though the galley's gun port doors. The leaves were to decorate bars. However, while laid in the gun port door, huge stick insect things crawled out of the palm leaves. Cooks picked these up, waving them in queens' faces. Pandemonium broke out. Queens screamed their tits off, dropping what they were doing and fleeing, with cooks chasing them. The fat chef went berserk, screaming, "Get back to your stations!" It was hilarious.

Easter occurred during one cruise. Again we laid on a show, an Easter Eggstravaganza. Most of us bought drag ashore. Some went to dress shops, saying, "I want a frock for my sister. She's *exactly* the same size as me." Others visited thrift shops, which were wonderful places to buy drag, especially high heels in size seven or eight. I helped produce programmes again and made a bona Easter *capella* (bonnet). This was a straw hat covered in bright paper flowers, like asters, lilies, and roses, in which to perform 'Easter Bonnet' from *Easter Parade*. Others did Easter-themed numbers, wearing Easter outfits. Sometimes we sang, sometimes mimed: it depended upon the complexity of the number and singers' skills. I can't sing to save my life, usually consuming too much gin anyway. But we did our best. It was great fun.

Some Aussies were invited. Even more found their way to the crew bar, even though it was strictly out of bounds to passengers. Surprisingly, young Aussies loved drag. The Pig was heaving with happy people. Holding my basket of plastic flowers as I sang, 'Easter Parade', I tossed my fake blooms into the audience. Some splashed into pints of beer, much to everyone's amusement. A wonderful evening.

While Aussie cruising we had great nights out at the Cross in Sydney. It was always busy, with an eclectic range of bars, restaurants and clubs for all tastes: gay, straight, whatever. Oxford Street was the main gay area, with the Trolley Bar, Barrel Inn and a rough trade bar, the Bottoms Up. A lot of the gay bars, clubs and a sauna at this time were started by Dawn O'Donnell, an Australian entrepreneur and supporter of the LGBTQ+ community. They included a well-known gay club, Capriccio's, which became famous for its drag shows and was visited by celebrities from all over the world. Eating out in Australia was cheap then, and wonderful. I seem to recall massive steaks stuffed with oysters.

Terry, ex-*Arawa*, took me to Bondi Junction, near Bondi Beach, to a fabulous gay bar, Chez Ivy, packed with gorgeous Australian *dolls* (hunks). Nearby, above a bakery was a gay sauna, a good place for cake and arse. Terry talked me into going with him, saying it was hot and they'd private rooms for sex. After drinks in Chez Ivy, we visited the sauna, enjoying an amazing night. It was packed with gorgeous Aussie men wandering around in flimsy towels. I took one back to my room. We had a great time: he was clean, sexy and unbelievably *hot*. Thankfully there was not yet such a thing as AIDS; it only hit ten years later, in 1982.

The Pacific Island cruises came to an end. We returned to Sydney for a few days and another hard turn around. *All* sheets, pillowcases, and towels had to be changed. Linen bags weighed a ton as we lugged them to the laundry. The lads and queens had told me about wonderful tablets known as *sweeties* that you could buy in Lisbon and Madeira. They gave you masses of energy, useful for a turnaround, or if tired. They were actually amphetamines, or 'speed', with names such as Preludin and Dexedrine. I tried them, and suffered dreadful, weird side effects. They gave you masses of energy but you couldn't stop talking, plus your mouth became so dry. Also your willy shrank – mine so much that I'd a job finding it! Afterwards I suffered a terrible come down, with horrible feelings of doom and gloom. Experimenting with sweeties a couple of times was enough for me; I never did again. Others loved them, especially those we call *sweetie queens*.

After a final night out in Sydney, in early April the ship sailed back to the UK. Our return voyage to Southampton was busy, though we managed to stage another show. The queens wanted to try production dance numbers, where we'd look similar in a line up. We 'borrowed' sheets, dyeing them in the pantry, to make outfits. I remember one number, 'Up, Up and Away'. We made a balloon backdrop, then, wearing identical loose-fitting sheet-frocks, we held a balloon in our hands, dancing to the music. It was corny but fun. Crew seemed to enjoy it. Another number was 'Sur La Plage', from the 1954 Sandy Wilson musical, *The Boy Friend*. We wore bathing costumes, dancing around with beach balls, which also went down well.

Gracie performed a John Denver number, 'Leaving on a Jet Plane'. We made a silver foil airplane backdrop, with Gracie on stage with a suitcase, belting out the song. Just for a laugh, one of the lads, shouted, "Well, f—k off then!" We even talked the Scouse ship's football team leader to let the boys take part in a show. Gracie with Lady Gambol performed 'The Man in the Moon' from the musical *Mame*. The football team were the chorus. It was *good craic*; they all enjoyed it. After shows, we'd mingle in drag with the crew in the bar. One of the lads told me I looked really gorgeous. I made him giggle when I said, "Sadly I have my mother's features but my father's fixtures!"

Towards voyage end we were informed that, due to the difficulty of getting waiters, the company proposed employing waitresses. (They were already employed on many ships, including with Union Castle, where they were called stewardettes. In reality, very few women worked on ships at that time, apart from cabin stewardesses.) These twenty-four or so women incomers were to be housed in six cabins at the bow, with exclusive use of the forward bathroom. This caused upheaval. It meant that in Southampton some crew would have to move cabins. One cabin was very miffed. They'd an A/C leak in a top wardrobe locker where they stored beers, chilled to perfection. A lot of queens, including me, thought having women on board was going to change and ruin everything. Nothing would ever be the same again. We were in for a big surprise.

During this time, we heard the dreadful news about the *Royston Grange*, a Houlder Brothers 10,262-ton refrigerated cargo ship on the South America run. On May 11th, 1972, she'd just departed Buenos Aries, bound for London. As she transited the Punta Indio Channel in dense fog, at 5: 40a.m. she'd collided with the fully laden twenty-thousand-ton Liberian tanker *Tien Chee*. The resulting fireball instantly killed all seventy-four aboard the *Royston Grange*, including women, a five-year-old child and the pilot, plus eight crew aboard the *Tien Chee*. It was a most heart-wrenching disaster, especially as Denise, ex-*Arawa*, perished aboard. He had shared an apartment in Canning Town with Kiwi Liz, who passed the sad news on to us and had the unenviable job of sorting out all of Dennis's personal belongings for return to the family.

Les told me the sad story of how Dennis should never have sailed in the first place. While on leave, Dennis bumped into an old friend, Joy, staying in the seaman's mission, Anchor House. Joy invited him aboard the *Royston Grange* for a drink. While Dennis was aboard, the chief steward (for whatever reason) sacked the Old Man's tiger. He stuck his head in the cabin to ask Joy if he had any friends looking for a job, before he contacted the Pool. Dennis either decided to sail, or was talked into it. Sadly, his fate was sealed. He perished with all the others aboard. May they all rest in peace. According to *Nautilus* and *Wikipedia*, the Houlder Brothers flew 130 relatives to Uruguay for a mass funeral. On May 20th, the victims' remains were buried in the British cemetery in Montevideo. Further to this, on June the 8th, a memorial service was held in the Parish Church of All Hallows by the Tower. One of the windows there now includes a stained glass memorial, commemorating all those who perished in the terrible tragedy of the *Royston Grange*.

# 11

# 'The Strange Case of Blondie' – Unforgettable Lee

May 16th, 1972, *Northern Star* docked in Southampton for nine days, before a summer season of two-week Medi cruises. Crew left. New crew joined. Some changed jobs. The waitresses arrived and appeared to be a friendly bunch of women. With passenger service being hard work that brought few tips, Alice took a job as radio officers' steward. I did the same, moving into a cabin with Alice, joined by new captain's tiger, Big Dave, and a strange, funny old queen, Bimbo. Elaine's friend Bernie, Flo, also joined. We hit it off immediately. He was tall, with wonderful posture, and extremely good-looking. Women swooned over him, but were 'barking up the wrong tree'. Bernie's a funny, extremely kind man, although somewhat of a paradox. He doesn't have much time for humans, but *really* loves animals, especially birds. He usually had one in his cabin. He adored cockatoos. People found that amusing. "Flo *loves a cockatoo.*" He also loved jewellery and was always smothered in gold and diamonds. That meant he got other nicknames, like Gold Finger and Diamond Lil. We had our moments, but he became another lifelong, dear friend.

Instead of staying in dockside seamen's missions waiting to join, he stayed with his good friend Lee, who owned a guest house in Hill Lane, Upper Shirley. Bernie said Lee was great fun, camp and interesting: I would love him. I was enjoying a drink in the Lord Roberts one evening when Lee walked in and Bernie introduced us. I took to Lee immediately. Good-looking in a pretty way, with striking blonde hair, a la Lana Turner. He'd great presence, a star quality, highly amusing and instantly likeable. Later he gave me his card and I promised to stay with him overnight next time I was in Southampton.

I loved listening to Flo's stories about *Southern Cross*. Not long after joining, he'd got boxed off with a bona homie, who turned out to be an *actual* gangster. Apparently he said something to Flo like, "Stick with me, honey, and you'll always fart through silk." "Yes, dear," said Flo, "I was a gangster's moll that trip." Flo could be extremely bold and *cod* too. On ship he lived next door to a waiters' cabin, where they selfishly played their eight-track tape player far too loud and far too late. He'd an assortment of pass keys and could stand it no longer. While the waiters were serving lunch, he let himself in, with a pot of honey. He pulled out a tape, smeared it with thick honey, and rammed it back in. Later, when the waiters tried to play it, out came a sorrowful 'woo woo' noise and it conked out.

*Northern Star* sailed May 24th, 1972, for a season of Medi cruises. This time I was officers' steward, sharing with radio officers' steward Alice, and the Old Man's tiger, Dave. It was easier than being a cabin steward. You got even more time off, with the same pay, though you were rarely tipped. It was great to be Medi sailing again: glorious sunny weather, brilliant ports, enjoying boozy lunches ashore. Evenings in the Pig were lively as ever. Now, with female crew members on board, spirits were served. At that time men mostly drank beer and ladies drank spirits. Booze was cheap too: a large gin about 8p, adding to the merriment. I took an unpaid job as crew librarian (dishing out library books and making a note of who borrowed them). I loved being first to see new crew and talent joining. The new female crew also enjoyed visiting the Pig for a drink. They were a friendly lot, mixed in well and were treated, quite rightly, as just another crew member. I became friendly with quite a few of them, especially Janice and a mature lady, Kitty. When the subject of a crew show came up, some were keen to get involved.

A whole bunch of new queens joined the ship too, including a Welsh queen my age – Tony, or Winnie. We became friends, though it was not a deep friendship; he never wanted to get close to anyone, including me or homies. A section waiter in the restaurant, he was also extremely amusing. Della, Derek, a rough Manchester queen, joined. He *really* enjoyed a drink and sweeties. He was kind, funny, sometimes rather heavy going but we got along fine. He was never interested in drag or appearing in shows. In fact a lot of queens weren't, including Fanny, Dusty and Kiwi Liz. They'd join in camp and Polari, even helping with shows– lighting, music and so on, – but they *never* dragged up. I asked Liz why he didn't drag up. He told me it was just not his thing, nor was it for some others. I enjoyed drag just for a bit of fun, not for sexual reasons, and I certainly had no interest in becoming a woman or transitioning. Drag didn't turn me on either. I did it for fun, although it seemed to turn on a lot of guys.

Another queen joining was Horseface Thelma. He was tall, and strong, built like a brick shithouse: not the prettiest queen, but good fun with a great personality. I had to laugh when I heard Thelma dragged a bit of trade to his cabin, saying in bed to the homie, "You will be gentle with me, won't you?" The queens sharing his cabin were in absolute hysterics. In another story I loved, Horseface was having a bit of trade and mistakenly picked up Deep Heat or Vicks vapor rub instead of lube. It was mentholated. They both leapt off the bunk screaming their tits off. Thelma said to the homie, "I don't know what you're f—ing screaming about. At least you can *blow* on yours!" Two other queens joined at this time. He became big friends with Candy and Desire. They all had a lot in common. Desire was tall and thin, nicknamed A Street Car Named Desire, which was later shortened to Desire.

I loved the officers' steward job. The officers were a great bunch, especially the chief officer and Old Man, Captain Morrison, ex-*Arawa*. Alice was great fun, with a wicked sense of humour, giving everyone nicknames, which I'm guilty of too. He nicknamed a plump radio officer Bessie and the chief radio officer the Toad. On a previous trip Alice was in a relationship with Chico, a Belgian boy with a massive cock. Alice always loved to be boxed off, but was now single. Along came Big Dave. A former guardsman, he was married, big and butch, definitely Alice's cup of tea. She quickly went about charming Dave. Very soon they were having a mad, passionate relationship. Dave disliked Bimbo, who was small, with sticking out ears, and nicknamed him the Chimpanzee. Bimbo drank heavily and was a dirty cow. In the bathroom one afternoon, Chico stepped out the shower, his enormous long cock hanging down. Bimbo grabbed it, saying, "How the f—k did Alice manage to take all that?" "You'll never find out," replied Chico, laughing and pushing Bimbo's hand away.

One middle-aged plump and regal queen was Millie. In drag she looked just like the Queen Mother. Our Old Man visited to watch crew shows and one night Millie in drag was standing near him. One of the lads asked the captain would he like a drink, then pointed to Millie, asking, "And your wife?" "Good grief," the Old Man said, laughing. "That's not my wife, it's one of the stewards." We organised other social charity events in the

Pig, like horse racing, and once tried an evening fair. There were a few stalls, a book and magazine stand, raffles, tombola and so on. Aussie Flo and I, wearing full ekes/bona capellas, ran a hot dog stand. Millie said she told fortunes, so we set up a Romani tent, with a large bulb in a vase as a crystal ball. That night we made quite a few bob. After consuming bucketloads of gin, Mille told outrageous fortunes. Anyone she didn't like, she told them dreadful things would happen. At the end of the evening she pissed off with the takings. Next day she denied all knowledge of the handbag: "Don't know what happened to it, dear."

Medi cruising was great for most stewards. Finishing work at about 12:30 lunchtime, we didn't start again until about 5:30p.m. There was no such thing as room service or afternoon teas in the cabins on this ship! We'd plenty of time ashore to go to the beach or do our favourite thing, have a boozy lunch, especially in Málaga. I'd wander into town with Gracie and a couple of queens and find a nice local restaurant. We'd have a few drinks, then lunch, often on fresh fish, a rarity on board, with a drop of local vino. We'd roll back to the ship. If there was time we'd have a snooze, then start work at 5:30p.m., trying to look sensible. Most of the waiters had also had a few drinks ashore, so the chaos at the galley hot press was very funny. No one seemed to mind in those days; it was part of daily life. These days if you turned to smelling of drink, you'd be sacked and thrown off at the next port, which I suppose is right.

Despite frequent ports when cruising, we managed to squeeze in crew shows choreographed by Flo. They were marvellous. He was a strict teacher too; he needed to be, with us bunch of reprobates. Flo dragged up to compère all the shows and was extremely witty and hilarious. We called one show something like No Reservations. Waitresses joined in. I can't recall all acts. They were mixed – straight and camp – as usual. With Flo in charge of dance routines, they were imaginative, with better timing and musicality. Routines included 'Perfect Young Ladies' from *The Boy Friend*. This was a mix of girls and queens dancing, which made it fun and confusing. Some guys, like Sean, sang numbers. I did a duet with stewardess, Janice. Gracie was Bassey and Elaine, Dusty. One of the ship's entertainers, Chris, performed. Dear old Kitty closed the show with a singalong. For a finale, the cast formed a semicircle at the rear of the stage, queens and girls with both hands on one knee, posing. Then, with the song 'A Pretty Girl Is Like a Melody', Chris walked us to stage front for audience approval, a fantastic finale.

August 12th, 1972, with my twin brother we celebrated our twenty-first birthday. Symbolically getting the 'key to the door' (parents' front door) was a big deal in those days. I must have taken a cruise off. My parents organised a big party for us. All our relatives attended and we had a wonderful night. I signed off *Northern Star* August 25th. When my leave finished, I phoned Lee, booking into his guest house in Southampton, while looking for a ship. I remember arriving in tight black and red flared hipsters, with a big zip, bright stretchy top and platform shoes. In the 1970s fashions were quite outrageous, with flares, bell-bottom trousers, hipsters, tight or flowing garish tops and platform-soled shoes.

A young-looking bearded man, who at first I thought was one of the guests, answered the door, taking me to the back room. I was somewhat surprised. Lee was wearing a kaftan. (Later I learnt he always wore kaftans indoors, finding them cool and comfortable; they hid his large tummy.) He was impressed by my outfit, saying he made clothes, and would love to copy mine. I said of course, and he invited me for drinks in the kitchen. Thus began a beautiful, loving, slightly doomed friendship. He introduced me to Roy, his long-time lover, who at first I'd thought was a guest. Fairly good-looking, smooth, well-built, with slightly bowed legs, Roy was well hung, with a pert bum. Though bearded, Roy was strangely sexy.

We sat chatting, having drinks. Lee was extremely funny. He found me amusing too; we really hit it off. He'd the air of a movie star, like Bette Davis, especially when smoking cigarettes. He told me he'd actually made a movie (that explained it!), one of Edgar Lustgarten's Scotland Yard films entitled *The Strange Case of Blondie*. The plot involved a touring variety star (Lee) who dragged up to 'case', then rob, houses. It was quite a racy story for those days, when drag was *never* seen on the silver screen.[4] Roy and Lee had written and recorded a song too, 'Love', hoping Lee would break in the recording industry. Sadly he failed to land a record deal, though I heard the demo disc. It was an enchanting song, and Lee's voice was beautiful.

Lee talked about his life. He was brought up in a massive house in Weston-super-Mare. His mother was a blowsy blonde, who had no problem with Lee being gay. She knew all the gay Polari too, though she could never remember gay people were called *homie palones*, she referred to them as *farter polarters*! As a child Lee was involved in a serious car accident, resulting in skin grafts, with terrible scars on one leg. This experience gave him a morbid fear of hospitals (and dentists). While trying to get into show business, he was called up for National Service. He absolutely hated the army. Marching and drills were definitely not him, although, being extremely pretty meant he'd have fun after lights out. To get out the army he attacked his scars with a knitting needle. (He loved knitting.) The scars festered. Consequently, he was discharged as medically unfit. Though this got him out the army, the knee scars caused him trouble for the rest of his life. They wept, needing constant dressing. He just referred to it as his *cod lally* when anyone asked, jokingly referring to it as woodworm. Lee found humour in everything, even in bad situations. He said he got his vodka from Rentokil,

---

[4] I've actually got the DVD, and I find it's really rather good, still.

the pest control experts, saying the vodka was only to treat the *lally woodworm*.

Next day, job hunting in Canute Road Shipping Federation. There were none, nor in the afternoon. Back at the guest house, Lee invited me to join him again, as Roy was taxi driving. Like the previous day, we sat in his kitchen chatting, laughing and enjoying a few drinks. Lee drank rather a lot, although we all did in those days. Lee told me he'd met Roy when they were both working as cooks on the old *Queen Mary*. To begin with Lee loved sea life, and together they'd joined the new super liner *QE2* in 1969, sailing on the maiden voyage. Eventually he began to dislike sea work, wanting to settle ashore. Their last ship was *QE2*, which he'd enjoyed, as it was a brand new ship and called into New York frequently. Lee absolutely loved New York. He'd tell me stories about wonderful times there: Broadway shows, superb restaurants. I'd never been, and it really didn't excite me. Eventually they left *QE2*, buying this large house for conversion into a bed and breakfast business, so Lee wouldn't have to go to sea. Roy took to driving a taxi to bring in extra money until business was established.

Visiting the Pool the next days and weeks there were still no ships. Lee was delighted. "Never mind dear," he said. "Sign on the dole and stay here with me." I think this was the first and last time I ever signed on the dole. I hated it, found it utterly humiliating, and received little money. With Roy out taxi driving, Lee was lonely, so he really enjoyed my company, especially as we shared the same sense of humour. He loved musicals and classic films: we'd spend hours watching them. He particularly loved Bette Davis movies. Over the weeks I became extremely fond of him and it was mutual; we'd crack each other up.

Around this time, I bumped into Terry the Scouser from *Arawa* and *Canberra*. Despite everything, we were thrilled to see each other, and got back together. He was staying in the

Southampton Docks Seamen's Mission on Queens's Terrace. I introduced him to Lee, who took to him (he could be endearing), inviting Terry to stay there with me. While at Lee's, one day Terry and I went to London for the day, visiting the mixed Salisbury pub in St Martin's Lane. We were drinking a beer when in walked the actor Rupert Davis. Terry recognised him and walked over, saying, "I recognise you, mister. You're Migraine." Rupert was not amused: "You mean Maigret. Get it right, sonny." I felt rather embarrassed, though amused. This was typical of Terry's sense of humour.

Lee was a complex personality; open-minded and liberal in so many ways, yet in other ways quite a prude. Extremely permissive regarding sexual matters, he could be rather prim in other ways. He was very dignified, disliking swearing and crudeness. If ever he swore, it'd be just a string of mild profanities like "frig, shit and piss." Disliking lavatory humour, he referred to poo as a *goggy*, the lavatory as a *gog box*. There was a toilet off the kitchen. Can you believe, sometimes he'd light a cigarette and sit there, on the *gog box*, just for peace. He always lit a cigarette for dramatic effect (Bette Davis style) before absolutely everything: using the toilet, answering the front door, even before answering the telephone. He was a very spiritual person too. I didn't understand that at the time, though years later Lee was to surprise me. I became quite spiritual too. I quickly became extremely fond of Lee, with his happy personality. He was always so overjoyed to see me when I arrived home. He'd be sat in the kitchen in a kaftan, usually in slimming black (though he owned multicoloured ones too), with a cigarette in one hand, a large drink in the other. As soon as he saw me his little face lit up with big smiles and we'd start chatting, having fun. We always enjoyed each other's company.

It was around this time I discovered the joy of douching. Lee regularly did, recommending it to me. Near the Lord Roberts was an old-fashioned medical supplies shop. They sold all sorts of things, like bed pans, pee bottles, wheelchairs and douches. After a couple of drinks in the Roberts I ventured into the shop, buying myself a douche – a rubber bulb with a long attached nozzle. I proudly took it home to show Lee and couldn't wait to use it. In the meantime, I wrote my name on it, so it wouldn't get mixed up with others. When Lee found it he couldn't help himself, he wrote on it, "Mish's gog extractor" and was in absolute stitches. He even showed it to people, laughing and chuckling. Again, even I had to laugh.

Finally the Pool offered Terry and I waiters' jobs on a Union Castle, Safmarine ship. We were obliged to take it; you were only allowed to say no three times, or be disciplined. October 3rd, 1972, we joined SA *Oranje* as first-class waiters. It was a regular five-week Cape trip. Lee was so upset, you'd think I was sailing away for five months. Built in 1947 as Union Castle Line's *Pretoria Castle*, 28,700 gt, the ship was sold in 1966 to South African shipping company Safmarine and renamed SA *Oranje*. It was old and tired; crew accommodation was extremely basic. We lived in four-berth cabins, with no air conditioning. Terry and I shared with two middle-aged queens, Georgina and Charmaine. I tried to be friendly with them, however I don't think they liked either of us, especially later in the trip. Georgina wore a *syrup* (toupee), which he took off before going to bed. Practical joker Terry hid it one night. When George awoke and couldn't find it, there was uproar; he'd *never* appear in public without it. Tony thought it hilarious of course and eventually the hairpiece was found. Suspicion fell on us both. The atmosphere was distinctly frosty thereafter.

The waiters' uniforms were very smart and the passenger accommodation luxurious, especially the dining room, with wonderful air conditioning. Restaurant food was truly excellent (we crew ate it too) though it took getting used to. First morning a passenger asked me for mortadella (a large, cold, spicy Italian sausage). I thought, *Strange*, going to the cold pantry and asking for it. "I think you mean *Maltabella*, mate" said the cook. "It's over there by the porridge." Sure enough, it was a sort of chocolaty porridge. South Africans, Yarpies, as the waiters called them, loved it. In fact Yarpies just loved food, eating like horses. Thank goodness we only had one sitting of six passengers to feed, so the work wasn't too hard.

In hot weather our cabins were like furnaces, unbearable. We sweated our tits off. We'd put wind chutes or cardboard beer boxes in the porthole to get fresh air. Sometimes there'd be a commotion in the night, when a flying fish flew in the porthole. I had a top bunk, lying underneath hot asbestos-covered pipes. The ship was alive with cockroaches. They crawled along these hot pipes, falling on top of me. Vile! The crew bar served only beer, 9p a pint. The atmosphere cliquey, as we were *new crew*. Heat in the bar was unbelievable. As you drank beer, sweat pissed out of you. We called into Las Palmas for bunkers, then on to South African ports, including Port Elizabeth and East London. None of these interested me much.

In some of the ports, Cape Town/Durban, gold bullion was loaded/unloaded, with armed guards standing by. This was due to a daring robbery in 1965, seven years earlier, on the *Cape Town Castle*. Gold bullion worth £100,000 went missing when, it was suspected, two crew members climbed through a ventilation shaft. When the ship docked in Southampton, there was no sign of it. The ship was watched for months and undercover officers travelled on board. Police thought it was an inside job. A watch was kept on crew members. This finally paid off when the gold was found cemented in the bottom of large emergency sand fire box; two crew were jailed for ten years.

On the homeward-bound leg of the voyage of *Oranje*, with few passengers, only regular 'company' waiters had a *show* (passengers on their tables). Us Pool men were merely given a morning job and afternoon teas, meaning no tips or overtime. With no access to the galley, we ate in the crew mess, where the food was fine. However, Terry wasn't happy with it. One meal he said was disgusting (he who was allegedly raised on scouse and jam butties). He became extremely angry, storming up the galley demanding a passenger meal, having a violent confrontation with a chef. At the end of the trip his services were 'no longer required'. I'd no intention of signing back on either. I hated the ship. November 13th, 1972, we both signed off in Southampton.

Around this time Lee started drinking whisky and water, thinking it would be more slimming than tonic. However, there was an unfortunate side effect: bright red veins appeared on Lee's nose, which he was very conscious of. During the trip I'd made friends with Gary, a young South African queen who worked in the beauty salon aboard the *Oranje*. I told him about the veins on Lee's nose and he sold me some expensive cream he hoped would fix the problem. He was looking for somewhere to stay in Southampton so I found him a room at Lee's.

On arrival we went at Lee's place. They got along famously, though Lee couldn't resist giving him a camp name, Garelda Gobble Off! I went home for some rest, returning to Lee's when my leave was ending. While I was away Lee had tried the cream on his nose. I asked him how he'd got on. As usual he was in hysterics about the whole thing. When he applied the cream, his nose began to glow and glow red, "Like a Belisha beacon, dear," only ten times worse! However, after a while it settled down. The veins were much improved. As usual he found the whole thing highly amusing: another story to tell people.

We'd spend hours in the kitchen, drinking and having a laugh. I met many more queens staying there. Lee's friend Debbie (David) Boaz worked on *Reina del Mar* and became another good friend. Great fun, always laughing and chuckling, he lived locally in a static caravan home. He also owned a villa in Spain. I first met Rosie at Lee's too: a kind, tough, camp London queen, hard as nails. Rosie had a camp, high-pitched voice, though if anyone took the piss, he'd soon sort them out and could be extremely violent. I also met Big Tracy (another Terry) who became a lifelong friend. Tall and well-built, Tracy was another queen who wouldn't stand any nonsense. Scouse Terry continued to lose his temper about nothing, and in a rage one evening he started on me. Roy immediately sorted him out with the help of Tracy, who actually sat on Terry to calm him down. Roy later suggested it'd be best if My Terry departed in the morning. That's exactly what happened. It was sad. I was truly fond of him. I thought about him often, and still do, and tried to contact him. But I never saw or heard from him again.

Meanwhile, I'd no luck getting a ship. At that time of year most vessels were away for the winter. Lee was delighted and the fun continued. We'd have a few drinks at home, call a taxi and he'd make a Grand Entrance at the Lord Roberts, our favourite gay pub. We were so close he'd get upset when I went home to see my parents. Lee absolutely loved Christmas, which was getting near. He hoped I wouldn't get a ship and would spend the festive holidays with them. However, *Northern Star* was due back December 17th, 1972. When I visited the Pool, they offered me a bedroom steward's job, which I had to take. It was a relief really, being short of money. It solved a dilemma too: upset Lee if I spent Christmas at home, or upset my parents if I didn't. Lee was unhappy but understood. You could only say no three times with the Pool.

I rejoined *Northern Star*, signing on December 18th, 1972, pleased to see lots of old friends. Even before the *Star* departed, we were having fun sailing day visiting the Lord Roberts with Gracie for a few drinks. The pub looked beautiful with all the Christmas decorations. As we left, landlady June gave Gracie a small decorated

Christmas tree for his cabin. Two hours later we turned to for embarkation, sucking mints, trying to look sensible, greeting passengers and showing them to cabins. Another memorable Christmas, although I remember little of it. Booze flowed freely, and everyone had a ball. I can't even recall what ports we visited!

A few days before Southampton, BRSs were told that on the next voyage our sections were increasing to five five-berth cabins, plus five six-berth cabins: a total of fifty bunks. It sounded like extremely hard work, so I handed in my notice. Later Chief Officer Ken Rakin said he was sorry to see me leave. I explained why and he said a hospital attendant's job was available with a single-berth cabin. I asked what it involved, as I'd no medical knowledge. He said I'd be looking after the surgeon's cabin, cleaning the hospital and so on. It sounded good to me, especially the bit about a single cabin; I could get up to all sorts of mischief. I called at the hospital and introduced myself to Dr Saxton, the senior surgeon. We had an amiable chat after which he told me, "You've got the job, Michael. Welcome to the team." The hospital was staffed by a senior surgeon, who mainly cared for passengers; a junior doctor, baby doc, who mainly took crew surgeries; and two nursing sisters. I soon learnt that, like crew, senior officers, including the medical team, were fond of a drink in those days, although it *never* interfered with work.

January 3rd, 1973, *Northern Star* docked in Southampton. I quickly stripped my section, took linen to the laundry and finished off. I reported to the hospital, to be shown round rapidly by the departing hospital attendant. He introduced me again to surgeon Dr Saxton, a dear old gentleman, and the two nursing sisters. On promenade deck he showed me round the isolation hospital, brig and his (now mine) single cabin, handed me the keys and departed. Reporting back to the hospital, my uniform was sorted: a white smock-like jacket, with hospital attendant epaulettes. As there was nothing further for me to do, I finished early.

# 12

# 'Florence Flightingale'

Home at Lee's, as we enjoyed a few drinks, I excitedly mentioned I'd taken the hospital attendant's job for the world voyage. He fell about laughing, thinking it positively hilarious. "They're never going to let a lunatic like *you* loose in a hospital?" He chortled and, as usual, he got me laughing too. Later, we visited the Lord Roberts. He made his usual entrance and ordered drinks. Trying not to collapse in hysterics, he pointed at me, saying to landlady June, "Have you met my friend, Florence Flightingale?" Cackling with laughter, he thought it hysterical. Later when Roy arrived home Lee was still chuckling about it; he did have a strange sense of humour at times. After Lee went to bed, I sat chatting with Roy, having drinks. I was shocked when he asked if I'd like to sleep with him. "Definitely not," I said. "What would Lee think?" Roy said Lee would be fine, as long as it was a friend. I thought it wasn't right; I'd better check with Lee next day. Sure enough, he was more than happy about it, in fact positively encouraging: "I don't mind bona friends like you making my

Roy boy happy." From then on I slept with Roy occasionally. He was well-equipped, willing, versatile (took it like a toast rack) and extremely hot. This cosy arrangement suited us all, until my Dominic came along!

It'd be an understatement to describe their open relationship as unconventional. Although they truly loved each other, Roy was promiscuous, and bisexual, with a proclivity for young men. Lee was happy for him to sleep with other guys he liked, especially young ones, as it kept him away from women. Lee was fond of women, with many female friends. But he most definitely didn't want Roy to have sex with them. They were both slightly kinky voyeurs and enjoyed watching sexual activity. Initially I was rather appalled. However, though slightly ashamed to admit it, I enjoyed watching porn, thinking, *What is so wrong about watching it live?* Apparently there were a few peepholes around the house. Roy would also bring young men to their downstairs bedroom, where we could watch a live performance through a crack in the curtains. It was a right turn-on. I laughed one day when Debbie, who was stood on the window ledge for a good view, got so excited, he fell off!

Over a relatively short time we'd become very close. I adored Lee and it was mutual. I'd never met anyone so interesting and amusing. He said one of the things he most liked about me was that I wasn't always on the lookout for sex. Most of his gay friends were like *bitches on heat*, he said: all they thought about was cock; I didn't. Which was true. I'd rather have a night out, a bit of camp fun, or a good meal, than go hunting for dick. Another thing he loved laughing about with me – my eyes swivelled a little when I'd had a few drinks. I was born slightly boss-eyed, having an eye operation to correct this. After the op I only looked out of one eye at a time. Consequently, when I've had a few drinks they'd start to swivel, which Lee found absolutely hilarious – the swivelling ogles!

Daytime alongside on the *Star*, I worked by on board, usually 9:00a.m. to 5:00p.m. I decided to give the hospital a good clean and polish. The day before sailing, Lee said he and Roy would meet me on the ship around 4:00p.m. for a look round. I met them at the gangway, showing them my cabin, and left them there while I went back to work. Later Roy went for a wander, and Lee met me down the hospital while I finished the last of the polishing. To my surprise, Lee told me they loved my little cabin, and they'd tried out the bed for sex. I was pleased, as it didn't happen often.

Later Lee was sat by the hospital door talking to me, when it opened. The captain, in civvies, put his head through. He asked Lee, "Are any of the medical staff about?" "Only *her*," said Lee, pointing to me. "Hello, Michael," the master said, smiling. "Nothing important. I'll call again tomorrow." When I told Lee it was the captain, he was in absolute stitches. "Only her." He laughed, adding he hoped it wouldn't cause me any trouble. I told him not to worry, our Old Man would be fine.

January 5th, 1973, I sailed as hospital attendant on *Northern Star* on a usual round trip to Australia. The hospital had male and female wards with six beds each, a waiting room, consulting room, operating theatre, X-ray machine, dispensary, sluice and such. On promenade deck aft of my cabin were male and female six-bed isolation wards. On the opposite side of the deck was the brig (ship's prison). It had a metal sink and toilet so that occupants couldn't hurt themselves. This place was the master at arms' responsibility.

My single cabin was isolated aft (at the back end) of the promenade deck, with a porthole and a bunk high off the deck (useful later). Before sailing, I decided to make it cosier: more elegant, comfortable, but modern and bright. I bought a colourful rug, soft bedspread, cushions, and a table lamp. Pleased with the result, I invited Gracie and Elaine to join me for a drink, to see what they thought. After a couple of drinks, I said, "Well, what do you think?" Gracie replied, "It'd be very nice, dear, if it was a *kitchen*!" *Bitch*, I thought. *She's only jealous I've got a single cabin!*

My job involved keeping the entire hospital clean, plus taking care of the senior surgeon's cabin. I also collected and served patients' meals. I'd give the old boy an early call with a tray of tea. Dr Saxton later held morning and afternoon surgeries. When finished, I'd tidy up the consulting room, emptying bins, cleaning and changing covers on the examination table. We'd an out of hours bell, manned by whoever was on call. Sometimes that was me, although there was always a doctor or nurse available. Passengers paid for consultations, medicines, and injections if they were seasick. However, to passengers with D&V (diarrhoea and vomiting) I gave a bag containing a bottle of K&M (kaolin and morphine), Lomotil tablets, and a short course of antibiotics. (Can you believe!)

K&M was wonderful stuff: morphine eased cramps and kaolin thickened up the poo a treat. I believe it contained actual morphine. Maybe that's why it made you feel so good. Not surprisingly, it's banned now.

Plenty of lads visited my isolated cabin. I didn't exactly have a turnstile, shouting, "Next," but nevertheless I had many visitors. There was a cute, young, well-built, athletic, dark-haired waiter. He was absolutely uninhibited. We'd get naked. I'd lay on my bunk, then he'd sit astride me on my dick while I enjoyed his muscular physique and smooth skin. Eventually we'd both climax: a happy ending, so horny and exciting.

In the Pig, crew would ask me about medical problems, or visit my cabin to ask (perfect excuse). One evening a good-looking mate of Chico's, who allegedly had a bigger dick than him, dropped in. It was obvious he was conspicuously horny, and interested. I was surprised, as he was dating a girl at the time. I thought it would be a blow job only; he'd probably be far too big and long for me to take. We stripped, and he sat on the edge of my tall bunk. I stood between his legs, going down on his beautiful cock, which I struggled to get in my mouth. It was enormous and of considerable length. Gently, he leaned back and to my surprise I felt my cock press against his arse and slide in. It was sensational; the way he moaned and squirmed, he loved it too.

One day a young queen, another (Slack) Alice (Alan) called to see me, saying she'd a sore dish (arse). Would I take a look? Being so popular and a *size queen*, I wasn't surprised, but was not relishing the thought of vardering her slack, heaving gash. I suggested she attend crew surgery, to see our understanding baby doc. Next time I saw Alice, I asked how he got on. "Well, dear," he said, "I told the doc I'd a sore bottom and he asked me to take my trousers down to examine me. He asked exactly where was it hurting, and I said at the entrance. He told me it's an exit, not an entrance, and you'd do well to remember that. In the meantime he gave me some ointment."

"That's bona, dear," I said, trying to keep a straight face.

The Pig was always busy and we arranged some great crew shows during the voyage. We staged another February Frock-Along with old routines like 'Thoroughly Modern Millie', plus new ones like 'Perfect Young Ladies' from *The Boy Friend*. Queens *and* the ladies performed, which always added to the fun and a little confusion. Mark the Stripper did a couple of routines and was extremely entertaining. There were various other acts. Horseface, with Desire and Candy, performed 'I Feel Pretty' from *West Side Story*. He mimed singing while looking at his *cod eke* in a mirror. It brought the house down. Other shows during the voyage were very ambitious, like 'The Ascot Gavotte' from *My Fair Lady*, which included some of the lads dancing with us. We also performed 'His Love Makes Me Beautiful' from *Funny Girl*. I played the Pregnant Bride. Again, some of our lovely young crew members joined in as singing, dancing bridegrooms, bless them.

Although having lots of fun and sex, I still yearned to be boxed off and in love with someone special. I though this had happened when I met Barry, a good-looking guy, who was excellent company and a talented artist. We had a fling for a number of months, in Sydney visiting Les Girls for drinks, dinner and so on. Some of the queens called him Barry Birdcage, which refers to rimming; I think he'd been caught *in flagrante delicto*. He did have some very strange ways. Inevitably, it all sort of fizzled out; I wasn't particularly heartbroken.

Hospital work varied. With no patients, easy. But with more than four patients, hard work. Outward bound I'd had kids with chicken pox in the isolation hospital, which meant feeding them, extra cleaning, sanitising. During the voyage a lady who became a bit bonkers was admitted. I'd never encountered anyone like that before, and I found the poor woman hard to deal with, especially at mealtimes. One week an old gentleman was admitted. He was so ill he was only allowed to suck ice. I took him some ice one day, cheerfully saying, "Here's your lunch, sir," but couldn't wake him. I fetched a nurse, who said, "Don't worry, Michael, he's passed. You can help me lay him out." I was absolutely horrified. I'd never even seen a dead body before, never mind help *lay him out*. I was feeling a little hysterical. Nurse told me to go to the 'medical comforts locker' and have a glug of brandy. After a couple of good swigs, I thought, *Let's do it*, and went to help her. I won't go into details, though it felt strange shaving and washing him so he'd look presentable for his poor wife.

Working in the hospital was a real learning curve. An Irish nurse, Mo, showed me how to take X-rays wearing a lead apron and how to develop them, though they were quite primitive. She also taught me many medical bits and pieces. We'd clean operating theatre equipment with ether, which made me feel wonderfully high. I discovered a good sniff of oxygen worked wonders for dreadful hangovers, although it didn't last long. Sister Mo seemed ferocious but deep down she was a really good, caring nurse. I laughed one day when Flo (Bernie) came down with chest pains, saying, "I think I'm having a heart attack." Mo examined him, declaring, "No, you're not." Flo was most indignant. "Oh yes, I am. And if I die, it'll be all your fault," he said, flouncing off. Mo was right, Flo only had bruised ribs.

We would take turns covering the afternoon emergency bell, usually 3:00 to 5:00p.m. One afternoon, a young Aussie girl rang the bell. When I asked if I could help, she looked embarrassed, saying, "No, it's personal, mate. I need to see a doctor." Calling at the surgeon's cabin, I told him a young lady wanted to see him. "Oh hell, Michael," he said, "can't you deal with it?" "No," I said. "She wants a doctor." After consultation, she left looking even more embarrassed. Tiding up the consulting room, I 'accidentally' read the open log book: "Removal of Tampax from vagina." No wonder she looked embarrassed. Answering the emergency bell I also saw a few gruesome things, especially crew injuries. I just had to deal with it and, with the rest of the team, do our best for our patients.

Waitresses on board turned out to be great fun. They certainly knew how to party. I befriended many. Jeanie, who also stayed at Lee and Roy's, became a close friend.[5] There were some great characters among them, too. Helen was very posh, with a double-barrelled surname and a rich, camp sense of humour. We had a lot of laughs and became extremely fond of each other. One evening when the crew bar closed, we went to my cabin for a nightcap, both rather drunk. She was telling me how she adored me, prompting me to tell her I felt the same

---

5   She still calls round to see us now.

way. We kissed. Mother Nature intervened, we became aroused, and our kisses intensified; the next minute we were stripping off and climbed onto my bunk. I knew exactly what to do this time, fondling her breasts, sucking her nipples, and we indulged in passionate sex, despite the large amount of alcohol consumed.

Next day I was absolutely mortified. Other queens considered it totally taboo and shocking for a queen to have sex with a female, worse than *tootsie trade* (sex between two passive men). I worried what they'd think if they found out. Would their attitude towards me change? Would I be ostracised? Thankfully Helen was extremely discreet, keeping our little secret. We stayed the best of friends. The encounter made me think I must still be a little bisexual. It gave me a better understanding of straight/married guys who indulged in sex with gay men.

It happened again with another stewardette, who was a sweet girl and adored me. She would join me in the bar. I asked her why didn't she sit with the lads. "They're only after one thing. You're different." I thought, *I'm definitely different*, though that isn't what she meant. Once again, after too much drink, the same thing happened. We finished up enjoying sex in my cabin. I assumed she was on the pill. As I was climaxing inside, she suddenly said, "Be careful, I'm not on the pill." By this time it was too late and I was mortified. This time I was doubly worried and there were a few anxious weeks until I could relax. It was the last time it happened on the *Star*. I made sure it didn't happen again.

Finally, the voyage came to an end May 19th, 1973, and *Northern Star* docked in Southampton. I paid off, spent a brief time with Lee and Roy, then went home, for a welcome, though short, leave. I enjoyed catching up with events at home and abroad; we sometimes missed out on things being away. The Vietnam War, thankfully, had come to an end that January. Britain joined the European Economic Community. And a new tax known as VAT was introduced. In the charts were Dawn and Tony Orlando's 'Tie a Yellow Ribbon Round the Old Oak Tree'. The best-selling album at the time was released, Pink Floyd's *The Dark Side of the Moon*, which was listened to on ships for many years. At the movies people were watching *The Godfather*, and *The Poseidon Adventure*. They hadn't shown *that* one on the ship yet!

# 13

# The Focks Mutiny

Leave finished, I returned to Southampton, spending a few happy days at Lee's. Another place to go on nights out was the wonderful Bishops Waltham Country Club. It was run by Norman Evans, who was to become a dear friend, even going on cruises together later, until he passed away. Norman was a most interesting man, clever, highly amusing and endlessly kind. He didn't have a camp name, though he was known as Prinnie when he ran 'Prinnie's Nightclub'. He had an amazing life, served in the Merchant Navy and went on to run many successful businesses. He had a very quirky home in Portswood, Southampton, with sloping floors and pissed windows, holding wonderfully outrageous lunches for crowds of friends. He also later had a home in France. When he ran the Bishops Waltham Country Club in the 1960s, it was extremely popular with everyone: gays, straights, even police. At that time, by law, bars were forced to close between 3:00p.m. and 5:30p.m. Not Norman's club, though. Being in the sticks and a club, they kept it open most of the time; apparently even cops popped in for an afternoon drink. Stars like Diana Dors appeared there in cabaret. There was also a resident drag act, Lee

Sutton, who was a truly amazing funny man, with a hilarious act. He even recorded some long-playing records in the 1970s.[6] We spent many happy evenings there, from what I can remember!

I rejoined *Northern Star* May 29th, 1973, again as hospital attendant, sailing May 31st. It was good to be back on board and cruising down the Medi. New crew joined: Dusty, another queen with an outrageous character, became a lifelong friend. Stocky, half-Irish, half-Canadian, had ginger hair, and mischievous twinkle in his eyes. He swore like a trooper and was incredibly funny. We were friends until his death a few years ago.

Dear old Dr Saxton was again the surgeon in charge of the hospital. Next to his bed he'd a table lamp turned on by the socket switch, where the back of the plug was hanging off. One morning as I served his morning tea, bearing in mind he often had a hangover, I fumbled in semi-darkness to turn the light on. I didn't notice the back of the plug had fallen off. My finger touched the live wires. I screamed my tits off. The tray flew in the air, landing on his bed, and the poor man was covered in hot tea, milk and sugar. Rudely awakened from his slumbers, he jumped up, yelling, "Oh my good gawd! What's happening?" I apologised, explained and quickly cleaned up. The plug was mended the same day, and looking back, it was so funny. *Northern Star* was cruising down the Medi and good times as usual: glorious weather and great ports. Evenings in the bar were fun, even managing to squeeze in a few shows.

Between cruises overnight, I'd see Lee and we'd go out. It was around this time with Lee I discovered an outrageous restaurant in Palmerston Road, German Edie's. German Edie owned and ran the place while drinking brandy out of piss pots and male urine bottles, to shock customers. She only had three things on

---

6   One of these can be found on YouTube: *Lee Sutton (A Near Miss?) - Drag For Camp Fo'lowers.*

the menu: steaks, omelette, and 'homosexual chicken' (chicken in a pale creamy sauce). Her poor, long-suffering husband cooked. It was unbelievable some of the things she did. If you wore a tie she liked, she'd snip it off and hang it in the restaurant! She also emptied dirty ash trays out the front door of the restaurant, indiscriminately tossing the contents out, regardless of passersby. A truly outrageous woman.

Another place we visited at night in between cruises was a nightclub, the Continental. It was upstairs in Southampton High Street, more or less opposite the old Dolphin Hotel. The premises were on two floors: a disco on the top floor and a bar with booths on the second floor. As far as I can remember, the booths had telephones and you could call a nearby booth if you saw someone you fancied. It was here for the first time I met the famous Pagan, ex-*Caronia*, *Andes* and *QE2*. (While on *Caronia* he dragged up as Cleopatra and was carried ashore in Norway by crew dressed as Nubian slaves!) He was on the dance floor in drag looking absolutely fabulous, dancing to a current disco hit, the 'Popcorn' song by Hot Butter. I was well impressed. Though I never sailed with him, I met him many times over the years. A good-looking, mixed-race person and a kind, sweet man. He lived in a nearby suburb, Portswood, near a busy *cottage* where he was pretty much a fixture!

I recall hearing sad news in June 1973 when P&O announced *Canberra* was unsuitable for world cruising and was to be sold for scrap. How wrong they were to be proved. During our second cruise, I was sent for by the accommodation officer. The captain's tiger (Elaine) was going on leave and would I like to take over for three cruises? It was lovely Captain Morrison. I jumped at the chance. Elaine was pleased it was me. On July 1st, 1973, I took over as tiger. I knew what was expected; he was a great old man and very amiable. All went well, and I loved the job, especially passenger cocktail parties held in his cabin. An officers' steward helped me, usually Alice. We had a great time. When the Old Man went to the salon for dinner, a waiter served his table and we tidied up the cabin, taking the chance to chuck a few gins down our screech! During the trip, Captain Morrison told me he was going on leave in Southampton and a Captain Focks was taking over. Elaine had already warned me he was due, having previously sailed with him on *Andes*. She didn't have much good to say about the new captain, except he was old-fashioned and strict. 'Old-fashioned' can mean many different things; I felt apprehensive.

When the new captain joined, everything went fairly well at first, although I felt he didn't like me. Perhaps he thought I was too young to be a tiger, after the older ones on *Andes*. He made me feel uncomfortable. On the evening of the captain's cocktail party, I'd prepared and laid out his evening uniform as usual. When changed, he brusquely told me I'd pinned his medals on incorrectly. Apologising profusely, I admitted not knowing the correct way. He looked at me with utter contempt, and showed me how to pin them the right way.

Things were about to go even more downhill! *Northern Star* visited Venice, docking alongside, far nearer the centre than ships do today. It was the first time I'd been to Venice and I looked forward to going ashore. After lunch I politely asked the Old Man if it was acceptable for the officers' steward to serve his afternoon tea, as I'd like to go ashore. "No," he said coldly. "That's what the company pay *you* to do."

I went for a stroll anyway, stopping for a drink in a bar near the ship. Crew going ashore asked if I was going into town. "No," I said. "That miserable old sod insists I serve his afternoon tea." Dusty joined me for a drink, having a good laugh as usual, then another drink and another and another. Before long I was becoming extremely intoxicated. For the first time in my life, I rebelled, deciding I *wasn't* going back to serve the miserable captain his sodding tea. I fell into a dreadful drunken state, not remembering anything until waking up the next morning, feeling extremely hungover, embarrassed and slightly ashamed. I realised I'd not only missed his tea, I'd missed the rest of the whole day!

Turning to next morning, I shakily took in the Old Man's tea tray, apologising profusely. I explained I'd got carried away ashore and was extremely sorry. His reaction was frosty and sullen. I didn't blame him really, I'd let him down and myself. Later, a deck officer visited me. I knew them all well and almost apologetically he told me I was to be *logged* that morning, meaning face a disciplinary hearing in front of the captain. My misdemeanour: "being absent from duty without suitable reason." I could be docked wages. This and my appalling behaviour would be noted in the ship's Official Daily Log.

The hearing took place in the officers' wardroom, with captain and senior officers seated behind a flag-covered table. A master at arms called me in to stand before them. The charge was read out and I was asked if I had anything to say. Being guilty, I didn't. The Old Man decided my punishment was forfeiting a day's pay. Not a severe punishment, however I was so upset he'd actually logged his own tiger. It was unheard of; there's usually such a bond. Departing, I tearfully muttered to myself, "Rotten pig." Judging by the way a few officers smiled, it must have been louder than I thought. He was to be captain the following cruise; I immediately handed in my notice. He was extremely frosty towards me the remainder of the trip. The atmosphere was dreadful. I was relieved to pay off July 29th, 1973. Happily, crew discharge books had changed in November 1972. They no longer bore ships' stamps for ability and conduct. My dear captain friend was unable to give me a 'double DR' (declined to report – meaning a bad discharge).

Little did I know my next ship was to be one of the most famous, iconic liners in the world and is now a floating hotel, albeit not sailing.

# 14

# 'Queen of the Seas'

The year 1973 was another with excellent music and films, with a Roberta Flack chart-topper, 'Killing Me Softly with His Song'. At the movies was a scary horror film, *The Exorcist*. I paid off *Northern Star* July 29th, 1973, which made Lee extremely happy. We'd become extremely close. If he didn't have a room for me, there was a spare bed in their private bedroom. This was extremely kind but not ideal. Lee snored like a warthog! After I'd been home to see my folks, I returned to Southampton and Lee's. It was easy to find. You walked out the north side of Central Station, crossed Commercial Road and straight up Hill Lane. I could do it with my eyes closed. I was getting to know Southampton well, liking the city a lot.

We had wonderful days for weeks, sitting in the kitchen, drinking, having a laugh, going to the Lord Roberts pub and so on. We slipped back into our happy routine. I'd visit the Pool in Canute Road, to see if there were any ships. The Pool was near the Canute Hotel, where a sign reads, "Near this spot in AD 1028 Canute reproved his Courtiers." (Southampton has much interesting history.) I only worked on passenger liners then and was particular about what ships I sailed on. Around this period I met Roy's brother Tony, who was gay, though not a queen; a *gay homie*. Lee would loved to have boxed me off with him. "You'd be my sister-in-law, dear." But although he was a kind, good-humoured guy, he *definitely* wasn't my type.

Lee loved musicals. When he heard Angela Lansbury was appearing at London's Piccadilly Theatre in *Gypsy*, Arthur Laurents's musical fable about Gypsy Rose Lee, the world-famous stripper, Lee instructed Roy to book us tickets. Show night, we took the British Rail train to London Waterloo, then the underground to Leicester Square. It was a short walk to the mixed Salisbury pub in St Martin's Lane for a few drinks, of course. Then on to the Piccadilly Theatre to see the show. I'd never seen a live musical before. It was a new experience for me and I absolutely adored it, starting a lifelong love of stage musicals. Strangely at this time I saw a newspaper picture of Liberace and Danny La Rue backstage at the Piccadilly Theatre with Angela Lansbury in December 1973. In later years I would get to know Danny, with an odd connection to them both.

During this period Lee was drinking extremely heavily during the day, which would upset Roy if Lee was drunk before he arrived home. I suggested therefore we invoke a new house rule: *No drinking before 5:00p.m.* I even made a poster to this effect to stick on the kitchen wall, where Lee drank, next to the clock. All went well for a while. Later, Roy was asked to wallpaper upstairs at the Lord Roberts pub. I went along to help him. (I'd helped Dad, can you believe.) The pub owners, Mike and June (Flicker), knew me by then. Finishing about 4:00p.m., we drove home. Finding Lee had already had quite a few, I reprimanded him. "What about this house rule? No drinking before five?" He started laughing, pointing to the clock; he'd stuck *fives* over every number! We had to laugh too; he was utterly incorrigible.

As usual Lee didn't want me to ship out when my leave finished. However, money was running low; I had to do something. He kept saying how I'd be much better off working in the galley (ship's kitchen). Money was good and I wouldn't have to depend on tips. "You'll be the only queen in the galley. All the cooks will adore you, darling." He talked me into visiting Cunard, to see if there were any jobs on *QE2*. He said it was the best ship in the world, a proper *Queen of the Seas*. It also called regularly into New York, which he absolutely adored, always telling me how wonderful a place it was. I'd never been interested. New York sounded crowded and noisy to me but I was curious to see it. Eventually I paid a visit to the Cunard office in the massive South Western House on the corner of Terminus Terrace and Canute Road.

This magnificent building was constructed 1865 as the Imperial Hotel, adjacent to the terminus docks railway station. In 1871 it was acquired by the London and South Western Railway, to be renamed the South Western Hotel. Being adjacent to the docks, it was ideal for passengers joining ocean liners. In fact, some passengers and officers from the ill-fated *Titanic* spent their last night here before joining the ship. During WWII it was acquired by the government and used as a military intelligence establishment. It was renamed HMS Shrapnel, after Henry Shrapnel. (In 1784 he invented the exploding shell; the fragments were give the name shrapnel. Although born in Wiltshire, he ended his days in Pear Tree House, Southampton.) After WWII the building was acquired by Cunard, later by the BBC, and finally in 1997 sold to be converted into luxury apartments.

I visited the Cunard crew personnel office, showing them my City and Guilds Cookery Certificates. However, the only galley job available next trip was night baker. Thinking it would be a foot in the door, I accepted. Following a strict medical and visiting the Canute Street Pool and Latimer Street Seaman's Union for clearance and so on, I received joining instructions. Lee was absolutely thrilled and we had a celebratory drink. I took a train home to retrieve my chef's clothes. I broke the news I was joining the famous *QE2* to my parents; they were impressed.

*QE2* was 70,000 grt but looked absolutely massive on joining on August 18th, 1973. I found the crew office down in the Burma Road (working alleyway), was given a boat card and cabin key, and a two-berth latty, sharing with another night baker. Our working hours were 7:00p.m. to 7:00a.m. Later that evening I turned to for our night's work. First job was making a huge bread mixture for the next day's rolls and loaves. We tipped flour sacks into a huge mixer, plus dry ingredients, yeast, salt, shortening and so on. Mixing it well, we added warm water until it became smooth and elastic, then tipped out a massive lump of dough. I struggled to carry it to a work surface. We weighed pieces to put in 'coffin loaf' bread tins, making bread rolls using a machine, picking them up four at a time, to place on baking trays (I soon got the hang of that). Left to prove (rise) in warm proving ovens, they were then placed in main ovens, using long-handled flat shovels. Opening the oven door, intense heat scorched my eyebrows; I soon learnt to stand well back.

Work went on much like this all night long, making about 1,800 bread rolls and hundreds of loaves for the 1,800-plus passengers and 1,000-plus crew. We also made fresh bagels, which I'd never heard of. They were unknown then, not like today. To my knowledge Southampton didn't have any kosher restaurants, though there may have been kosher shops in St Mary's Street, an area I rarely frequented. *QE2* carried a small percentage of Jewish passengers from the US. They were attracted by the kosher kitchen, restaurant area and even a synagogue!

We cooked other things, like croissants and bloomers for other chefs, who made sandwiches for private customers (*bloods*), like barmen. Chefs were paid for this. They paid us for the bread; everyone got a cut. I realised later it was a big thing on board. Money was king, trickling down, everyone getting a share. Even deck crew had money-making schemes by screwing down large opening portholes and windows. To dump gash, barmen had to pay deckhands to unscrew them to throw out the gash. (It was all thrown in the sea then, though that's now illegal.)

During the evening we were given a break, a chance for a pint. I noticed the bar also served spirits and to my surprise also served it in bottles. There were a number of busy crew bars; a couple of ordinary Pig & Whistles on decks 1 and 2. One was open most of the day. The other one opened different hours for watch keepers. Plus there was the Dhobi Arms near the laundry aft down the Burma Road. It was only a dispense bar; you sat on beer barrels in the Burma Road to drink. Drinks were available most of the day. Crew from certain areas sat together. For example, there was a Scouse table and a Belfast table, with all the usual banter and rivalry. It felt strange sitting in a crew bar in chef's clothes. I thought if only the *girls* on the *Star* could see me now! After I left *QE2* another late-night bar/nightclub opened, The Castaways, allegedly with a reputation as a gay bar.

Being a night worker, when we docked in New York five days later, I'd all day free ashore. What a place! All I'd heard about it was true and more, with an unbelievable atmosphere. It was like no place I'd ever been. So much to see, to do. With wonderful people, some of them quite bizarre. No wonder Lee loved it. It was a place you'd want to visit again and again. I wandered up Manhattan's infamous 42nd Street, awash with movie houses, including porn cinemas, peep shows, sex shops and so on. A notorious porn movie, *Deep Throat* starring Linda Lovelace, had just been released and banned in twenty-six states. I just had to watch and it was a hoot! She was supposed to have a clitoris in her throat, deep-throating cocks. I don't know what all the fuss was about. Us queens had been deep-throating for years! I wandered up to famous Times Square, seeing the Empire State Building, Chrysler Building and other sights. Truly amazing. I too fell in love with New York and the American people, who were extremely kind, friendly and generous.

I loathed working nights though, finding it impossible to sleep during the day. I'd hear crew walking along alleyways, doors slamming. Plus while working at night, everyone was up the Pig enjoying themselves. Departing New York, I gave notice, after just one trip. The head chef, who was always charming with me, invited me to his office. He'd guessed I didn't like nights, mentioning next trip a vegetable cook's job would be available. I jumped at it, saying "Yes, please. I love cooking vegetables." Back in Southampton we docked for an overnight stay (*QE2* did in those days). I changed to a day cooks' cabin. My new cabin mate seemed pleasant, but again, he was straight. That evening I had drinks with Lee, telling him all about my trip, huge lumps of dough, singed eyelashes and so on. As usual he was in stitches about the whole thing. Next day I sailed back to New York.

On my return to the ship, I fully expected to be preparing large amounts of vegetables, but not bloody mountains of the stuff. We prepared sackfuls, filling large plastic bins with carrots, peas and the like. These we dragged to huge boilers to cook. They weighed a ton. I needed help just to tip them in. After work I'd go for a beer, noticing a few queens in the bar, sitting with them for a chat. It appeared there wasn't much social life on this ship. It was all work, work, and money. Because they finished so late, most hadn't even changed out of their work clothes. Docking in New York, the chief veg cook instructed me to fill the boilers and turn them on to boil; *Port Health*, I thought. Wooden crates arrived dangling with seaweed. I asked cook, "What's in them?" (I should have guessed.) Prising open the lid, he pulled out a large *live* lobster, waving it in my face. I jumped back, screaming my tits off. Then he told me to boil them, alive! I said "Sorry, I just couldn't. You'll have to get someone else to do it."

At some point I saw the *Canberra* in New York, thinking she looked so beautiful and wishing I was there instead of on this thing. P&O must have changed their mind about scrapping her. She was also cruising from New York, though it wasn't a great success. Marketing was by Cunard and bookings for *Canberra* extremely low, probably because the bulk of the passengers were put on *QE2* instead of *Canberra*. She was laid up for a while, then continued, finishing her New York cruising season. Although P&O were going to scrap her, there was an upsurge of UK cruise bookings in 1973. Later that year *Canberra* went for a ten-week refit to be converted for full-time cruising, taking over from *Orsova* for a busy 1974 UK cruising season.

I really disliked working on *QE2*; such long hours and little social life or fun. I also hated the veg cook job and handed in my notice again. Chef sent for me again, making me sit almost on his lap, asking, "What's the matter this time?" I told him cooking veg wasn't me and as for cooking those hideous lobsters, I just couldn't. He asked would I like a pantryman's job? I'd be preparing melon, grapefruit, making coffee, tea, toast, that sort of thing. It sounded fine. I accepted the job.

Arrival Southampton. I went to Lee's, telling all about the veg cook's job and hideous lobsters. He thought it all hysterically funny as usual. Later, having drinks in the kitchen, he surprised me by saying I'd look marvellous as a blonde. Foolishly I let him talk me into it, bleaching my hair white, then dyeing it ash blonde, fairly unusual for a man at that time. Next day on board looking so different, everyone thought I was a new crew member!

The tourist cold pantryman's job was fine. First evening: preparing starters, fruit, coffee and so on for dinner. Next morning I was behind the tourist galley breakfast press, again preparing fruit, plus urns of tea/coffee, toast and flapjacks. Toast was cooked in a revolving toaster, halved, placed in two-way hot drawers; waiters helped themselves. I also made white and wholemeal flapjacks, again placing them in two-way hot drawers. This was all done simultaneously and was extremely hectic, with me singing *Gypsy* numbers. The chefs all thought a singing blonde cook amusing, nicknaming me Baby Jane. This was a reference to the Bette Davis and Joan Crawford movie *Whatever Happened to Baby Jane?* They had it slightly wrong though. I was actually singing about Baby June from *Gypsy*. It was just too hectic, so once again, I saw the head chef, asking for a job change. He almost sat me on his lap! I wasn't sure if he was gay or bi – unusual for a head chef. I think he just a *camp homie*. I'd met many guys who were straight, but loved gays, all the camp, even learning Polari. Today I still meet guys I knew on the ships, coming out with things like, "How bona to varder your dolly eke," and the like. He asked me if I'd like an especially good, easy job available: pantryman in the Queen's Grill. I said, "Yes, please."

    Back at Lee's, I told him about my hectic trip in the cold pantry. As usual he found it highly amusing, chuckling, "You need to be like the Hindu *palone* with multiple arms (Durga) in *that* job, dear." I had to laugh, confessing cooking aboard ship really wasn't me. And being the only gay in the galley, sharing with straight guys, would make trade almost impossible. I'd probably sign off the next trip. But my Queen's Grill pantry job turned out to be brilliant: sedate, classy and easy, with just one-meal seating. I was just preparing little silver toast racks, filling delicate bone china tea and coffee pots, and so on. At the end of the voyage I also received a bona *dropsy* (tip) from the waiters. It was a one-trip relief job though. The regular guy was due back, which suited me. I was leaving anyway, wanting a waiter or steward job. I handed in my notice. The hotel officer heard I wanted a steward's job and said positions were available. October 2nd, 1973, I signed off, signing on again as a waiter.

Cunard supplied most of the waiters' uniforms, which were smart, dark red jackets with Cunard ties and bowties. Cabins were very basic: two- and four-berth. Being new, I was allocated a four-berth one down on deck 6. Only the indoor pools on deck 7 were lower! Thankfully crew come and go, so there'd be a chance to get a two-berth cabin. A few queens worked in tourist, many more in first class, making it relatively easy to arrange a gay cabin mate. Instead of *peak boys*, Cunard actually employed *glory hole stewards*. (Old liners' vast crew dormitories, housing as many as thirty-six, were called *glory holes*.) These guys had enormous influence allocating cabins. Once more it was all about money. Give the glory hole steward a good dropsy, and he'd arrange your choice of cabin and cabin mate. It was the same all over the ship. If you didn't give platehouse men a dropsy, they'd make it difficult for a waiter to get clean crockery.

As a new waiter, I started in the tourist-class Britannia restaurant. As normal, new staff were given tables furthest from the galley, an area nicknamed the *brickyard*. (The waiters walked with trays on their shoulders like bricklayers.) The best tables were near the galley; food would be hot and fresh. The brickyard being furthest to walk to, the food was lukewarm when it got to passenger tables. We worked in teams of two, serving two sittings of sixteen passengers, with help from a commis waiter. Despite food being mainly plated, not silver service, it was hard work. With two sittings, meal service was hectic. The galley was a tiny service galley; it was the former Look Out Bar. You should have seen faces of the cooks when they saw me the other side of the hot press. They were astonished, saying, "Here, how come you's a cook one minute, a waiter the next? I expect *Miss*

*Fillips* gave you the job." Mr Fillips was the outrageous gay chief catering officer, who had much influence. He wasn't very popular. However, he was kind to me, when I later got to know him through mutual friends Bobby and Patsy.

Lee had a good friend, Jewish Amber, Tony, from the cruise ship *Andes*. Lee asked me to connect with him: he'd be working in the first-class restaurant. I tracked down this fat little queen, saying to him, "Lee said to say hello and sends his love." Amber gave me a withering look, saying disinterestedly, "That's nice, dear," and wandering off. I thought, *Bold cow. Obviously he doesn't like younger queens*. Later we became good friends. He was extremely witty, with a wicked tongue and great fun. He understood and spoke Yiddish fluently working in the kosher section of the restaurant. I picked up some Yiddish from him. Lots of Polari is Yiddish. For example, wig was shyckle. (Sheitel is a wig worn by married Jewish women.) Schwartze is a Jewish, not racist, term for black people.

While at Lee's he'd told me about his long-time good gay friend Sherry. He lived in New York and if I got the time, I should go and visit him. Lee would call him and let him know I might. Next trip, when the ship docked, I had lunchtime off, so I gave Sherry a call, asking if he was free. He was. I had his address in Queens. Lee previously told me to take the Blue Subway train to get there. Sherry told me which station to get off at and that he'd meet me there. As we'd never met, I told him I'd be wearing blue flares and a lavender shirt. Arriving in Queens, as I left the station Sherry waved to me, introducing himself. "You managed to spot me then?" I said. "Honey, I couldn't miss you," he said, laughing, "Leonora's got to your riah; you like a f—ing Belisha beacon!" We went to a local bar for a few beers. He was a charming, amusing man. He'd worked at sea previously, obtained a job on a US ferry, and was now living in New York. We had a lovely afternoon, and kept in touch for years.

Between trips the *QE2* was in Southampton for long overnights. I'd visit Lee and Roy, of course. We'd have drinks in the house, then call in the Lord Roberts. On one trip, the landlady, June, asked me to buy her some extra-long eyelashes in New York. I bought six pairs, two for me. Next time we docked in Southampton, Lee and I had a few lunchtime drinks. He suggested we both wear a pair of the eyelashes to the pub *for a bit of camp*. Being tipsy I thought, why not? We ordered a taxi. The driver was absolutely astonished, and on our arrival we made a big entrance, killing ourselves laughing. Customers laughed, but it went down like a lead balloon with Madam June. She was *not* amused at us two silly tarts falling in the door at lunchtime wearing long black eyelashes. I think at first she thought we were taking the piss and wearing *her* eyelashes. Later when I gave her the unused new ones, she realised it was just *a bit of camp*. She forgave us and we had a good laugh about it.

Some evenings we'd visit a gay nightclub, the Magnum in St Mary's Street, Southampton. It opened in 1969 and was thought to be one the oldest gay clubs in the UK when it closed in 2004. Our dear friend David, who'd been to sea, ran it for many years. He became good friends with Danny La Rue and they both dined at our home in later years. We became friends with Danny.

One night in the club, we'd all had quite a few drinks and were dancing to a latest hit song, 'Monster Mash'. Tony, Roy's brother, was extremely drunk, dancing in the most peculiar manner, jerking violently and waving his arms around excitedly. Lee said loudly, "Varder the monster," and we were in stitches. Because it was so amusing, Tony became known by us all as the Monster, though not in an unkind way and not to his face.

Around this time, at Lee's I met Pearl, who said he was a Romani Gypsy. His family were actually fairground people, with rides, stalls and slot machines in Battersea Park Fun Fair, London, since the 1951 Festival of Britain. He was fairly tall with dark hair, good-looking and extremely amusing. He lived in a large, classy mobile home in Rownhams, a leafy suburb of Southampton. He told me that his father, like mine, hated him because he was gay. When Pearl was young, fairground men sexually abused him in private, although in public they'd verbally abuse him for being gay. How true this was, I don't know. But the way things were in those days, it's quite possible. Pearl was a lovely man, though a terrible hypochondriac, always dying of something or other. Lee and I'd listen sympathetically to his 'maungeing', then Lee would say, "Oh how awful, dear. You poor thing. How you suffer!" In the end we'd start giggling and tittering, including Pearl.

While I was at Lee's, he introduced me to many friends, including Sharon (Barry), who'd worked on cargo boats with his mate Tuesday (Billy). Sharon was slightly older than me, good-looking, well-spoken, extremely cultured, and with impeccable taste. In the 1970s, when Royal Viking Line was formed, he took a job on that line. Their beautiful ships were exquisite, with one-meal seating throughout, sailing on exclusive world cruises. Following that he went on to work as butler in many rich, famous households in the UK and US. Later, he bought his own beautiful little boutique hotel in Torquay, where he's now retired. We are still dear friends to this day and we visit him in regularly in Torquay: such a delightful place. Thanks to him we later became friends with the celebrated prolific author Lesley Pearse, a delightful, amusing lady who also lives in Torquay. Billy, Tuesday, went on to become an extremely successful and world-renowned clairvoyant. He now lives in Babbacombe, Devon, still working as a famous medium.

*QE2* was really geared up for the large number of American passengers carried. They were demanding, but very generous. Ice was plentiful, and iced water was served every meal, to every passenger. Coffee was available at all times; some Americans drank it throughout their meals. Food was very good for tourist, with plenty of smoked salmon and even beluga caviar. Station head waiters served specials, like beef wellington, plus flambés like duck a l'orange, crêpes suzette and so on. Waiters had after-meal jobs. The worst jobs were allocated to newcomers like me. My job was hoovering what felt like an acre of the Britannia restaurant *brickyard* with a monster vacuum cleaner. It really was hard work *and* you had to wait until all passengers departed. I'd get so annoyed; other waiters were given easy jobs. One guy cleaned dumb waiters, which we all cleaned anyway. I muttered and mumbled loudly about hoovering being a "Japanese torture," much to Janis Joplin's amusement. (This was ex-P&O John, who'd joined and who was also hoovering.)

Sailing transatlantic (the so-called western oceans) in October, I found the sea was often rough. So after five days at sea it was a treat to dock in New York. I loved going ashore, to marvellous market diners, serving delicious food, beers, wine and cocktails. Some old New York waitresses were *so* rude and funny. If a customer left no tip, they'd say something like, "I guess you didn't enjoy the food sir, right? And I guess your mother probably wasn't married either?" Shops were full of things unavailable in UK: walkie-talkies, posh telephones, rare LPs, cheap Levis and so on. A large Salvation Army thrift shop, not far from where the ship docked, sold old furniture, including occasional antiques, old clocks and paintings. Queens bought these back to the UK, furnishing their homes, even selling some on. Amber's house in Mayflower Road was filled with beautiful antiques. He even built a sort of Roman-style porch with fake fibreglass marble pillars. It's still there today.

On board I befriended many well-known, infamous queens from the old *Queen Mary*, and Clarence House on the *Andes*. I'd heard about them on P&O and Shaw Savill, from people like Elaine, who'd sailed on *Andes*. Also, from gossip in the Pig, they'd become urban myths over the years. Sid (Cynthia/Slippery Sid) was a waiter in the Queen's Grill and became a good friend. Charming, elegant, well-spoken and smart, he always wore a tie. If he'd money, he was extremely generous, though sometimes he pulled strange stunts like forgetting his wallet when it was time to pay. He was also something of a mystery. Deeply into art and antiques, he claimed to be friends with Oliver Messel, the artist and interior designer, linked to royalty and to Cecil Beaton. Sid had 'suspect' friends too; I later unwittingly became involved in one of his dubious deals.

Bobby (who never had a camp name) was another Clarence House queen. So elegant and extremely good-looking, women swooned over him and men were instantly drawn to him. He worked as a butler in the luxury suites, and was highly respected on board. His flat in London was furnished with beautiful antiques, furniture, and paintings. Rumours abounded over how they were acquired. Previously Bobby had indulged in a long passionate love affair with an aristocrat, Sir Keith —, who told his family that Bobby was his private secretary. Sir Keith died of a brain tumour in Bobby's arms (some say during sex), leaving Bobby everything. The family were not happy. Because of the cause of death they successfully disputed the will. Apparently, in revenge, Bobby telephoned an East End mate to collect him in a van, along with quite a few choice antique pieces for his home.

Bobby shared his London flat with his friend Patsy, a wine waiter on board. A charming young man, tough, though kind, with dark Irish good looks. He was immensely worldly, with an outrageous sense of humour. He'd extremely good taste in clothes (and young men). I remember he gave me one of his T-shirts; I treasured it for many years. I'd thought he'd find me provincial and boring, but we got along fine, becoming good friends.

I met another dear friend while on board, my mate Martin, who'd been working on *QE2* since the ship's launch. He told me a funny story about when he worked as officer's steward alongside a lovely queen Jane, who always wore slap and had bleached blonde hair. I later met Jane, who was a delightful, amusing, sweet man. Everyone loved him. One day the staff captain called the pantry to ask for a tray of tea. Jane replied, "Not at the moment, Chief. I'm busy dyeing my hair." The staff captain sighed, saying, "When you've got time then, please."

Life on the *QE2* was very different to what I'd been used to. Everyone on board was obsessed with money. I found little social life, nor crew entertainment, nor Sods Operas. There were occasional movies, plus rare shows, sometimes with passenger entertainers. I recall the ship laid on a show for crew one evening with Count Basie and his orchestra, in a passenger area. We were told to make our way there just before it started and not to wander around the strictly out-of-bounds passenger accommodation. I went with Patsy, who insisted we smoke a joint before the show. Odd for me, as I didn't smoke, but it made me feel fantastic. I really enjoyed the sensation. It seemed to enhance the show. Colours on stage seemed to dance to the music; it was brilliant.

The ship was truly geared up for drinking. There were even shelves in the galley for us waiters to stand our pints/drinks on, to guzzle while serving dinner. Even the bar sold bottles of spirits. Because booze was so easy to get, many drank in their cabins as well as the bar, as did I. I'd invite queens round for drinks before dinner and we'd have a good laugh before turning to in the restaurant. Passengers often said to us, "You boys always look so happy." (No wonder!) When I'd have drinks with Patsy, he'd tell me off for letting queens drink my booze so often. He'd say they were a bunch of freeloaders. They all had houses and were saving for more houses to let out and earn even more money. I just enjoyed their company, but Patsy was right in the end. A lot of them ended up with pots of money, although they rarely seemed to go on to enjoy it. Once you get into the habit of scrimping and saving, it's very hard to let go. Spend and enjoy life.

At one point I shared a cabin with Mandy (Andy from the *Star*). Decorating it very 1970s style, we stuck wood effect Fablon on the tin clothes lockers, to make them look like wardrobes. Plus we had posters, mirrors, bedspreads in avocado green, bean bags and a shag carpet. We bought an antique commode in the Salvation Army, turning it into a cocktail cabinet – so funny. It all sounds hideous now, especially the shag carpet. We'd also transport antiques to Southampton in our cabin for other queens. I recall Sid asking me to bring an antique table home for him. We managed to squeeze it in our tiny cabin and held a dinner party during the trip. You really felt how small our cabin was with a large thing like that filling it.

It was hard work in the restaurant. Again, my after-meal job was vacuuming carpets. Tank-like vacuum cleaners were stored in a locker, with a miserable old sod guarding them. Always last to finish, I'd go to collect a hoover and he'd say, "They're all out." I'd ask about the ones at the back of the locker and he'd say they were broken. I think he was just too lazy to empty them. He'd leave the key in the lock. One day someone pushed the door shut, locking him in. He had to shout for a long time until he was let out. When he told me, I said, "That's dreadful. How could anyone do such a terrible thing," trying to keep a straight face. I think he suspected it was me. After that he always had a machine ready and waiting. Next trip *QE2* was due to sail from Southampton, for a repositioning voyage, operating a season of Caribbean cruises from the US for five months, November to April 1974. Boys in the restaurant said it'd be easy, as there was only one sitting cruising, instead of two transatlantic. I'd already served four months and didn't fancy another five, so once again I handed in my notice, paying off when we docked in Southampton November 8th, 1973.

I stayed with Lee. It was our usual merry routine, although as I'd changed jobs, I didn't have much leave. I spent a brief time with my parents, then returned to Southampton. First day visiting the Pool, I found the only jobs available were on *QE2*. Finally leave ran out and so did my money. As *QE2* seemed the only job I was likely to find, I accepted. Lee was upset again. I'd be missing a second Christmas, but he understood, promising we'd have another Christmas on my return in April. (We did.) I was to join *QE2* in Boston, which meant I needed a US visa; I believe Cunard obtained it through their agent. I didn't notice it at the time but on my visa description, the *female* box had been ticked. With long curly blonde hair, I did look rather camp. But *female* was a bit much! (I've still got my fifty-year-old visa.)

# 15

# A Caribbean Queen's Brush with Death

Cunard organised a crew coach for November 18th, 1973, Southampton to Heathrow, where we booked into a hotel for an early Boston flight. We were miffed hearing we'd be sharing a room (and king-size bed) with another crew member. Some raised hell. Others, like me, went along with it. I'd seen my roommate around the ship. He was about my age, clean, straight – I thought – and acceptable. Later, after a supper and drinks, I retired to our room, sliding into my side of the bed, trying not to disturb him, laying there awaiting sleep. After a while his hand wandered across the bed, touching me. I went along with it, indulging in mutual *hanky panky*, without a word spoken. It was weird, though exciting. Next day he acted as if nothing happened. I never hooked up with him again, although I saw him around the ship occasionally. Next morning, after breakfast, crew boarded an early flight to Boston, arriving later that morning, joining *QE2* about noon. I was pleased to see familiar faces. As we weren't required until dinner, Sid kindly asked me to join him for lunch in the famous

Anthony's Pier 4 Cafe. Though I was shattered, I found it was truly enjoyable, with a fabulous menu: oysters, lobster, steaks, the works. We tottered back to the ship for a snooze before dinner.

Sure enough, there was one seating of meals in all restaurants, plus excellent food for our American passengers, who were a joy and extremely generous. Tips for a fortnight's cruise would be about $10, or £8, from every passenger, about $60 or £40 a week. Our wages were about $60 or £40 a week, so we doubled our money. I heard an amusing story about later world cruises. If one of your passengers passed away, you missed out on their end-of-voyage tip. To make up for this, the waiters contributed $5 weekly to a 'death kitty'. If one of your 'bloods' passed away, you got the kitty. I expect when some passengers appeared without their husband or wife, the waiters rubbed their hands with glee, thinking *yes* regarding the kitty! Cruising around the Caribbean was brilliant. With many passengers on day tours, waiters were divided into three watches: red, white and blue. In port, one watch took turns to have lunch off, meaning time off after breakfast until dinner. We spent days on beautiful beaches, notably on St Thomas, with its cheap booze and jewellery.

I moved to the first-class Columbia restaurant on the next leave party change over, again serving one seating of sixteen passengers between two waiters. The restaurant décor was classier than the garish red, white and blue colours of the Britannia restaurant. Columbia was contemporarily furnished in rich shades of beige and natural wood colours. Plush carpet with a stylish design. Dining chairs were modern, elegant and extremely comfortable. At dinner, tables were laid with a beautiful kind of light-refracting crystal table lamp, lit from below. Only they weren't crystal, they were made from a heavy, clear resin; the overall effect was extremely clever and attractive.

There were many queens working in the Columbia: South African Tina and I became great friends. Highly amusing, mysterious about his age, his dark riah obviously dyed. He was also a big friend of Sid (Cynthia). I also became friends with Scottish Julie/Queen Juliana. Slightly older than me, he'd worked on the infamous *Andes*, telling me hilarious stories of all the camp and carry-on that happened on board. He told me some queen friends on *Andes* lived in a plainly decorated six-berth cabin, which posh Clarence House queens referred to disparagingly as the 'railway carriage'. One day a queen knocked on the door of Clarence House, asking to see Bobby. Without allowing admittance, Sidney said snootily, "Bobby, there's one of *those* railway carriage queens to see you, dear."

Clarence House was one of the few six-berth cabins with a porthole. Apparently before turning to for dinner service the royal queens would enjoy a cocktail or two. One evening they were regally sitting having a drink when a wave slopped in through the porthole, soaking them. None of them moved a muscle or commented; too royal to be seen to look undignified!

To start in with the Columbia, I worked on a station with any waiter, eventually teaming up with Julie, who was great to work with and a good laugh. I recall one lunch. Meal service was about to end, when we'd wipe down, finish work and take a nap. At the last minute in walked an American Southern gentleman, who looked and dressed like Colonel Sanders (Kentucky Fried Chicken), saying loudly to the table, "Howdy, folks." Julie was furious, seething. He quietly said to me, "You'd better serve that finger licking c—t, dear." I struggled to keep a straight face.

Once again my after-meal job was the loathsome hoovering. Jewish Amber was 'cruet queen', in charge of a team maintaining condiment trolleys of salt, pepper, mustards, pickles, jams and so on. Mustard, for example, was made fresh every day, a job I'd have loved; it was easy-peasy. However, the cruet team were hand-picked by Amber. Only guys he fancied or his best friend queens stood a chance. Although the ship was supposed to be one-class cruising, the food in Columbia was even better than the Britannia: endless amounts of beluga caviar, special dishes and table side flambés. Beef wellingtons were amazing, the crispy duck à l'orange unbelievable. It was cooked in steam ovens, I believe. The flesh melted in your mouth; the skin was crispy and delicious. I've never found it that delicious anywhere else.

QE2 I think was the last liner ever to offer *genuine* first-class silver service. All food at dinner was served separately. Hot dinner plates were placed before passengers and everything was presented on silver dishes. Waiters served the main courses and vegetables with a special spoon and fork. Gravy and accompaniments, such as hollandaise, mustard, and Béarnaise sauce, were presented and served separately. Even starters were served with style. We'd a wonderful smoked salmon trolley, with brown bread, capers and lemon. Lobster, crab and prawn cocktails were served in silver dishes, sat in a silver bowl full of crushed ice. Even fruit juice was served in a silver dish of crushed ice. Truly first-class service, the like of which will never be seen again – the end of an era.

Although officially not allowed, we also ate off the passenger menu, instead of eating crew food. Many of us put on weight. Amber made such a pig of himself, he'd visit the crew mess with plates full of beef wellington, lobster and crêpes suzette. He'd become so enormous on the ship, he'd spend much of his leave at expensive health farms, starving to lose weight. Then he'd get back on the ship and stuff himself, putting weight back on. This constant yo-yo dieting is *so* bad for you. I think that's what contributed to his diabetes and ill health, which prematurely stopped him from going to sea. Even *I* put on weight. Dear Patsy said to me, "You're gonna end up a fat queen like those others if you're not careful, dear." I thought, *Oh no I won't*. I'd studied nutrition at college and knew exactly what to do. I immediately gave up large plates of food, as well as fattening things like desserts, biscuits, cakes, and sweets. My weight went back to normal, where it's stayed pretty much to this day.

Not long after joining, a few queens suggested organising a Christmas pantomime. I offered to join in. I thought it was a great idea, a chance for 'dragging up' and fun. We met in a small disused room that'd previously been the bar for a grill room above. It was decided to put on *Cinderella*, a wonderful show for drag, costumes and funny lines, with Ugly Sisters. I'd some good ideas for the script. I'd seen a panto script used on the *Reina del Mar*, with funny lines like

"To marry the Prince it is my duty

I've seen his cock, and what a beauty."

and

"Off you pop to the ball, my pet.

We'll get the Prince to f—k you yet!"

There were howls of outrage from some queens. They protested that we couldn't use such foul language in front of female crew members in the audience. I suggested we could tone it down a bit, like, "We'll get the Prince to shag you yet." No, they said. Still too vulgar. I thought a crew pantomime without rude and funny lines was a waste of time, and withdrew from the project. It was never staged.

With Christmas 1973 imminent, most crew decorated their cabins with plenty of tinsel and the like. While ashore in New York, I bought a couple of LPs. One was the Patti Page Christmas album; the other, for some weird reason, was Walt Disney's *Cinderella*. Strangely, there was a queen known as Patti on board. He was a big, strong man. Rumour was that he'd previously been a Royal Marine. He could be extremely aggressive, though with the amount of gin and sweeties (speed tablets) he consumed, it was no wonder. He was a waiter and also took care of large potted plants in the restaurant. His other hand-picked job was to visit the cold rooms before dinner to collect the restaurant manager's boutonnière (buttonhole flower). Patti always seemed moody, galloping about. I nicknamed him the Wildebeest, behind his back! (He was bigger than me and prone to be extreme violence.)

Christmas at sea was always fun on ships, despite all the extra hard work. I'd get into the Christmas spirit, playing the Patti Page Christmas album to death. I'd visit Patsy's cabin, we'd have a few drinks, play music, really get to know each other. He was into pot, but being a nonsmoker I rarely indulged. When I told him about my Cinderella album, he said, "Bring it round." We played that to death too. I don't know if he'd slipped something in my drink, but one evening while playing Cinderella, I acted out *all* the roles, including the Fairy Godmother's song, 'Bibbidi-Bobbidi-Boo!' (It has just made a comeback in a TV commercial.)

Being usually the last to leave the restaurant at night, Patsy asked me to plant some weed seeds in the potted plants, which he harvested before they became too noticeable. Patti would have gone berserk if he'd known there was *pot* in his pot plants! Gin and speed were fine by him, but definitely not weed.

Every so often people flew home for reasons like a death in the family or a medical problem. New crew were flown out. One evening who should I bump into in the crew bar, but Roy's brother Tony, the Monster. He was extremely pleased to see me, which was probably the reason he took the job in the first place, as he had a soft spot for me. He would have liked our friendship to have gone further. So would Lee. Sadly, he was a sweet guy and good fun, but rather overweight and sweaty, not my type at all. Thankfully he was in the Britannia, so I didn't see too much of him.

QE2's itinerary was great for crew – cruising round the Caribbean, sunbathing, swimming, duty-free shopping and so on. Then we turned around in New York, sometimes overnight, which was amazing. As mentioned, American passengers were very generous with tips, so we had a ball in New York, shopping and going out for fancy meals. Shopping was fantastic. It was here I discovered the disposable douche, ready filled with water, antiseptic and fragrance, so convenient to use. Many queens went to the sauna baths (*tubs*), where they enjoyed getting well-serviced. Initially, I didn't go, thinking they may be like *cottaging*; sex in public toilets was not my thing. When I heard how much fun queens were having in the tubs, and also that there were private rooms, I tried them.

Alongside in New York one day I visited the legendary gay sauna Everard Baths at 28 West 28th Street. It was certainly an eye-opener, considering homosexuality was illegal in New York at the time. Everard's was a huge place, with a pool, whirlpools, steam rooms, saunas, private rooms with beds and subdued lighting. Leaving your clothes in a locker, you wandered around in just a towel. Private rooms were $1, which I happily paid. I wasn't into public sex, though I understood lots of guys were. I walked around checking the place out, noticing naked guys in rooms with doors ajar. That was an open invitation, whether laid on their front, or back; that's what they were *into*.

I made eye contact with a hot guy, returning to my room with him for a hot, steamy time. After dressing, I went shopping. I've never been one for multiple sex partners; once I've had sex, I'm done. I wasn't a prude. If other guys enjoyed multiple partners, that was fine. I noticed there weren't many black gentlemen in the baths, though they were hugely popular. Eventually I met a black guy with skin so smooth and sensual. He came to my room for amazing, exciting sex. He *did the lot too* and was a big boy. No wonder they were sought after. Later I too began to enjoy watching guys having sex in public. I still didn't like being watched myself, old-fashioned thing that I am.

*QE2* usually sailed in the early hours of the morning from San Juan, Puerto Rico, allowing us to visit gay bars that weren't busy during the day. Hispanic Puerto Rico was known as rather dangerous. One night I went ashore with Tina, starting in his cabin for a few gins. "I know a bona little disco dear, called the Abbey," she said. "You'll love it, dear." Next, out came weed, more gin, then a couple of sweeties, which I disliked. I said no thanks. Tina insisted. "Go on, dear. It'll get you in the mood to dance, dear!" By the time we went ashore we were *off our tits!*

We found the Abbey, down the back streets. It seemed like a church with disco lights in stained glass windows. We had a riotous night. After an evening of drinking, dancing and flirting, we headed back to the ship. As we staggered along back streets, two men suddenly grabbed us, attempting to mug us. Struggling with my attacker, I kicked him hard in the balls and he ran off. I was so wasted, I didn't realise he'd stabbed me in the back until Tina saw blood and started screaming, "Help, police, murder!" "Hang on, dear," I said. "I'm not dead yet." Next thing I was in an ambulance, then in a city hospital getting the wound stitched. Next day at work the stitches on my back were sore. I remembered the hospital doctor's words. I was lucky, he said. Any deeper and the knife would have pierced my lung. I could have died. I promised myself I'd take more care in future.

*QE2* visited Haiti, another interesting island. It was wonderful: hot weather, with beautiful beaches and cheap bars. Local people appeared poor, selling home-made voodoo dolls for a few dollars. The boys purchased these and brought them back on board. One of the head waiters at the time was a most unpleasant man. Most of the waiters actually hated him. For badness, some of the lads wrote his name on voodoo dolls, sticking pins in his heart and brain. Sometime later I heard he'd actually passed away. I'm not sure if it had anything to do with the dolls, or just a coincidence?

Although *QE2* was somewhat a party ship, some crew went overboard. They partied in their cabin into the wee small hours, which was annoying when we had to start work at 6:30a.m. Queens with cabins near me were extremely noisy, especially

Shirley. He was a pretty thing, with long blonde hair, and named after Shirley Temple. Was he camp or what! He was so camp that passengers asked, "What's your name, your *other* name?" He'd admit it was Shirley and passengers called him Shirley. He was sweet, but lazy, and always in a vile mood in the morning and often very *cod*. We never really hit it off. I think he thought I was a *Shaw Savill slut*, whereas he was a *Cunard queen*. One night he held a very noisy cabin party, which went on and on, with dreadful loud music. I was pissed off and remembered Yorkshire Barry's trick on the *Canberra*. My cabin mate was out, so I took a dime (ten-cent coin), placed it in a cabin plug, pushed it into the wall socket and flicked the switch. There was a small bang, a little smoke, and all noise ceased immediately. I quickly wiped soot off the plug and socket, turned out the lights, and leapt into bed. Next day everyone wondered what caused the fuse to trip. "Probably a short circuit, dear," I said, laughing to myself.

One day at sea, April 3rd, 1974, between New York and the Caribbean, I woke up to find the ship eerily quiet. Only the emergency lights were working; the cabin was hot and airless. In the washroom I discovered no hot water and the toilets wouldn't flush. (This wasn't a huge drama then, you could flush them with a bucket of water.) Turning to in the dining room, I was informed by the head waiter that three of the ship's boilers were contaminated with oil, resulting in a total breakdown. The ship was drifting. With absolutely no power, and emergency electricity only, the galley was reduced to serving cold food. No toast was available. And – Americans' worst nightmare – there was no coffee. We served fruit juices, tinned meat, fruit and bread, all of which were cold or warm. The situation on board was extremely unpleasant for all. It was stuffy with no air conditioning, plus our vessel was drifting helplessly.

The situation needed fast, drastic action. As we weren't far from Bermuda, Cunard New York office managed to charter a cruise ship, the Norwegian *Sea Venture* (later *Pacific Princess*). Luckily it was in Bermuda between sailings. Later she rendezvoused a safe distance from the *QE2*. The plan was to evacuate passengers by tender using the *Sea Venture* boats. Strangely most people were pragmatic about it, even though transfer was quite a hazardous operation, considering the sea state and age of the passengers. However with the co-operation of the British and Norwegian crews, it was a complete success.

Being a world-famous liner, the story quickly made international headlines. The headline in the *New York Times* read, "QE2 Passengers Arrive, Joking About Adventure." The article went on to say there were tales of good cheer and the gallant crews, regarding their rescue. Some said they "would do it all over again." After the ship drifted for three days, tugs towed those of us remaining on the *QE2* to Bermuda for repairs. There are excellent shipyards there.

The accommodation was stifling hot. As we no longer had passengers aboard, we were allowed to sleep on the upper decks. The ship's musicians also laid on entertainment for crew on the top open deck. Crew bars served as usual, but with no ice. We mainly bought bottles and cans, to drink on cool open decks while enjoying entertainment. One afternoon I was in my cabin getting ready to go up on deck, when Roy's brother Tony, the Monster, came round, initially for a chat. He started making sexual suggestions, pouncing on me. I felt sorry for him and rather horny, going through the motions. It was relatively enjoyable. He was another one who *did the lot*. However, he *really* wasn't my type. I had to keep him at arm's length after that. That evening we were up on deck, drinking dark rum and coke for a change. We were low on booze, so I gave Tony the money to go down the Dhobi Arms for another bottle. He came back with a bottle of Bacardi white rum. When I pointed out it was the wrong rum, he rushed back down for dark rum. He failed to return, so I went below looking for him, finding a broken bottle of dark rum in the Burma Road and a trail of blood! I followed the bloody trail upstairs until I got to Tina's cabin. He shared with Patti (the Wildebeest). They hated each other's guts. Their door was open, so I asked had they seen Tony? "Yes, dear," said Patti. "He came in here, dear, dripping blood." "Oh, how awful," I said. "What happened?" "I told him to get out, dear, he was getting blood on the carpet. I told him to piss off to the hospital, dear," said Patti, without a grain of sympathy. It turned out Tony tripped carrying the bottle, sustaining a few nasty cuts. But after a few stitches and treatment he was fine.

Tina told me a story about sharing with Patti, although he was prone to embellishing stories and rather economical with the truth. Patti kept staying up late and playing endless Shirley Bassey music loudly on his record player. One night Tina was trying to sleep and Patti was at it again, guzzling gin and playing loud music. Tina became enraged, eventually jumping out of his bunk, going into the alleyway to collect a heavy brass fire nozzle from the emergency locker. He returned to the cabin, raised the fire nozzle over his head, and sent it crashing down on to the record player, which collapsed in a shower of sparks. Tina said to Patti, "Now play the f—ing thing, dear!" Even Patti, when he regained his composure, had to laugh. They had a few gins and a giggle together.

Sid also told me an amusing story regarding Patti. They were in a New York market diner, smartly dressed as usual: jackets, ties and overcoats, enjoying a drink and a bit of *camp*. Two local burly longshore men (dockers) nearby were giving them cod varders (dirty looks). One of them, in a loud voice, heard all across the bar, said to the other, "That's one thing I cain't stand: big men acting like little fairies." A hush descended on the room. Patti took a sip of his drink, stood up, and took off his overcoat, saying, "Sidney, hold my coat, dear." He turned and faced the men. "I get very annoyed when people disturb me while I'm having a quiet drink." Being ex-military, he launched an extremely violent and ferocious attack on the two local men, knocking them both out. They fled, to loud applause from customers. Patti dusted himself off and rejoined Sid, saying, "I bet they'll think twice before bothering little fairies again, dear!"

When the ship arrived at Bermuda for repairs, with no passengers aboard we were offered the choice of staying on board, with limited facilities. Or we could have a week's unpaid leave ashore. No choice, I thought, a week in Bermuda sounded great. We went ashore on tenders. I stayed at the Imperial Hotel, which sounds grand but it was cheap and a dump. I shared a room with Tina, who promised to behave himself. We rented mopeds to explore the island, enjoying our week. Tina was always highly amusing. Bermuda is a truly pretty island. The weather was glorious, though certain things spoilt it for me. Food and especially drink were expensive (to keep riff-raff out?). When I saw the price of beer compared to petrol, I saw it would have been cheaper to drink petrol! I loved swimming then, but despite hot weather, the sea was always freezing. Bermuda is in the west North Atlantic. Personally, we didn't find the island particularly friendly either. We didn't find any gay or mixed bars. It seemed a little homophobic. Nevertheless, Tina managed to hook up with a sexy black guy, as usual.

Following our week in Bermuda, we returned to the ship, sailing back to New York. I can't recall if we completed another cruise. However, *QE2* arrived in Southampton April 22nd. I signed off and asked to return May 7th, 1974, giving myself two weeks leave. I went to Lee's. He was eager to hear all about the trip. He'd heard about the breakdown. When I told him about Tony's accident, he was in absolute hysterics, as usual. It wasn't meant in an unkind way, he just saw the funny side of things, even mishaps and disasters. My mum was a bit like that too. If

Dad dropped a plate and it broke, for example, she'd start giggling and start me giggling too. Dad would get the right hump, saying, "I don't know what you two think is so bleeding funny."

I later went home, then returned to Southampton May 5th, spending a couple of days at Lee's. He kept his promise. We had a full Christmas dinner in May. I mixed gallons of cocktails before we ate. Lee got overexcited and I got extremely drunk, falling asleep before we'd finished the meal. What I do remember was great fun. We had a good laugh about the whole thing.

May 7th, 1974, I rejoined the *QE2*, in the first-class Columbia restaurant. It was good to see old friends like Sid, Tina and George. The only aggravating thing was a shortage of crockery and especially teaspoons. (Passengers took them as souvenirs.) Cunard were making cutbacks due to the October 1973 fuel crisis. By 1974 fuel prices had increased 300%, making ships' operations more expensive. More cuts were introduced. Instead of putting milk, cream and rolls on the table automatically, they were only available when asked for. Caviar was less plentiful. A shortage of crockery developed too. Much had smashed in bad weather and Cunard were slow to replace it, to save money.

One highlight during this time was a party thrown on the Southampton Royal Pier at Town Quay, by two *QE2* queens, for their joint birthdays: Barry/Madam DuBarry, and Janis/John, who was twenty-one. It was held in the Mecca Ballroom, with its plastic palm trees. Post-war, the Mecca pier was a busy entertainment destination and hosted dances and many big acts. (Sadly it was destroyed by fire only thirteen years later, in 1987.) The party theme was America the Beautiful. Fancy dress was encouraged. Lee went as Mae West; Janis was an indigenous North American woman. I was Marilyn Monroe. I borrowed a tight-fitting satin dress and high heels from Big Marge, a stewardess, and finished it off with long evening gloves and a feather boa. Camp or what! Janis dressed at Lee's, sticking red glitter dust on his face, which looked good but like a glittery red graze. Everybody dressed up. Sid went as a dead ringer for Liberace, Barry as an American general, and there were all sorts of other American and UK celebs. Patsy appeared as Marc Bolan, complete with a fedora, carnation, silver trousers, platform shoes and a floor-length purple velvet scarf. Cabaret was supplied by queens performing numbers from the musical *Cabaret*, which was all the rage at this time. They did lively songs like 'Mein Herr' and 'Cabaret'. What a night! Booze flowed like water; everyone had a ball. It's still talked about today.

Later, Roy picked us up for the drive home. Feeling tipsy and ravenous, we stopped at a Civic Centre burger van. Walking back to the car, I tripped on my high heels, dropped the burger and sat on it! On inspection, there was a vile greasy mark on the arse of the frock where my bum squashed the burger. I confessed to Marge, who often stayed at Lee's. Quite rightly, she felt rather cross with me. Next day I took it to a specialist dry cleaners, hoping they'd get the stain out. Thankfully it cleaned up like new; all was forgiven.

On my first round trip to New York I worked with a great guy. But the second trip I was assigned to a large senior officers' table, and my workmate was difficult to work with. Our passengers were frightful too; some of them up were their own arses. Because they sat at a senior officers' table, they bragged about how many trips they'd sailed and such.

Social life on board was poor as usual. We didn't have time for fun. I wasn't getting any trade (sex). I wondered, was it the pressure of work, or was it that I was twenty-three, and no longer a chicken? Was no one interested in me? *Oh dear*, I thought. *At this rate I'll end up an Old Maid, or a Spinster of this Parish.* I decided it was time for a change. I'd had quite enough of *QE2* anyway. I handed in my notice, paying off in Southampton May 20th, 1974.

# 16

# Northern Star Revisited and 'Viva España'

I stayed at Lee and Roy's for a couple of happy days, then went home to my folks for a rest. Returning May 30th, I visited the Pool; they were looking for bedroom stewards for dear old *Northern Star*. I accepted, joining the next day. It was good to be back on a happy ship again and see lots of familiar faces, plus some interesting new ones. I was relief BRS. When guys went on leave, I took over their sections. This made a change. Instead of starting down on B deck, I covered sections on various decks, including slightly posh ones like Flo had on an upper deck. Up there cabins had private en suite facilities. That was unusual in those days on tourist-class immigrant ships.

Her Majesty the Queen Mother launched *Northern Star* in 1961, paying a visit to the ship on May 31st, 1974. She used one of Flo's slightly posher en suite cabins as a cloakroom. When she left the cabin to tour the ship and dine, her fur coat was hung up in the cabin. Us queens were naturally following her every move and couldn't wait to try on her fur coat. Some struggled to get it on. It was then we realised how tiny she was! (Imagine if we'd been caught! She'd have been OK but would her aides have been outraged?) She went on to enjoy luncheon with the captain in the passenger dining room. She got one of her favourite meals: roast trimmed rack of lamb, with fresh vegetables and new potatoes.

I sorted out a gay cabin and, when Tina joined as assistant barman, moved him in too. It wasn't ideal. He finished work quite late, but we were usually up having fun anyway. He worked in the Tavern Bar, the most popular on board, which had the longest ship's bar in the world and a jukebox. At this time the Three Degrees' 'When Will I See You Again' was a huge hit. Tina heard it so often on the jukebox, he'd sing it all the time, in his own inimitable way. He did make me laugh. I found life on board much the same as ever, relaxed and fun, especially the crew bar. How different it was from the constant graft on the *QE2*. We were Medi cruising again, but still managed to squeeze in the occasional crew show.

Around this time a huge hit was released: 'Y Viva España', by Sylvia. It became something of an anthem for Brits going to Spain. Spanish people seemed to love it too. This song played constantly on TV and radio. Talking with Debbie, who had a villa in Calpe, Lee said he'd love to go to Spain. He told us that he'd *never* had a proper holiday abroad in his life. I suggested we could book a package holiday at the end of the summer, maybe September. I'd have a couple of cruises off. It was more or less decided. As usual, Lee got *so* excited and never stopped talking about it. Sometimes he was just like a big kid.

Flo (Bernie) adored Lee, giving him one of his beautiful diamond rings for his birthday. Later, overnight between cruises in Southampton one evening, I had drinks ashore with Lee. I noticed he was already quite merry. After more drinks and laughs, Lee decided he wanted to eat at German Edie's restaurant. Roy drove us there. By this time Lee was extremely merry. After more drinks, we ordered food. Lee had steak as usual, falling asleep halfway through with his face down on his food. That happened sometimes. Edie was swanning around, guzzling brandy, being generally outrageous as usual. She also adored Lee. Noticing him asleep, she gently woke him up, admiring his diamond ring. He was grateful, drunk and emotional, telling her, "You can have it, my darling," giving it to her. Oh dear. Next time I saw him, he was worried sick in case Bernie noticed it missing. I told him Flo would be fine about it. (I've since spoken to Bernie/Flo. No, he had never noticed the ring missing and yes, he'd have been fine about it if he had.)

In July the chief steward advised me that Lady Gambol/Dennis was due leave. Would I like to take over as CCOs' (Chief Catering Officers') steward? I graciously accepted and felt *made up*. It was an easy and prestigious job. I basically looked after the chief catering officer, Mr Frank, a plump middle-aged man who was rather formal and abrupt. He called me Rudd, not Michael or even my surname, Rudder. As he was a bit scary, I didn't correct him. From then on I was just Rudd. He occupied a spacious cabin on the main deck square. Like the captain, he held cocktail parties for the more affluent passengers in his cabin. As he hosted a table, after the party he'd go on to the restaurant. I loved these parties. It gave me a chance to guzzle a drop of his gin, while tidying up, although I was terrified that he'd return and catch me at it.

Sometimes he dined in his cabin. He'd mark his requirements on the menu and I'd visit the galley to see the head chef, who'd supervise his meal. The chef at the time was very amusing, with a wicked camp sense of humour. He'd say to me, "What's *she* having for *her* dinner tonight?" I'd start giggling, handing him the menu, saying madam wants the consommé, lamb chops and the rest. I thought if Frank heard us talking like this, he'd blow a fuse! He'd never have understood it was just a bit of camp.

He was married and supposedly straight-laced, though I'd see an attractive stewardess spend time in his cabin, with the door locked! Mr Frank would also visit the galley to make sure all was going well and check on the waiters. One evening he asked Horseface if he was wearing make-up. "Who me? Oh no, not me, chief," he said. Frank rubbed his finger across the horseface; the finger was coated in slap! He raised his eyes, saying, "What's this, then?" smiled and carried on.

Mr Frank's cabin was extremely cluttered with 'knickknacks'. His own collection of souvenirs made cleaning a nightmare. One ornament, a blue and white Dutch ashtray, was decorated with little glazed clogs. Being a nonsmoker, I hated emptying ashtrays. I would turn them upside down over a rubbish bin, give them a gentle tap on the bin to dislodge ash, then wipe them with dry muslin. However, when I tapped the Dutch astray, one of the clogs hit the bin, falling in. I had the disgusting job of fishing it out and get Chippy (the ship's carpenter) to glue it back on before his lordship noticed! Some of the furniture was also intrusive. As I crashed the huge Sherman Tank vacuum around the room, I struck the leg of a wall cabinet, which bent out of shape, nearly falling off. I quickly straightened it out, hoping he wouldn't notice. With his strict formal attitude, my nerves were getting bad by this time. It was a relief when he finally took leave and our regular chief catering officer, the Red Baron, rejoined.

He was wonderful to look after: relaxed, good fun and easy-going. He called me just Michael, (like most captains did). First day when I took his tea tray in 7:00a.m., he said, "Michael, I've had a *hard night*! Fetch me a beer please and don't tell Dennis" (Lady Gambol, his regular steward). This happened most days. When his cocktail parties finished, he'd tell me to help myself to a drink. I didn't need to be told twice. It was happy days! When Dennis returned to the ship, I told him about the Red Baron's cold beer some mornings. "He has the same thing every day with me, dear," he said, laughing. I returned to my relief cabin steward's job.

Life aboard drifted happily on. The bar was busy; my love life busy too. John, the blonde deckhand, drifted into my life again. I was extremely fond of him but it wasn't exactly *love*. On board was a blonde young queen, Kenny, who took a fancy to John and relentlessly pursued him, trying to do what us queens call a *Maggie snatch* (stealing your husband/boyfriend/trade). John wasn't interested, telling me all about it. He said Kenny asked him, "What do you see in Michele? I'm younger and much prettier than she is." He was actually, but I thought, *Bleeding cheek!* and confronted him. "Just a bit of camp, dear," he told me. I told him I didn't think it was, and proceeded to do what us queens call *clean her*, or *wipe the deck with her*. I told Kenny in no uncertain terms that John just preferred me to her! He didn't know what to say. John and I found the whole thing highly amusing.

I'd renewed my friendship with Welsh Winnie, who also stayed at Lee's. Like everyone, he adored Lee. We'd all talked about the upcoming holiday in sunny España and decided to go to Benidorm. It had a reputation for fun and was near Calpe, where Debbie owned a villa. Deckhand John wanted to come along and so did Winnie. Debbie said he'd come too. He couldn't wait to show us the delights of Spain and his villa. We booked a ten-day package deal in Benidorm late September and Debs kindly organised a stretch limo to transport all six of us to and from Gatwick Airport.

I paid off September 8th, 1974. After a day or two at Lee's, I went home to my parents, returning to Lee's when the big day finally arrived. As always, Lee was like a big kid. He was *so* excited. After a couple of drinks we piled into the stretch limo: Lee, Roy, myself, John, Debbie and Winnie. We had more drinks on the way up, boarding a Dan-Air Comet to fly to Alicante from Gatwick Airport. We arrived at our hotel early evening, dumping the bags in our rooms, and went out to explore. We went to the nearest bar, of course. Lee loved lots of ice in his drinks and was determined to get plenty in Spain. He'd learnt *mucho hielo* (*much* ice), pronounced *moocho yellow*. We sat chatting with our drinks. Nearby, a glass cabinet contained large dishes of food. One was a small mountain of potato salad. Lee started giggling, saying, "Varder the flies dancing over that potato salad." "Yes, dear," I said. "They're probably singing 'Climb Every Mountain.'" We all started giggling and laughing. It set the tone for the holiday. We never stopped laughing, and enjoyed the most amazing ten days.

Our hotel was on the side of a steep hill. As we'd all had a few drinks, when we were dropped off outside the back of the hotel it didn't seem very tall. Next morning with John I called in Lee's and Roy's room, walking out onto the balcony to see the view. Lee shouted, "Get off that balcony, you raving lunatic." "It's quite safe, Lee," I said, jumping up and down. "Just a bit of *stone worm*." John and Roy started giggling. Lee was screaming; I didn't realise that he had such a phobia. His fear of heights was so bad that he had to change rooms. Strange thing is, now I'm older I'm terrified of heights too. Later we all met in the hotel garden bar. Lee said, "Now we're in Spain, let's drink the way the locals do. Coffee and cognac." Then we went for a stroll around Benidorm and the Old Town.

One evening Debs took us out to a feast of local slow-cooked baby lamb. It was truly delicious. At that time, as a gimmick, the Spanish waiters poured wine directly into your mouth from a strange triangular shaped bottle. We also guzzled gallons of sangria and local plonk. Later Debs also took us to the obligatory flamenco show. I sat next to Lee, knowing what his reaction would be. He found flamenco dancing hysterically funny. To the Spanish it's a serious dance. However, as soon as they started dancing and stamping he started tittering. He started me giggling too. Our eyes started streaming. We tried to suppress our helpless laughter. He couldn't help cackling, "They look like you with those lobsters, dear." The others didn't understand why we were convulsed with mirth. It was our private joke; we enlightened them later.

It must be remembered that at this time, fascist dictator Franco was head of government in Spain. Debbie visited Spain often, and warned us to behave ourselves. Homosexuality was illegal in Catholic Spain and frowned upon by many people. There were no gay bars as such, but in the Old Town there were some mixed bars, which usually had a statue of David on display to indicate they were mixed or gay-friendly. This dates back to the Biblical times of David and Jonathan. In his famous lament, David said unto Johnathan, "Your love to me is wonderful, surpassing the love of a woman" (II Samuel 1:26). In Biblical times the modern idea of sexual orientation didn't exist, so this may not have been a sexual reference. However, David became something of a gay icon. His statue in bars dropped a subtle gay-friendly hint. I'd had my hair streaked for the holiday, was looking very fit and we had a wonderful time, especially in the Old Town bars. We enjoyed the new part of town too, with English pubs. 'Viva España' was playing everywhere. The weather was sunny, the atmosphere incredible, and everyone had a ball. Roy hired a car, driving us all to Calpe for lunch. We visited Debbie's villa, swimming and sunbathing.

One day by the hotel pool we were sunbathing, drinking and laughing. Winnie observed I had extremely large teeth. I was dumbfounded, as Winnie's were bloody huge, like a horse. (I believe that's why he was called Winnie.) I told him so. He said he didn't think his were large, then Lee joined in, saying he agreed with me they were huge. Winnie said to Lee, "Don't you start, dear. Your teeth are like tilting tombstones!" (They were.

Lee had a fear of dentists.) We all cracked up laughing, having a great time with plenty of banter, more of which I can't recall.

We enjoyed a marvellous time. Sadly the holiday came to an end. We flew back to Gatwick, where our limo awaited to whisk us back home to Lee and Roy's place. Along with the others, I rejoined the *Star* October 20th, 1974, again as cabin steward. The ship was sailing on its final Medi cruises, before departing on its usual round the world trip to the Antipodes in early November. Life on board was much the same as ever: great nights in the Pig, the odd bit of trade, and days ashore. Little did I know that during the ship's last cruise, my life was about to change *forever*!

# 17

# Dominic Comes into My Life

During that final summer cruise, *Northern Star* docked in Lisbon October 28th, 1974. My old ship *Oriana* was berthed there too, quite near the *Star*. At lunchtime a small deck crowd, who'd heard the *Star* was a fun ship (it was), came over from *Oriana* for a beer. I bought a pint and, seeing a free seat, joined their table. I soon noticed one of them near me was gorgeous, good-looking, with dark brown hair and well-built. He was looking at me in an interested way and I returned his look. In fact I couldn't take my eyes off him. Little did we know at the time, but it was love at first sight.

We sat chatting, drinking, laughing, and exchanging the usual seamen's banter. I discovered his name was Dominic. He had a strong Belfast accent, so I knew where he was from. (Queens called Belfast homies *Turkish* or *Turks*; I never did find out why.) When it was time for the *Oriana* crowd to return to work, Dominic stayed. Apparently he'd had a row with the bosun's mate, deciding to go *adrift* (skip work). We talked for ages, drinking more beer, then retired to my cabin and to bed. We had the most amazing sex. He had a lovely, muscular body and smooth skin, all the things I like. I was in heaven. Dominic asked me what I was doing that night. Would I fancy a run ashore with him? I agreed. He said he'd be back on board to meet me when I finished work.

That evening I finished a little early. He hadn't arrived yet. I went for a shower, wondering if he really would turn up. Then his beautiful head appeared in the bathroom. He said he'd wait in my cabin; it was all open houses in those days. I think we had a drink in the Pig, then walked into town for a drinks and dinner. We found a local restaurant where the passing trams made it uniquely Lisbon, rather romantic. Our meal wasn't particularly good. The waiter kept loudly clearing his throat. However, we enjoyed ourselves and never stopped talking, about his life and mine. It was an absolute fluke we met, Dominic told me. He usually only sailed on cargo ships, sailing on *Oriana* by default, as no suitable cargo ships were available on the London Pools. We finally tottered back to the *Star*, returning to the Pig for more drinks, and eventually going back to my cabin for some more fun.

When I awoke next day he'd gone. I turned to as usual, bumping into Terry, ex-*Arawa*. "Eee girl, did your homie get off last night?" he said. "I saw him running round looking for the gangway but I think we'd sailed!" I rushed aft to look through the brig (ship's prison) porthole on prom deck, to see if Dominic was there. Sure enough, he was! I waved to him, thinking, *Oh dear, what happens now? He's a stowaway,* my *stowaway. A punishable and possibly sackable offence!* Later that morning the chief officer, who I suspected was a BMQ, called me to his cabin. He was vile, saying I'd harboured a stowaway and he was going to "throw the book at me!" I didn't know quite what to do, so I went to see my mate Big Sheila, one of the steam queens (laundry maids). She was extremely sensible, saying, "Have a talk with Captain Murrison. You've been his tiger. Just explain what happened."

Lunchtime, as usual, I went up the Pig. To my relief Dominic was there, having a beer. I joined him. He told me he'd found the brig in a vile mess, so early that day he'd asked the master at arms for cleaning gear. (MAAs were kind of a ship's police/security officers, not popular with crew.) Dom scrubbed and polished the brig until it was gleaming. They were so pleased and impressed by him, they let him out, advising him to eat in the crew mess, visit the crew bar, and make sure he was back at 10:00p.m.

I asked Dom what'd happened the previous night. Apparently he awoke in my bunk, realised he had to get back to his ship, and rushed to find the gangway. When he got on deck he realised the *Star* had sailed. It was in the river Tagus, heading out to sea. He was tempted to dive over the side to try and swim ashore but decided it might be too dangerous. Just as well he didn't; the Tagus is deep with strong and fast-moving currents. He would surely have perished! He bumped into a kind, friendly quarter master. When the QM heard what happened, he asked Dom if there was anything he needed, like money or fags. (Dom didn't smoke.) Then he took Dom down to the master at arms near the brig. We both recall the QM well but can't remember his name. He had bad skin, and needed to put medication on his face that looked like make-up. It must have been very embarrassing for this kind man, as I suspect he was a manly gay, definitely not the type to wear make-up.

Early that evening I made my way to the captain's cabin and knocked on the open door. He saw me, saying, "Come in, Michael." I explained how I'd 'accidentally' stowed my friend Dominic away on board and asked, "What will happen to him and me?" He smiled, telling me he'd already been in contact with *Oriana*. They confirmed Dominic was one of their best ABs (able-bodied seamen) and to send him back to *Oriana* when we docked. I asked if we were going to get into any trouble. He said, "Don't worry, Michael, I've sorted it all out. Just don't let it happen again." What a wonderful man, what a relief. I was thrilled, and when I told Dominic he was relieved also. He told me luckily the *Oriana* was on a Medi cruise. Lisbon was its last port and he was pretty sure his ship got back the same day as us.

I'd have meals with Dominic in the mess room, making sure he had everything he needed. He was allowed out until 10:00p.m., spending nearly all his time with me when I wasn't working. First evening about 21:45 Dom said he'd better get back to the master at arms, to be locked up in the brig for the night. Next day he told me when he got to the MAA's alleyway, they were sat drinking whisky and so surprised and pleased to see him, they asked him to join them for a drink! Usually they'd have to go to the Pig to collect a stowaway, getting abuse, even pelted with beer cans. They couldn't believe that he'd voluntarily gone back, and felt so pleased with him. We enjoyed an extremely pleasant couple of days on board. Dom asked me did I fancy shipping out with him on a cargo boat? Of course I would! He'd always been on cargo boats, mainly the marvellous Port Line. He said I'd like it: less pressure, more laid back. I agreed, giving him Lee's guest house number, so he could ring me when he signed off.

*Northern Star* docked in Southampton October 31st, 1974. That morning Dominic was taken to the gangway. The MAAs shook his hand, then he walked back to the *Oriana* at 106 berth. Later that morning, our ship's company signed off. Those sailing next trip would sign on the following day. Later, back at Lee's, we had drinks and I told him all about the trip and the beautiful young man I'd met. I said he was going to call me, as we planned to ship out together. Innocently, I failed to realise what might be going through Lee's mind, and the consequences of finding my own boyfriend.

By the next day, before returning to work, I hadn't heard from Dominic. Thinking he didn't really want to see me after all, I signed back on. Sadly I got on with my work and then returned home to Lee's. While I was there the hall payphone rang. It was Dominic. He'd tried to call many times but the line was either busy, or no reply. I told him I'd signed back on but knew how to arrange to be signed off! (I later often wondered if the phone was deliberately busy using an extension line, or unanswered on purpose?)

Dr Burke ran a surgery in Oxford Street not far from the Pool, where seafarers were able to temporarily register if they had a medical problem. You visited him with a sob story, saying you felt unwell, depressed, suicidal and such. He'd sort you out, give you a prescription and, if needed, a sick note. I persuaded him to write me a sick note, bless him. This is how I managed to sign off November 4th, 1974. Dominic and I were over the moon. It meant we could ship out together. He came back to the guest house to stay. I naively hoped Lee would be happy for me that I'd met a handsome man. I wanted him to like Dominic for my sake. Initially Lee appeared to be kind to him. I didn't realise Lee saw him as a threat to our cosy, loving relationship, as did Roy (unlike placid AB John). I suppose Dominic was a stranger to Lee and Roy. Sadly things would never quite be the same again, although I still adored Lee, until his untimely death in 1981.

At the time I didn't make allowances for the fact Dominic was a butch AB. He was shocked by Lee's outrageous personality and drinking. Also he was shocked by all the queens coming and going in the house, the outrageous camp, and the Polari. He'd never known anything like it. I also failed to make allowances for his age, only twenty. Being an AB, I thought he was older. (At the time he was one of the youngest ABs in the Merchant Navy.) Like me, he'd bypassed the National Sea Schools, by taking a job on a coaster (small coastal cargo ship) in 1969 at fifteen. That way he'd accumulated sea time for his young age, which allowed him to enter the Merchant Navy. In the days that followed Dom and I got to know each other better. I soon realised he was not much of a hugger or kisser. This was due to his terrible childhood. He was unwanted by his parents, and consequently raised by his granny. He too soon realised I was not the saint he thought I was when we first met in Lisbon!

We visited Canute Road Pool every day, trying to get a cargo boat together. But we were only offered passenger ships. Dominic suggested we go to London, to try one of the Pools there. He'd previously shipped out of Tilbury, saying it was a friendly Pool; we headed to London. We stayed at the Stella Maris seaman's mission, near Tilbury Docks. Visiting the pool, the jobs board had nothing for two. So I mentioned to the counter guy that Dominic and I were hoping to ship out together. "What do you think this is," he said in a London accent, "a bleeding marriage bureau?" I blushed but he just laughed, winked, and said, "I'll see what I can do." Next day we called in and he told us he had a BP (British Petroleum) tanker job for both of us. *Middle trade* articles (for shorter voyages), going to Scandinavia to deliver central heating fuel; we'd probably be home for Christmas. At that time there were TV adverts showing new BP super tankers. I thought that hopefully we'd be on one of those, in a delightful single cabin with en suite bathroom. I was excited as I had only been on passenger ships. Tankers were new to us both, so we were both a little apprehensive. Tanker crew had the reputation of being rather nuts, due to long periods at sea. But I thought, what the hell, Dominic's been on lots of cargo ships.

The pool man told us to stay the night in the seamen's mission. "Tomorrow we'll come and get you." *Get you* sounded a bit ominous, although I thought no more about it. Next morning a bus arrived outside the mission to collect us, plus the rest of the crew, taking us to the ship berthed in an oil refinery, a place I'd never even heard of: the Isle of Grain. I looked around the bus and saw the usual mixture of crew. Near us I noticed what looked like two queens. One had dyed hair, a bold eke, and looked cod and evil. We arrived at the refinery on the Hoo Peninsula in Kent. To us *tanker virgins*, it looked like we'd arrived on the surface of the moon. Soon we saw gleaming BP tankers in the distance, and thought they looked wonderful. However, the bus stopped at a rusting old heap of a tanker slumped against the jetty. Was this our ship?!

'Oriana' My first ship, 1969

Author with passengers, Christmas 'Oriana', 1969

'Northern Star', 1971

My first drag show, 1971. L-R: Flo, Alice

'The Strange Case of Blondie'. My friend Lee Publicity photo, 1972

Drag Shows 'N.Star', "Funny Girl" 1972-4

Author singing (badly!) 'Northern Star', 1972

QE2 'Queen of the Seas', 1973

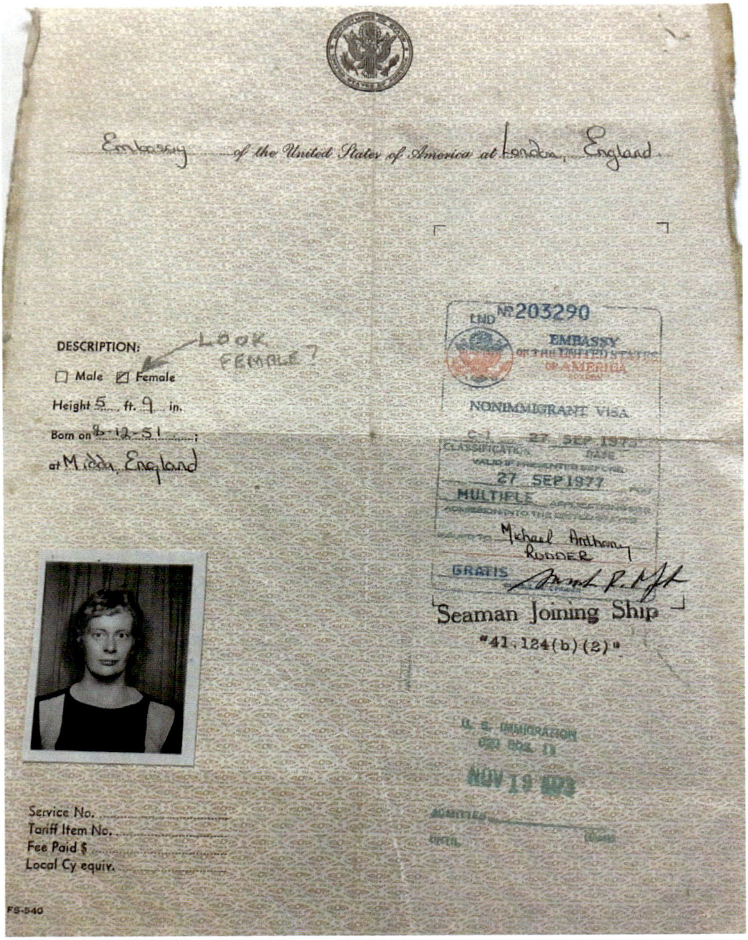
Embassy of the United States of America at London, England

DESCRIPTION: LOOK FEMALE?
☐ Male ☒ Female
Height 5 ft. 9 in.
Born on 8-12-51
at Middx, England

Service No.
Tariff Item No.
Fee Paid $
Local Cy equiv.

№ 203290
EMBASSY OF THE UNITED STATES OF AMERICA
NONIMMIGRANT VISA
27 SEP 1973
CLASSIFICATION DATE
27 SEP 1977
MULTIPLE
Michael Anthony RUDDER
GRATIS
Seaman Joining Ship
"41.124(b)(2)"

U. S. IMMIGRATION
NOV 19 1973

FS-540

My US Visa to join QE2. (My blonde period- note US Immigration ticked female!)

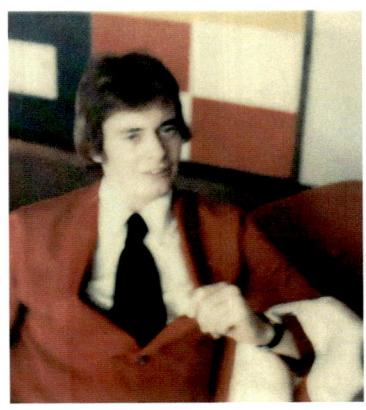

Author in QE2 waiter's uniform, 1973

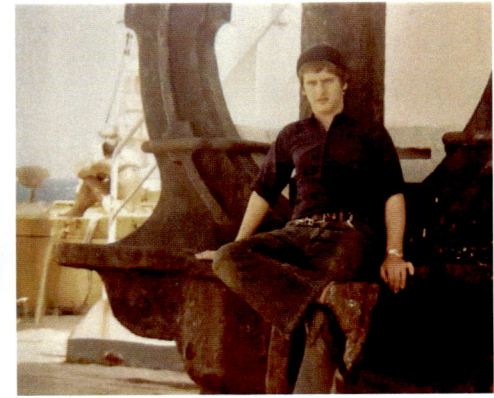

Dominic (on 'Oriana') when we met in 1974

Author (aboard 'Northern Star') when we met, 1974

Author as ships cook, tanker 'British Merlin' (Note snow to my left)

RFA 'Resource.' Where Author found his Faith, 1976

1981, Driving through a riot Falls Road, Bobby Sands death Belfast

Dominic in Costa Rica aboard Banana Boat 'Manistee', 1981

Dominic as Coxswain driving lifeboat tender 'Sun Princess' in background

Shipmates relaxing, Crew Bar, 'Sun Princess'

Dominic driving lifeboat tender in St Martin, Caribbean. The day he collided with a mooring buoy

Dominic as Crew Club Chairman with Star Rosemary Clooney (George Clooney's Aunt), 1985

'Royal Princess' named by HRH Princess Diana 1984

Author with Rosemary Clooney. L-R: Goddess, Mary, Author, Rosemary Clooney

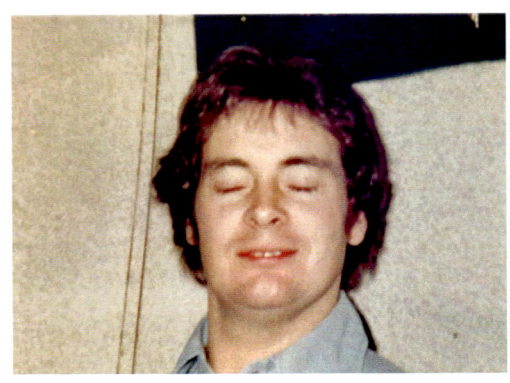

Author after a hard days work

Our Civil Partnership, Southampton December 2005. Author (seated) and Dominic

# 18

# Shanghaied!

As we drew closer, we saw that the tanker was the *British Merlin*. A 1961-built, 11,000 grt BP tanker, with fore and aft accommodation, and steam-driven winches, which Dominic loved, being a steam enthusiast. He reported to the bosun. I reported to the chief steward in his cabin. The two queens I'd seen on the bus introduced themselves: Jeff and George (Hester, and another Georgina). Hester was second steward, and was delegating catering jobs. He gave me the crew mess man's job, signing on November 10th, 1974. He later told me he'd clocked us on the bus, guessed we were a couple. He thought that as a mess man I'd see more of Dominic. Although Hester looked like an evil queen, actually he was a good man, with a great sense of humour. They'd both previously served on various ships, including doing many years on the old Orient liner *Oronsay*. Our crew cabins were all single-berths, with communal bathrooms nearby. My job a doddle. I just took care of the crew mess, and cleaned the chief steward's cabin. No uniform. I wore what I liked, jeans and T-shirt even.

I can't recall much of my work routine, I was so happily in love. As I looked after crew I got to know them all. They were a smashing bunch, liking me too. At night I'd leave out food for the watch keepers; bread, cold meats, salad, pickles and so on. At first in the mornings I'd have a mess to clean up, dirty crockery, crumbs and such. After a few days the night watch keepers cleaned the mess for me, so when I turned to, it was all clean. I'd sit with a cuppa before getting breakfast ready. The master actually looked like a proper old-fashioned bearded sea captain. His hobby was knitting. Passing his cabin, I often saw him in his comfortable chair, needles and wool in hand.

One evening the officers invited some of us to their bar for a game of darts. Unlike the crew bar, they also served spirits. As the evening wore on some of the lads, including me, got hideously drunk. I think everyone enjoyed themselves too much. We weren't invited again.

As Christmas drew near, it dawned on the crew that despite the fact we'd signed *middle trade* articles, we probably wouldn't be back to celebrate Christmas. Shipping companies found it hard to find crew over the Christmas period. To get over this, BP sent UK-crewed tankers sailing around Scandinavia and foreign-crewed tankers sailing around UK. This way crew couldn't pay off over this holiday period; we'd all been shanghaied! Most of us typical seaman were pragmatic about it. We laughed and got on with life. A few made desperate efforts to be flown home. One AB went to the centre castle store, put one hand on a vice, hit it with a hammer and was paid off. He was flown home at the next port. (As they couldn't get UK ABs, he was replaced by a Somali chap.) A week later he was followed by the bosun, a tall, upright, distinguished man. The bosun was proud of his war service, when he apparently drove Maiale torpedoes. These were straddled by two men in frogmen's outfits, who guided them to attack enemy targets before swimming away. Now he had a much younger wife and was anxious to be home for Christmas. In port, a gangway was rigged overboard. While he and three

ABs were positioning it by hand, he claimed to have hurt his back. Consequently, after a doctor's visit, he too went home for Christmas.

The chief cook suspiciously developed a chronic ulcer. He was sent to a shore doctor and flown home. Naturally, the company couldn't find a chief cook just before Christmas. When the chief steward told me, I foolishly informed him that I'd trained to be a chef. He asked if I'd help out in the galley, *just until they found a new chief cook*. I agreed. Little did I know what I was letting myself in for!

In the past, when the company had a bad reputation, seafarers referred to the initials BP as 'bags packed'. Most crew couldn't wait to get off. To counteract this, BP offered better conditions, pay and, as I was to find out, plenty of food with many choices. There were large menus for breakfast, lunch and dinner. The second cook and baker thankfully carried on making bread and desserts. (I was hopeless at bread.) Being a first-time ship's cook, I found it rather daunting, though quite enjoyed cooking and creating menus. However, the fridges were a terrible mess. The embittered previous cook hadn't rotated fresh produce. It broke my heart to throw rotten food overboard, as we did in those days. Meat came in carcasses, whole sides of bacon and so on. The last cook didn't like roasting shoulders of lamb either (too hard to carve). So he roasted just the legs, leaving carcasses with only shoulders. I'd never really been trained in butchery, so I struggled getting enough chops for meals and so on. Even the bacon needed to be sliced by hand.

Thankfully, my Dominic helped me, he found a bacon slicer in pieces, assembled it and screwed it to a wooden bench, making it easy to slice rashers. The crew seemed happy with the menus and enjoyed my cooking. I tried using fancy college names, like calling cauliflower soup *creme du Barry*. (It was named by Escoffier after Comtesse Du Barry, mistress of Louise

XV.) I was highly amused when an old greaser asked me, "Ere, Michael! What's this cream doobry?"

I cooked the Christmas lunch, which went down well. We were in port that day and Missions to Seamen bought us all little Christmas presents. It was all rather sweet and jolly. Dominic and I stored cans of beer in our port boxes, chilled by the cold air penetrating through the steel. We'd sit in the cabin having a beer before lunch and dinner. New Year's Eve, we were in a little harbour again and went for a walk ashore, for some more expensive beers. We'd become friendly with a Belfast radio officer, who smuggled us down a bottle of whisky, bless him, to see in the New Year. At midnight all the vessels in the harbour sounded their sirens and fireworks exploded. It was so cosy sat in the cabin having a dram, thinking what 1975 had to offer.

After Christmas, BP found a chief cook. He flew out and I reverted back to mess man. Then we'd good news. In January the ship was due to change Articles. These ship's Articles of Agreement were for certain periods of time – one year, eighteen months and such. (Even though I've googled it, I'm not sure what these periods were/are.) When Articles changed, you weren't forced to re-sign and the company were obliged to get you home. Would we stay? Dominic and I liked the ship. It had a pleasant happy crowd. This being my first tanker, I had wondered at first if they'd accept an openly gay man like myself? I'd heard conflicting stories. Due to long periods at sea, some tanker men were considered a bit strange. Some queens said they'd had a ball. Others said the crew were *cod* (not pleasant) toward them. I needn't have worried. Everyone was fine. I was treated with great respect. I can only conclude that queens who were treated cod were probably cod queens! Nevertheless, sailing around Scandinavia was cold and dreary, compared to the Mediterranean, New York and so on. Along with most of the crew, we decided not to re-sign. January 18th, 1975, we flew home from Gothenburg, landed in Heathrow, and made our way back to Southampton.

After a few days at Lee's in Hill Lane, I took Dominic home to meet my parents. My mother, as usual, was kind and welcoming. Dad was unsurprisingly not so forthcoming, although polite enough. In the 1970s the IRA started a bombing campaign in England. I suppose some people thought *anyone* from Northern Ireland was suspect. I talked with Dominic at length about the Troubles, and understood more than most why these terrible events happened. However, most people in England had no understanding of what it was all about. The press and the government made sure of that. It took some time for my parents to realise what a kind, caring and good person Dominic was. As usual at that time, we had to pretend Dominic and I were just good mates. Sadly, any mention of any other kind of relationship strictly taboo.

We returned to Southampton and Lee's. He was sat in the kitchen, in the usual black kaftan, a cigarette in one hand, a large vodka in the other. As previously mentioned, things had changed. I was with Dominic now and couldn't possibly spend so much time having fun with Lee and keeping Roy happy. Dominic had a low opinion of Roy, who he thought was greasy and a younger version of Rolf Harris. In later years that turned out to be the case. This led to an atmosphere at times, although I believe Lee continued to be kind to both of us, and we still enjoyed a certain amount of fun. I suspect that deep down Lee hoped things with Dom and I would fizzle out.

Certain queens visiting Lee's place either didn't like it, or were jealous of the fact I was now boxed off with Dominic. They made their resentment quite clear. One of them cruelly said to me, "Just because you're *boxed off* you've abandoned poor Lee. But let me tell you something, my dear. You mark my words, THAT BOY won't stay with *you* for very long!" I still see these people after all these years together. I wonder if they remember their harsh words? I haven't forgotten, but I have completely forgiven. Good friends are too precious to abandon if you don't see eye to eye occasionally. Plus it's all in the past, a long time ago.

A lovely queen Debbie/Dave visited Lee's too. Due to the 1973–4 oil crisis, cruise lines suffered, especially thirsty old cruise ships. Debbie's old ship *Reina del Mar* was to be sold. He found a job with RFA (Royal Fleet Auxiliary), telling us it was well-paid, interesting working aboard tankers/supply ships. RFA ships are manned by civilian Merchant Navy crew, and follow the Royal Navy fleet to supply and replenish them. At this time passenger fleets were shrinking. Many seaman from liners were joining RFA, who then had a fleet of about twenty-plus ships. (The Royal Navy, at the same time, I believe had about sixty vessels.) Debbie gave us the telephone number of RFA, whose offices were in the Empress State Building, West Brompton, London. (RFA crew nicknamed it the Mad House.) At the time when built in 1950 it was one of the tallest buildings in London, accordingly named in honour of the Empire State Building. We telephoned the Mad House, asking if there were vacancies for a steward and an able seaman. They had two jobs on a small fast fleet tanker, *Blue Rover*, 16,000 gt and built in 1969. They'd contact the Shipping Federation, advising them we had jobs with the RFA. We just needed to visit the Pool for medicals, Union clearance, rail warrants, and joining instructions.

# 19

# Interesting Time with RFA

We were issued with rail warrants to North Shields on the Tyne, where *Blue Rover* was in dry dock. Dominic knew of a seamen's mission in South Shields, at 53 Mill Dam. On March 2nd, 1975, we took a British Rail train to Waterloo, and then went to Newcastle via Kings Cross. Finally a local service took us to South Shields and the mission, an old-fashioned, basic, though clean, place. When we arrived the weather was positively freezing. In the bitter howling wind we both caught colds. I remember us going out for a few beers that night, as there weren't many restaurants. Dominic said, "Let's have fish and chips," which we ate while walking back. In the mission we warmed up with some whisky macs (scotch and ginger wine). It was all incredibly romantic.

Next morning we took a small ferry to North Shields and onto *Blue Rover*. Even in the 1970s you could see how antiquated the shipyards were. The ship was actually afloat in wet dock. We'd be working by until the ship was ready to sail. It didn't involve much: cleaning, loading stores, preparing cabins, dining areas and so on ready for main crew to rejoin. As it wasn't possible to live on board, we were given daily subsistence: a generous payment for food and lodgings. An average weekly wage then was about £50 a week, or £7 a day. Our subsistence was over £17 a day! At lunchtime we'd go to a local pub, which was heaving with shipyard workers packing the public bar in their dirty work gear. We'd have a couple of pints and a pub lunch, just as everyone did in those days. Dockyard pubs were basic. Their main function was serving quick pints with food and a well-deserved pint on the way home. I remember seeing a guy sink a pint of Guinness before it had even settled.

Finally, preparations began for the rest of the crew to join. To our dismay the two-berth cabins were to be occupied by two crew. Normally on cargo ships, including most RFAs, the adult crew occupied single-berth cabins. Only boy ratings shared a cabin to stop them 'getting up to mischief' or being led astray by ratings. Dom told me a funny story of a Port Line ship he was on. One day when the 4–8 watch keeper was on his rounds waking everyone, he caught two deck boys in bed together. He wasn't bothered; he was more concerned what was for breakfast! Deck boys' job was to prepare the mess room for meals. When word got out, as usual the crew took it in their stride. They were more concerned with whether the boys had washed their hands before starting work! No mention was made of them being queer or gay; it was just two boys shagging each other!

We signed on March 4th, 1975, sailing to Portland (Castletown) near Weymouth, Dorset. For *work up* we were testing all the replenishment equipment, plus boat, fire and NBCD (Nuclear, Biological, Chemical Defence) drills. Gas-tight double compartments were at all entrances and exits, with spray-cleaning stations. Airtight exterior metal dead lights covered all portholes or windows, which screwed tight shut. Water spray jets on the exterior of the vessel were there to wash away poisons, radiation and so on. Plus there were other devices to keep ships safe in the event of hostile attack.

*Blue Rover* was a great little tanker to work on, the routine easy. I took care of a few officers' cabins, serving meals in the officers' dining room. As the ship rolled somewhat, dining tables were equipped with large double-sided rubber place mats. These shiny mats clung to the Formica tables, holding crockery and cutlery in place; they were extremely effective. We returned to Portland in Dorset, where there were about six pubs right near the ship. They were frequented by Navy base workers and Navy or RFA ships' crew. Being new, we found our first RAS (replenishment at sea) extremely interesting. A Navy ship like a frigate or cruiser came alongside; both vessels held a steady speed of at least ten knots. With large ships like aircraft carriers, the tankers or supply ships came alongside ('held station') with the larger vessel. A small line was fired between the vessels. Lines and oil pipes would be hauled across on flexible rigs; nozzles were connected and replenishment commenced. During work up, deck crew were exercised in transfer of fuel, stores and personnel by this method, also in 'emergency breakaway'. Crew were also exercised transferring stores and supplies vertically by helicopter (VERTREP). Most RFAs were equipped with a helicopter pad (as was *Blue Rover*) and most had hangars.

Following work up we had a quick run to Gibraltar, to 'break the bond' for duty-free in the bars. Dominic and I went ashore for a romantic dinner. However, so many cockroaches were running around the floor that we had to keep shuffling our feet to keep them at bay. Although we liked the ship, we weren't happy with the accommodation. Being new to RFA, Dominic shared the only two-berth ABs cabin. All the rest were singles. (This was due to the fact that when entering service, it became obvious they needed two extra ABs. The solution was to get rid of two deck boys and use their cabin.)

There was only one queen on board, Phyllis, the Old Man's steward. He had a two-berth cabin to himself. He was a strange old queen, not sociable, and no fun at all! I remember him raising hell because his afternoon kip was disturbed for an NBCD drill. Nevertheless, we *all* had to take part in drills. No exemptions, not even for posh Phyllis. After a couple of months we decided to hand in our notice, to see if we could get a ship together with single cabins. We paid off in Portland April 29th, 1975. We took a train from Weymouth to Southampton, checking in with Lee at his Hill Lane guest house. I nipped home to my folks as usual. Only being away two months, we didn't have much leave accrued, and returned to Southampton.

Around the late 1960s a new company, Overseas National Airways, planned to build eight ships to use for fly-cruises. As Cunard's transatlantic business dwindled, Cunard bought fifty per cent of ONA shares, with a view to operating fly-cruises. As the first two ships were built, ONA ran into financial trouble and in 1971, Cunard acquired the company. They commissioned the first two ships as *Cunard Adventurer* and *Cunard Ambassador*, mainly for the US market. These two 14,000 gt ships were unsuccessful. Not up to Cunard high standards, they were badly built and not enduring. The first one, *Cunard Adventurer*, built 1971, was sold in 1976. *Cunard Ambassador*, commissioned in 1972, suffered a catastrophic fire in 1974 and was declared a total loss. Interestingly, the builder's number was 666, Satan's number!

*Cunard Countess* was their latest new small cruise ship. However, I believe the deal was signed in the 1970s. By the time the ship was built in Copenhagen, the shipyard was in financial trouble. To save money, the ship was sent to Italy to be finished. She was 17,500 tons and extremely popular for twenty-one years, sailing out of San Juan, Puerto Rico, with US, UK and international passengers. (We were to see her there in 1982.)

Monday morning we jumped on the bus to the Pool in Canute Road. On the jobs board was a 'run job' on *Cunard Countess*. That meant joining the ship, taking it from A to B, one port to another, then signing off. It was a quick, one-off job, and usually paid extra, as no further work was offered. We were sent to the Cunard personnel office, who had the final say. As I'd sailed with Cunard, they were happy with me; Dominic was unknown to them. They looked at his book and noticed he'd been with Port Line, one of their subsidiaries. For a reference they called Frank Butler, Port Line personnel officer in KGV Dock in London. He asked, "Is Dominic wearing a tie?" (When young, he always wore a tie.) They replied, "Yes!" Frank declared, "I know him well." Consequently, Dom was given the job. Cunard made it clear it was indeed a run job. We'd be paid a considerable amount extra (we can't recall how much). However, they didn't want to hear any moans on our return.

We were to fly to Copenhagen, Denmark, May 19th, join *Cunard Countess*, and take the ship to a shipyard in La Spezia, near Genoa, Italy. There the ship would be completed. Then we were to fly home. We were glad to get away from the strained atmosphere at Lee's. I travelled to Heathrow with another steward, John/June, a hard-drinking and rough Scots queen. Flying to Copenhagen May 19th with the ship's cooks, we prepared the vessel for the crew who were joining next day. It was quite a shock to find the ship was an empty shell. Decks and staircases were in place, with little else, except the bridge forward and a mess room aft. Our sleeping accommodation was made up of wooden partitions. We slept on temporary beds welded to the deck.

We were alongside overnight in Copenhagen. It was the first time I'd been to the Danish capital, so I went to see the sights, especially famous Tivoli Gardens. Next day Dominic plus the rest of the crew joined us. We all signed on May 20th, 1974.

The ship stayed one more night in port, a chance for Dominic and me to enjoy Copenhagen. Next day we departed for La Spezia in Liguria, northern Italy, for fitting out (finishing a ship's interiors).

The short voyage was fairly uneventful. During the trip, Dom celebrated his twenty-first birthday.

Now he was officially legal *ashore*. Eight years before, the 1967 Sexual Offences Act made homosexual acts in private between two consenting males over twenty-one legal. However, this did not include the armed forces and the Merchant Navy. I thought, *Now at least if we ever get into trouble ashore, they can't accuse me of corrupting someone under 21.* Nevertheless, I didn't think the Act would change homophobic attitudes ashore. As for life on ships, everyone seemed to accept each other anyway. As long as you were a good person, no one was interested in your sexuality. You were just another ship mate.

*Cunard Countess* docked in La Spezia May 28th, 1975. We paid off and were taken to a hotel for the night before a flight back to the UK. Our hotel must have asked the ship's agent what the British liked for breakfast and been told bacon and eggs. In the morning we were amused to be served a plate of bacon *mixed* with eggs, cooked *together*, with bacon sticking out of the yolk. It was served with strong Italian coffee.

We flew back to the UK, and had a couple of weeks leave split between our families and Lee's place, where things were still rather strained. Pearl visited one day, coming to our rescue. He saw what was going on, felt sorry for us, and asked if we'd like to stay in his caravan. We'd be looking after his dogs while he was away – one week on, one week off – on the Weymouth Sealink Car Ferry. We jumped at the chance. I asked Lee if it was OK. Of course it was. It was a joy staying in Pearl's large, luxurious mobile home in Rownhams, the genteel Southampton suburb. It was the first time Dominic and I were able to have time alone together. Neither of us could drive, so we took the bus to Southampton for shopping and a pub lunch in the Globe. We enjoyed a wonderful time together. I'd cook supper while Dominic took Pearl's two Pekinese dogs for walkies. It was bliss with no one to bother us.

We decided to return to RFA, as they were the only company who might let us to ship out together on the same vessel. However, we kept our relationship low key, especially as Dominic was on deck. We telephoned the Mad House and they offered both of us the RFA *Olmeda*, a 33,000-gt Ol-class fast fleet tanker. After clearance from the Union and Pool, and being issued with rail warrants, we got a British Rail train to Plymouth, making our way to the Devonport Naval Dockyard. Then the ferry took us out to Torpoint, where the *Olmeda* berthed at Yonderberry Oil Jetty. Thankfully there were single-berth cabins for all, as there were on most RFAs. We signed on 11th June 1975. There was a large crew bar right near our cabins, run by the crew. It served CSB, Courage Sparkling Beer, draught ale and lager, as well as spirits. Some deployments were extremely long, as much as eighteen months. This beer and lager was reputedly brewed extremely strong to last whole deployments. The crew gave it the nickname 'nerve gas' (and it was)!

I was officers' bar steward, taking care of the senior purser's cabin, and the officers' wardroom. Alfie Kendal, the senior purser, was a joy. I soon discovered he loved gays. I think he knew most of us were fun, good at our jobs, and kept everyone happy. A couple of years later he took a ship on an important sales tour, employing mostly gay catering staff. His friendliness was probably why I was given the bar job. He was married, middle-aged, plump, very jovial, and loved food, especially drink. Though straight, he was what we call a camp homie, and great fun. I'd take him morning tea, service his cabin and tidy up the officers' wardroom. I served pre-lunch and pre-dinner drinks in the bar. At night they helped themselves. Most mornings Alfie quietly told me he'd had a "hard night." I should bring him black coffee laced with a large brandy. He'd spray masses of air freshener around, in case anyone caught a whiff of his "special" coffee. It really didn't fool anyone. You still smelt the brandy, though no one mentioned it.

We were supposed to be the replenishment tanker for HMS *Ark Royal*, the veteran WWII aircraft carrier. However, she was delayed in refit. We spent six months on *Olmeda*, mainly sailing round the UK (*rock dodging*). We were exercising and refuelling Royal Navy ships and occasionally going to ports like Gibraltar, which was a great run ashore. (It was not much fun for the queens; it appeared a little bit homophobic.) Debbie joined the ship too. It was good to see him. Sometimes we had long weekends off and Debs knew how difficult it was for Dominic and me to relax at Lee's, so he'd give us the keys to his caravan home in Hedge End, Southampton. We'd go there to collect his mail and have a cosy weekend together, which was wonderful. It was kind of Debs and so typical of him. He was a delightful man.

Scots queen Morag/Bruce, who I'd sailed with on the *Arawa* and the *Northern Star*, was on board. He was rough and highly amusing. One evening in the bar after a few pints of nerve gas a greaser (engine room rating) *sent up* Morag for a laugh, using very colourful language, shouting, "Ere, Morag, when I shagged you last night, I ended up with shite on my dick." Quick as a flash Morag replied, "What did you expect dear, caviar?" Even Dominic, who dislikes bad language and vulgarity, had to laugh. Morag got his revenge on the greaser, who passed out drunk one day in the bar. With other crew members' help, he made the greaser's face up with lipstick, eyeliner, eye shadow, the lot. On waking, without even looking in a mirror, the greaser went straight to the mess to eat. It took him a while to figure out why the crew were all doubled up with laughter.

On one trip a new north country steward joined. We soon realised he was gay, though rather naive. He wore thick-rimmed glasses and because he had an extremely long, thin nose, Morag gave him the nickname Keyhole Kate, after the *Dandy* British comic character. One day before lunch Morag said to Kate: "Those thick glasses look so cod, dear. Leave them off." He little realised that the poor queen was practically blind without them. We were highly amused when Kate went to serve soup at lunchtime. His fingers slipped into the hot liquid. As he dashed to serve it and get his fingers out, he crashed into a large pillar, spilling the contents. The glasses were hurriedly reinstated.

RFA contract guys were the golden boys, getting the good deployments going to America, Australia and such. Alfie Kendal asked why didn't I take a company contract? It was very beneficial. I asked him to sort out the paperwork for me. During the trip I had a very tongue-in-cheek humorous interview with the assigned security officer, an amiable man. I'd heard that part of a company contract was signing the Official Secrets Act, and so I enquired if being gay was a problem. He asked me, did I suffer from homosexuality? "I wouldn't call it suffering. I rather enjoy it." By now he was smiling, trying to suppress a chuckle. Asking, "Are you a practising homosexual?" I gave him the usual answer: "How dare you! I'm fully qualified!" He started chuckling, telling me *they* may need to check me out, in case I got friendly with a couple of Russian sailors and gave away secrets. I cheekily told him *one* Russian sailor would be enough for me, and had a laugh about it. A few weeks later I signed a company service contract and the Official Secrets Act. Dominic wasn't interested in a contract. He wasn't that enamoured of RFA, though I thought it would give me stability, and maybe help me start saving for a deposit on a home for us both (which it did).

Alongside one day, in the cold store collecting lemons for the officers' bar, a Geordie steward said to me, "One of your *maites* just joined." I knew exactly what he meant; must be another queen. Later I bumped into Vera/Brian, trying to act butch and straight, wearing jeans. He saw me and was so pleased. "Hello, duck. What a relief to see another HP. I was worried to death joining this naval-type ship." I'd met Vera previously on *Canberra*. He was a section waiter, a leading hand, drinking in the PO (petty officers') bar. As I drank in the crew bar, we'd rarely socialised.

We soon got to know each other well. He lived in Brighton and was one of the funniest, kindest men I've ever had the privilege of having as a lifelong friend. Brian was stocky, plump, extremely jolly, with mad hair like Boris Johnson. It made him look comical. He was in charge of the officers' dining room pantry aft, making lots of friends with his larger-than-life personality and wicked sense of humour. As I served officers drinks forward prior to lunch, I missed the crew meal. After closing the bar, I'd go aft to collect my meal from Vera. One day in rough weather I ran along the deck clutching my coat, dodging waves to avoid getting soaked. On arrival for lunch I said to Vera, "I feel like Marilyn Monroe in *Bus Stop*." Vera said loudly, "You look more like the bus stop, dear!" Even I had to laugh.

Most evenings we'd go ashore with Vera in Plymouth, visiting a well-known pub, the Lockyer Tavern, a large pub with a mixed clientele, a gay back bar and an interesting history. It was a famous gay place in the 1950s, '60s and '70s. However, it's sadly no more. Local artist Beryl Cook frequented it. She was said to be amused by drag shows and gay people. A lot of her paintings were influenced by this place, immortalising the camp, welcoming patrons of the pub and buxom bar maid. Beryl Cook had a style all her own, which her painting *The Lockyer Tavern* embodies. Dominic, Vera and I would go there, have a few drinks, and enjoy the atmosphere. However, Dominic would rather it had been just him and I.

Previously Vera was in a drag act known as Bosom Buddies. The name of the act came from the closing song of the show *Mame*. It's a musical based on the 1955 novel *Auntie Mame* with music/lyrics by Jerry Herman. Vera got the name playing the Vera Charles part. I'd actually seen Vera's act many years before, when he danced along the bar in London's famous Vauxhall Tavern, but I didn't know him at that time. After a few drinks in the Lockyer, Vera began singing and dancing to the music, much to everyone's amusement.

Although Dom and I enjoyed our time together, our relationship really had its ups and downs. In Shakespeare's *A Midsummer Night's Dream* Lysander says to Hermia, "The course of true love never did run smooth," and this certainly applied to us early in our relationship when cracks began to appear It was both our faults, mainly me. We were actually completely different. Dominic was shy, quiet and reserved. I was the complete opposite. Dominic naturally wanted to spend time with just me. One of the main problems: Dominic was suspicious and wary of queens, who to him appeared to want to wedge us apart. They looked on Dominic as just another short fling that wouldn't last long. They were more interested in being entertained by me. When we first met, Dominic had put me on a pedestal. After spending time with free and easy Lee, and knowing I'd kept Roy happy, I fell off his pedestal, bringing about mistrust. I wasn't the jealous type at all. I also think I didn't make allowances for the fact that Dominic was younger than me. Before we'd met he'd had a completely different experience of being at sea.

We'd a fair number of fallings-out and eventually paid off *Olmeda* December 5th, 1975, in Birkenhead, both going on leave. I went home for Christmas and Dominic went home to Belfast. I was due to rejoin *Olmeda* in Birkenhead in January 1976. We met after Christmas, enduring another trying time in

Southampton. Things did not go well with Lee and Roy, again. When it was time to sign on, we'd talked. Dominic and I thought perhaps it'd be better if we were apart for a while, to see how we really felt about each other. Consequently, I signed back on *Olmeda* January 5th, 1976. Unbeknown to me then, Dominic bumped into a fellow Belfast AB, John, known as Mad Dog (ex-*Northern Star*) in Liverpool and found a job on a little coaster, *Frendo Hope*. He signed on the same day in Birkenhead. Both our ships sailed the same day, going separate ways.

Life on the *Olmeda* was not the same as previously. We had a new senior purser who wasn't fun like Alfie Kendal. Debbie had left too. I felt quite lonely, missing Dominic like hell. I hoped that maybe we'd both cool off, meet up again and things would be wonderful. While the ship was docked in Plymouth, I bumped into Flo (Bernie) in the Lockyer Tavern. He was on an ammunition ship, RFA *Resource*, telling me the ship was going on a great deployment to America with *Ark Royal*. It sounded wonderful. I contacted the Mad House, putting my name down for that deployment.

While in Plymouth I told Bernie, "You *must* meet my friend Vera. She's *so* much fun." We arranged to meet in the Lockyer Tavern. Vera and I arrived first and after a few drinks Vera started performing to the crowd. They were very receptive. Drinks flowed. Later, seeing Bernie enter, I went across to greet him, introducing him to Vera, who was dancing around, extremely drunk. I said, "Bernie, this is my good friend Vera." Bernie *clutched the pearls* (hand to throat), fixed Vera a withering look, and said, "Is *that* her?" Vera and I often had a laugh about it afterwards. "Is that her," indeed!

In the two years I'd known Dominic, I'd discovered what an extremely good, kind man he was. If only we could sort out other little problems in our relationship, like me thinking he was possessive. I felt love depended on freedom; it should be freely given. In its purest form it doesn't seek to possess, or ask to be possessed, as in Kahlil Gibran's famous book *The Prophet*: "Love possesses not, nor would it be possessed; For love is sufficient unto love."

Meanwhile, we regularly wrote to each other. As a prolific letter writer, regularly corresponding with Mum and others, I found writing easy. Dominic found writing hard, so I appreciated the fact he'd taken the trouble to send letters. They were romantic, heartfelt and often extremely amusing, which made me miss him even more. He was a Catholic, with extremely strong faith. I was an atheist. He told me he'd pray for me. I almost laughed, taking little notice as I'd no religion, faith or beliefs. That too was about to decidedly change!

# 20

# Run, Baby, Run

At the end of January 1976, a signal arrived from the Mad House to pay off *Olmeda* in Portland February 1st, and join RFA *Resource* in Plymouth February 3rd. I travelled to Lee's for a merry reunion. Then I took a train to Plymouth, joining *Resource* at anchor. Ammunition ships usually anchored far out, well away from the docks, due to the nature of their explosive cargo. I was thrilled to be sailing with my old mate Flo (Bernie). Not being on a 'passie boat', RFA crew called us Bernie and Michael, not camp names. Everyone knew we were gay but they treated us just as another crew member. On RFA ships we were usually more subdued, though not always. Everyone knew, and we still had a certain amount of camp, especially if there were a few of us! I was in charge of the officers' dining room, a job I didn't much like. I preferred cleaning cabins or bar work. Bernie was captain's steward, looking after a delightful Old Man.

*Resource* spent time in Plymouth storing before sailing. Evenings, as usual, we'd go to the Lockyer Tavern for drinks. Sometimes we'd end up in notorious Union Street, where matelots (Royal Navy sailors) and locals went to party. It was a street leaving with pubs, bars, dance halls and nightclubs. I can barely remember the pubs but I think there were the Clipper and the Doghouse. I also remember a nightclub, Diamond Lil's. The BBC were filming the evening before the deployment sailed. When we enquired, we were told they were making a major documentary series entitled *Sailor*. It follows the *Ark Royal* on our five-month deployment to North America, with Rod Stewart singing the opening theme music, "Sailing." *Ark Royal* crew were filmed enjoying a final night ashore before the deployment sailed. Union Street was positively jumping!

During the voyage we followed *Ark Royal*, spending days at sea replenishing and exercising. Although Bernie was great fun and good company, I really missed Dominic. We wrote long letters to each other, which were heartwarming, making separation even worse. The British Forces Post Office postal system was brilliant. I even received letters at sea by helicopter. *Resource* and *Ark Royal* met up in Puerto Rico and I had a smashing night out with Bernie. A good-looking matelot came back to our ship. I had fun with him but just went through the motions. Strangely I didn't enjoy it, missing Dominic. Back at sea, I became quite depressed, thinking we were going to be away from the UK for five months – five months before I could meet up with my beloved Dominic again. Classic songs like Ella Fitzgerald's "Ev'ry Time We Say Goodbye" made it more painful. Listening to the beautiful lyrics, I started drinking even more than usual, not eating properly and losing weight, which is quite unlike me. I was extremely low, tortured and lonely. I felt like a strange powerful force was chasing me, which I was running to escape from. Somehow, I couldn't quite put my finger on exactly what it was, or what was wrong with me.

We called into various Florida ports, including Fort Lauderdale, a place I've always loved. There was a fabulous seafront Gay Hotel and the Marlin Beach Hotel. Part of the classic 1960 Connie Francis movie *Where the Boys Are* was filmed there. Ironically it became a gay hotel, bar, and resort, appropriating the film title as its catchphrase. Hugely popular daily afternoon gay tea dances were held in the poop deck bar. Evenings it was packed with good-looking gay guys, drinking cocktails, having fun. We had some great nights there. Sadly in 1986 the hotel tried to attract college spring break students and thereby lost its gay trade. It went bankrupt in 1992 and was demolished.

*Resource* spent a long weekend in Norfolk, Virginia, a short flight away from New York. Unusually, Bernie and I were lucky enough to get the weekend off. We decided to fly to New York, as he'd never been. We stayed in an old-fashioned Times Square hotel, the Edison, having a great time in town and in gay bars and clubs, drinking far too much. Late-night, raunchy gay sex clubs like the Mineshaft and Anvil advertised in gay mags. One ad even read, "Be a whore. Check your clothes at the door." We chose the Anvil, on 14th Street, housed in a former sailors pay-by-the-hour hotel, The Liberty Inn. Inside there was a rectangular bar, a dance floor and a 'performance area', painted black. Gay porn was shown on a large screen. Behind this was a huge, dark 'wild back room' for sex and other things. We bought drinks, watching the show, our eyes nearly popping out of our heads. Naked men sitting on huge dildos and live *fisting* (fist f—ing) on stage, which we'd never seen before. I'm no prude. I was enjoying it, but was slightly shocked. It was a wee bit over the top, like Sodom and Gomorrah. Strangely, I didn't have sex that weekend. I just enjoyed drinking, dancing and watching the goings on.

During the deployment I met two charming young matelots off *Ark Royal*, Chris and Alan. I can't recall where – in a bar, or the Enlisted Men's Club? They were such delightful, gentle souls, and both gay. However, being in the Royal Navy, they needed to keep it well hidden. Homosexuality was illegal in the armed forces. Officers watched out for it in ships' companies. Ratings slept in large messes holding many bunks, making it difficult to get up to much, or to have privacy. Nevertheless, it still went on, though in secret, for fear of shame and dismissal. A bad discharge could really destroy the rest of a young man's life.

Homosexuality was officially illegal in the Merchant Navy. However, merchant ships generally accepted and tolerated it. Gays were seen as just another member of crew, able to be open about their sexuality. Single cabins on most cargo ships made things even better; one could entertain privately. Bi guys were easily available. Chris and Alan had a deep sense of peace about them, which I couldn't figure out. I met them a few times; they'd come back on board with me for a drink, looking around the ship. They couldn't believe we had single cabins and an actual crew bar.

We got along great. Both lads were so calm and serene, with a beautiful outlook on life. Eventually they told me they were both Christians, believing in God and Jesus. It meant nothing to me. I didn't have such beliefs.

However, they gave me a book, begging me to read it. Entitled *Run Baby Run*, it's the 1966 biography by Nicky Cruz, a man whose childhood in Puerto Rico is overshadowed by spiritualism. He moves to New York, becomes the leader of one of the city's fiercest, toughest street gangs, the Mau Maus, and is involved in drugs, knife fights, torture and murder. Cruz is proud, tough and feared on the outside. Inside, he's running scared, lonely, battling drugs and alcoholism. Eventually he meets a Pentecostal minister, David Wilkerson, the author of *The Cross and the Switchblade*. Wilkerson attempts to bring Christianity into Cruz's life, quoting the Bible. For example, "For God so loved the world, as to give his only begotten son; that whosoever believeth in Him may not perish but may have life everlasting." Although Cruz is extremely difficult, Wilkerson resolutely refuses to give up on him, until eventually Cruz finds redemption, accepting Christ into his life. The book is this amazing story.

Next few days at sea I read the book. I found it compelling reading, a classic testimony. Truly shocking, it was an amazing and extremely uplifting story. At the time I was feeling extremely low, still drinking too much, eating too little. Receiving Dominic's letters cheered me up but made me miss him even more. One night I went to bed, feeling very sorry for myself, with a rather peculiar sensation I couldn't shake off. Like someone or something was pursuing me. After drifting off to sleep, I experienced the most amazing, strange, vivid experience which to this day I still don't know if it's real or a dream. While lying in bed drifting off to sleep, my heart started beating harder and harder, then suddenly it stopped. I floated above my bunk and, looking down, I could see myself asleep in my bunk. Ahead I saw this amazing place, down a sort of enormous bright tunnel, full of light and incredible love. "Have I died?" I thought. "Will I never see my loved ones or Dominic ever again?" Then, as if my thoughts were heard, a beautiful voice spoke. "Now is not your time. Go back, with peace and love in your heart." I floated down to my bunk and to sleep.

When I awoke next morning, I thought, *Was that just a dream?* It seemed so real; I felt so different, so much better. My heart was full of love and amazing peacefulness. From then on, I believed in God, accepting Christ as my Saviour, something I thought truly impossible. I have a strong faith now. Though I'm not what you'd call an extremely religious person, it's *my* faith. I go to church occasionally but I don't broadcast the fact. Instead I have my quiet faith, just like my mum had. And I regularly say my prayers. Like her, I try to show my faith by being respectful, helpful and kind. When I told Dominic what'd happened he was so pleased that his prayers had been answered. I've never told anyone else about this experience before, except Dominic, as it's truly personal and private to me. It felt extremely difficult to actually set it down in writing. Nevertheless, I feel the need to mention all events that shaped my life, including this.

*Resource* returned to Plymouth July 26th, 1976. I proceeded on leave, spending time with my folks and at Lee's. After a five-month trip I had quite a few weeks leave. Meanwhile Dominic had written. He'd left *Frendo Hope* in March, joining *QE2* May 22nd, 1976, the year the starboard steam turbine exploded. The ship was delayed for weeks during repairs in Southampton. The summer of 1976 was extremely hot, with swarms of ladybirds all over the ship.

I'd written, telling him that I was paying off *Resource*. Dominic was due leave. He'd replied saying a deckhand friend, Joe Dunford, owned a cottage in Stoney Stratton, a village near Shepton Mallet in Somerset. Joe had told Dominic he could stay there with me for a holiday. It sounded great, as I was feeling fairly weak, and even washed out. It was all arranged. Dominic signed off *QE2* August 2nd, 1976, and we met up. I am not sure how we got to the cottage, as neither of us drove. I think we took the Penzance train to Bruton or Castle Cary, and a bus the rest of the way.

It was an idyllic cottage, set in a beautiful little village with friendly neighbours, who all knew Joe and each other. The weather was glorious and we spent a few extremely peaceful, happy weeks there. We'd travel to Shepton Mallet for lunch and go for evening walks to a lovely old country pub not far away. After having a couple of pints, we'd walk back and I'd cook supper. The air was fresh and it was so quiet at night, perfect for sleep. Absolute bliss. I soon got my appetite and strength back. I felt God had answered my/our prayers. Some evenings we'd take a neighbour's dog for a walk to the pub. First trip we discovered the dog had a taste for beer. We gave him a few clean ashtrays full of ale to drink. Big mistake. Dom had to carry the dog all the way home along the narrow winding lanes, mostly with no pavements. Luckily the lanes were quiet too.

At the end of leave Dominic was offered *QE2*. Being based in Southampton meant he could hop off at any time for us to get a ship together. This was a sensible thing to do, as *QE2* ran to a schedule. He signed back on September 5th, 1976. At this time, due to the situation with Lee and Roy, Dominic tells me he was of the opinion that he wasn't welcome there. Three's company, four's a crowd. Dominic was the fourth. Consequently, he now stayed with Terry and Jim, owners of the Amsterdam Guest House, who he met through Tommy Anderson. (Dom had sailed with Tommy previously on the *Port Houn* in 1971. Tommy was the first person to give him oral sex, even though Dominic was only seventeen!)

The Amsterdam was always busy with celebrities from Southern TV and the local theatre. Jim ran the guest house, while Terry was the director of ITV's *This Is Your Life*. He also directed the hour-long specials, like the famous ones with Lord Mountbatten and Danny La Rue, who became a close friend. Dominic said he was deeply indebted to Terry and Jim for letting him stay and dine when his funds ran low.

I was offered RFA *Engadine*, a helicopter support/training ship, based in Portland, Dorset. Hearing this ship never went far, I thought I could hop off if I needed to. Signing on September 8th, 1976, I was Old Man's steward again, but dismayed to find that catering crew cabins were two-berth. My cabin mate Chris was a gorgeous-looking young blonde, who I immediately fancied. Sadly he turned out to be rather dense, which rapidly cooled my ardour!

I soon discovered why *Engadine* never went very far. Despite being fitted with stabilisers (to make safer landing for helicopters), it could roll on damp grass. In rough weather it was all over the place. The Old Man was cordial, though exacting. I was fine with that; we'd a happy working relationship. He'd ask me for some thick slices of lemon to freeze, then pop one in his gin and tonic. It cooled the drink and imparted a rich citrus taste. He also kept empty sauce bottles, making his own vinaigrette dressing. Very good it was, too. However, life was boring based in Portland/Castletown, where the naval base is situated. There were a few pubs in Portland. Nearby was the excellent seaside resort of Weymouth, which I came to love. However, in those days when the season finished it was a dire place, so quiet. On weekends off, with Weymouth Station close, I'd go to Lee's and sometimes home.

During this time Lee and Roy took over a pub near the docks, the Davis's Hotel, in Terminus Terrace. They employed a queen friend of theirs off *QE2*, Ava (Derek) as cook. He was tough, good-looking, with gorgeous dark hair, and took his name from movie star Ava Gardner. (Queens did then.) He'd previously been a ladies' hairdresser (caring for Lee's hair) and was a self-taught cook. Like many self-educated chefs, he produced wonderful food. The pub became a roaring success, the talk of Southampton. On leave Bernie/Flo would often work behind the bar. Customers adored him. He was smart, funny, witty, so camp, and became something of a local legend. Ava, being stuck in the kitchen and out of the limelight, hated Bernie's guts, and pulled wicked stunts. Bernie would ask for a curry or chilli for his supper. Ava stirred in handfuls and handfuls of extra garlic, to ruin any chances of Bernie's potential trade!

One night Bernie and I attended a fancy dress party. I was Wonder Woman, I think. Bernie was wearing a home-made, extremely tight catsuit, complete with tail. While having a drink in the Davis's a woman stared at us, saying loudly to Bernie, "You've got a f—ing cheek wearing that!" Before Bernie could say, "I'll wear what I like, dear," the woman went on to say, "My husband bleeding fancies *you*." We all had a good laugh. It was a golden time for gay men in the 1970s and early 1980s. Most people had gay friends and we'd have much fun ashore together. In the '80s, this sadly all changed for many years when the dread horror of AIDS reared its ugly head.

The 1970s were also the golden era of fancy dress parties. I recall going to one dressed as Carmen Miranda, with a heap of plastic fruit piled on my head. Bernie and Stella came dressed as nuns, with *church keys* (ships' beer can openers) around their necks instead of crucifixes. They flatly refused to shave off their moustaches (another feature of the 1970s). Luckily the car had a sunshine roof. I was able to stick my tall fruit hat through it. People howled with laughter when we stopped at traffic lights; Carmen Miranda in the front passenger seat, accompanied by two nuns with moustaches! The Davis's pub was wonderful, one of the last of a golden era of dockside pubs. Lee quietly told me the pub would be the death of him. Sadly, his words were prophetic.

Many crew took weekends off, leaving a skeleton crew, which made life on board very dreary. There were no other queens on the ship to go ashore with. In the evenings I'd wander ashore, usually alone, for a drink in Castletown, Portland, pubs. At that time songs like "You'll Never Find Another Love Like Mine" by Lou Rawls and "If You Leave Me Now" by Chicago were top of the charts. They played constantly on the jukebox. I'd listen to the lyrics, which made me miss Dominic even more. I felt sorry for myself and extremely lonely. I hated the ship but decided to wait and see what Dominic wanted to do. He wrote saying he was paying off the *QE2* in November, before the ship went away for the winter. Then he planned to go home to Belfast for Christmas and New Year, a time he really enjoyed as a Catholic. (Being seafarers, it was quite rare to get Christmas and New

Year off, especially if on company contract.) I was stuck on the *Engadine*.

On board RFAs were signalmen who I believe worked in both the Royal Navy and Merchant Navy radio rooms dealing with signals, especially from the MOD. Most of them were real characters, some quite bonkers! I think it was due to listening to all those messages. A signalman on *Engadine* was like this and highly amusing. One of the catering boys aboard was huge, with strange features, and the signalman unkindly nicknamed him the Beast. At this time, Johnny Mathis had a huge, constantly played, Christmas hit with "When a Child Is Born." The signalman started singing loudly, "When a beast was born." Although slightly offensive to me at the time, I had to smile!

Fortunately the Old Man decided to go home for Christmas and New Year. I wouldn't be required and could go home too. Dominic and I kept in touch with regular phone calls and letters, which actually made separation even harder. After festive celebrations, I rejoined my ship and its boring routine continued during January. However, things were about to change!

# 21

# Far East Fun Run

Early January 1977, the captain sent for me, saying he'd received message/signal from Alfie Kendal, senior purser aboard RFA *Lyness*, asking for me to be transferred to *Lyness*. It was due to sail on a Far East defence sales tour. The Old Man said under normal circumstances, he wouldn't let me leave, as he was extremely happy with me. However, as he was due to go on leave himself soon, he'd allow me to transfer. I telephoned Dominic, telling him the exciting news, asking him to contact the Mad House to try and get a job there too. I paid off *Engadine* January 24th, nipping home to see Lee for the night. Next day I took a train to Portsmouth, joining *Lyness*, signing on 26th January 1977.

Alfie Kendal was pleased to see me, and appointed me captain's steward. Alfie said he'd wanted as many gay catering staff as possible for the deployment, to ensure drinks and meals served in various Far East ports were top notch (beautifully presented and served). Most catering staff, like myself, who'd previously worked on passenger ships, knew how to give good service. Gay stewards love to go the extra mile for their customers. That there'd be quite a few queens and gay men aboard always added to a happy ship's atmosphere.

I was made up to see some friendly, familiar faces, like Vera (Brian) and Trish (Trevor, ex-P&O). I'd given Alfie Trish's phone number; he'd contacted him with a job offer. There were other queens on board, like Ronnie/Dolly Potter and his Irish friend Cora. (I never did know his real name.) Ronnie was a typical tough cockney Londoner: gregarious, an undetermined age and extremely funny. The Scots second steward was gay, as was Alfie Kenda's right-hand man, deputy purser John L. Known as a *rice queen*, he adored East Asian men, which tickled me. Dominic managed to get a job on board too, signing on January 28th, 1977. We were happily reunited again.

*Lyness* was a 17,000 grt combat stores ship built in 1966, designed to carry large amounts of naval stores. As well as the normal Merchant Navy crew, it carried naval dockyard stores workers, who helped to move the military exhibition equipment around the ship. With huge internal lifts between decks, the ship was ideal to hold a defence sales exhibition on board. The lifts and decks were used to set up bars and restaurant-type eating areas, complete with carpets and potted plants. She had additional accommodation for military personnel. This is where the *squaddies* (army guys), and *boot-necks* (Royal Marines) were accommodated, who demonstrated the weapons systems, Scorpion light tanks and various other weapons. Shortly after loading we sailed for Alexandria, through the Suez Canal to the Far East.

The Old Man was a dear old Scots gentleman, Captain Andrews. Making beds, I always use 'hospital corners' (learnt from the *Star*; it means tucking sheets in tight, with four mitred corners). The first morning the Old Man asked me, "Michael, can ya nay tuck my sheets in soo taight. Last night I couldnae get into bed; this morning I couldnae get oot again!" I had a quiet giggle to myself, thinking, *This poor man, kicking the sheets up, just to get in and out of bed.*

Alfie Kendal and Ronnie Dolly were old friends, so Dolly looked after Alfie's cabin. Later, about 3:00p.m., I walked forward from our aft accommodation to get the captain's afternoon tea. Passing Dolly's cabin, to my surprise I saw he was putting curlers in his hair, getting ready for a pre-dinner nap. I asked, "Doesn't Alfie have afternoon tea?"

"Don't encourage them, dear," said Ronnie. "She knows where the bleeding kettle is." I had to laugh to myself: Dolly doesn't encourage afternoon tea. Camp or what!

Despite being senior purser, Ronnie referred to Alfie as TFOQU – That Fat Old Queen Upstairs. It didn't take long for everyone to copy this, with much encouragement from John L, who thought it absolutely hilarious. Later that trip the Old Man stopped me, asking, "Michael, why do crew refer to me as 'that fat old queen upstairs'?"

"Oh no, Captain," I said. "It's not you they're referring to. It's Alfie Kendal, the senior purser." "Indeed," said the Old Man, highly amused, going on his way chuckling. It turned out to be a mad hilarious trip with all these queens on board, which once again made Dominic unhappy. I spent far too much time camping it up with them!

First port was Alexandria, Egypt. Local dignitaries, army, navy and other top-ranking officials and so on, came aboard to inspect the weapons and weapon systems the UK had to offer for sale. There was a huge array of defence hardware, all sorts of weapons, even a little remote-controlled tank to defuse bombs. After viewing the hardware, drinks were laid on temporary bars constructed in the stores lifts. The stores decks were converted into marvellous drinking and eating areas, with excellent food served, taking into consideration local dietary customs and tastes. There were case loads of alcohol supplied.

This was hardly touched, Egypt being a predominantly Muslim nation. Of course, some of the opened bottles and cases of booze mysteriously found their way to our cabins. With pints of nerve gas, plus plenty of free bottles, the trip turned out to be one big party.

Vera had been promoted to catering store keeper by this time, and was a petty officer. RFA had a strict hierarchy: "Ladies, wives and women." Officers and their ladies used the officers' wardroom and dining room. POs used the POs' bar and dining room for themselves and their wives. Crew used the crew bar and mess for themselves and their *women*. Vera brought a case of drag with him for the trip, putting on her one man/woman drag show in the crew bar. He dressed in various outfits, such as Shirley Temple, singing "On the Good Ship Lollipop." As a waitress he sang Dora Bryan's '(Why) Because He Loves Me'. Vera was a tart for Joan Sims's 'The Spring Song'. He was also a girl guide for another number, 'Follow Me', and made quick changes between numbers. It went down a storm; the boys loved it. I think Trish and I donned frocks to join in the fun.

Not long afterwards the captain spoke to me, saying he'd heard Brian/Vera put on a show in the crew bar, and the boys loved it. He requested that I see if Vera would do a show for the officers. I asked Vera. "Yes, duck. Of course," he said. I relayed his response to the Old Man. Quite often on Sundays, pub lunch was laid on while we were alongside, when there were no exercises, with just a handful of duty crew. One Sunday it was decided to hold a pub lunch with Vera performing his one man/woman show in the officers' wardroom. He had the use of a cabin near the bar, next to John L's cabin, as a changing room.

Being invited to join the pub lunch was quite an honour. When it was finished, everyone settled down with drinks, waiting for the show to begin. Introduction music played, then in pranced Vera wearing one of his outfits. It went down a storm;

they loved it. When he'd finished his final number dressed as Shirley Temple, Vera joined us for a drink. Quite a lot of drink flowed. On Sunday evenings, a cold buffet was laid on in all eating areas, including in the officers', POs' and crew messes. Everyone could just help themselves. It required no staff. (I usually laid on a tasty cold spread, plus cheese and so on, in the captain's fridge.)

After a while Vera disappeared, supposedly to get changed. However, he'd caught the eye of an extremely handsome Rhodesian man, an army captain or similar, who followed him out the bar. Shortly after John L appeared, whispering that Vera was entertaining a gentleman in a next-door cabin. We flew there, listening at the bulkhead, hearing this man's voice saying firmly, "You've been a naughty girl," then a loud slap, followed by a scream. This was repeated. "In fact you've been a very, very naughty girl," followed by an even louder slap, a louder scream and Vera's voice shouting, "*I've done f—k all!*" We all fell about laughing. The thought of him calling her a naughty girl and slapping her fat arse! Even Vera laughed when I told him we'd heard the whole thing. Later we had a laugh when I reminded him, "You've been a *very* naughty girl!"

The trip turned out to be one of the most amusing trips I've ever sailed on. We went to some marvellous places, spending about a week in each, including Manila, Philippines, where Marcos was in charge, with a night-time curfew. Hong Kong, Indonesia, and Bangkok, Thailand. It was our first time there. The place was swarming with people. Ashore in the evenings, bar girls seemed very free and easy. If you didn't like girls they'd find you a man! Sembawang, Singapore, was our last port. Alfie decided to take the catering staff to dinner as a thank you for all our hard work. I seem to recall it was in one of those large outdoor eating areas the crew nicknamed the Sembawang Hilton. We sat at large tables. Naturally I was at Alfie's table with the other queens. When the main course arrived, it was huge platters of food garnished with chicken heads for chicken, fish heads for fish and so on. Some of the queens screamed their tits off when the food arrived. So funny; we had a wonderful evening.

This voyage wasn't without its ups and downs. Dominic and Vera fell out badly. Vera told me he wanted to make it up, asking me to tell Dominic he wanted to "bury the hatchet." I relayed this message to Dominic and his reply for Vera was, "Yes, right in her fecking head!" Even Vera laughed. They did make it up eventually, becoming good friends. Trish fell madly in love with a married service man on board. They too had ups and downs. One night, whilst serving officers dinner, Trish and I were talking about their turbulent relationship. Dolly, who was jealous, told Trish, "Why don't you act your age, Trish, dear? You're not exactly the epitome of eternal f—ing youth anymore." Trish replied, "Ooh, hark at Methuselah?" This didn't go down well; they fell out too.

Dom and I also had our moments. It was true, I did spend too much time having fun with other queens. An incident happened one evening in Manila which didn't help. I don't recall it, though Dominic remembers. Ashore with Dom and some queens, I apparently took a fancy to one of the local boys. I was holding his hand and appeared interested. Dominic understandably was extremely upset and disappeared into the night.

Later Dominic had a talk with Ronnie, seeking his advice. That was a bad mistake on Dominic's part. Ronnie may have been jealous our relationship. Ronnie told Dom to put his foot down hard, to stop me doing whatever I wanted and *make* me spend more time with him. This happened. Dominic called to see me. We had a discussion. Dominic's words and actions truly hurt and upset me. I made my mind up that when we returned to the UK I'd be leaving the ship without him.

Before arrival in the UK, we talked. But I stood firm, saying I felt he was too jealous, possessive and controlling. I'd go my own way, and have a long hard think about everything. Dominic was of the opinion that on board ship the other queens only wanted me to entertain them, which I was more than happy to do, leaving him "on the sideline." He said my trouble was, "I wanted my cake and eat it."

That year Captain Andrews was in command of *Lyness* for the Queen's 1977 Silver Jubilee Fleet Review. So on arrival in Southampton June 26th, 1977, I stayed aboard. *Lyness* prepared for the Fleet Review, with a full dress rehearsal June 27th. On June 28th in Southampton, official guests, including members of Her Majesty's Opposition Government boarded. At 11:15a.m. precisely, we sailed for the Review, which included *Royal Yacht Britannia*, many Royal Navy vessels, including HMS *Ark Royal*, THV *Patricia*, QE2 and many RFAs, including *Engadine*. It was a very moving spectacle to watch. As is usual for any naval or royal event, it was precisely, elegantly and beautifully carried out like clockwork.

On our return to Southampton, Dominic paid off June 29th, 1977, flying home. I stayed with the ship, taking it to the Tyne, paying off on 7/7/77, said to be the luckiest date in the calendar. Not for me. Taking a train to London with Ronnie and Co, we partied all the way to Kings Cross. I must have stumbled off the train, somehow making my way to Waterloo and boarding a train to Guildford. The next thing I knew, a police constable prodded me, saying, "You can't sleep here, sir." "Where am I?" "Haslemere, sir," he said. Oh dear, I was asleep with my luggage on the pavement outside Haslemere Station! It was only about twenty miles from Guildford, but it had added a lot of extra time to the journey and it was late for my parents to pick me up. I managed to get a train back to Guildford. Dad picked me up from the station, laughing when he saw the state I was in. Mum was not pleased and gave me a good talking to, which I probably deserved, bless her.

Dominic and I wrote. He said he regretted listening to Ronnie, agreeing he was probably jealous of us. The problem: I was a people person. I just loved mixing, enjoying company. Dom was a much quieter person, happy with his own company, extremely happy with mine. Three or more was a crowd to him. We both decided to write, give it time and see how things panned out. Dominic shipped out again on *QE2* 26th August 1977. He'd been on her before, with mates on board, and in 1978 she was doing her first world cruise.

Meanwhile, I spent a happy time at Lee and Roy's (wondering if Lee was pleased my relationship with Dominic was floundering, albeit slowly). Eventually I joined RFA *Tidepool* in Portsmouth, September 3rd, 1977. One evening in Portsmouth Dominic tells me he came down to see me, to discuss our unsure future. We met in a pub outside the naval dockyard. Dominic was hoping to have a heart-to-heart discussion. However, we were joined by a *Tidepool* crew member I knew, who Dominic felt was over-familiar. Dominic said I appeared to have little time for our discussion. Feeling like a "spare prick at a wedding," he jumped on the next train back to Southampton. (Again this isn't in my memory, but as Dominic has a better memory, it must have happened.)

Dominic remained on the *QE2*, which strangely became most fortunate for his sister, Veronica. While working in Germany she met and fell in love with Keith, a black American soldier stationed there. She flew home from Germany to apply for a ninety-day marriage visa and returned to the US, where they married. Sometime later, they were served a notice of eviction from their apartment.

So Keith could "get back on his feet," and find an apartment, she later flew home while pregnant, giving birth in Belfast. The baby was christened Nova. Following the birth, Keith stopped calling or answering her calls. Apparently, while travelling to Buffalo, New York, he'd met someone else. Veronica needed to fly back to America to get papers that would allow her and the baby a green card to become US citizens. There was a time limit. It appeared Keith didn't want to send the papers, nor did his mother, who lived in Washington DC. This is where Dominic came in; he was on the *QE2* when it dry-docked in Bayonne, New Jersey, December 1977, to have two new penthouses installed.

He called Keith's parents in Washington DC and arranged to travel there to collect the papers. He stayed with them and thinks they were so surprised, they meekly handed the papers over to him. When Dominic next went home, he handed those papers to Veronica. She flew back to the US to confront Keith. She believes when he saw the adorable and extremely beautiful little toddler Nova, it melted his heart and he just wanted life to go on as before. It was all fate, as I was to meet them later. Veronica and I are now extremely close, as she is with Dominic.

## 22

# Return to Oz

Joining *Tidepool* September 3rd, 1977, for the deployment, I found to my delight that my old mate Bernie/Flo was aboard. Michael B was the purser. I knew him vaguely, another amusing gay man. Also onboard was Mike M. I knew him from *Canberra* and the *Northern Star*. He was my age, tall, dark hair, and he spoke with an extremely posh accent. He never had a camp name, just known as *Oriana* (which he'd sailed on initially) or 'posh Michael'. There were also two older catering queens, Peter and George. They went everywhere together. Consequently, the crew christened them 'Hinge and Bracket' (a drag act dressed as two genteel older ladies, who played and sang comedy Gilbert and Sullivan, Noël Coward, and Ivor Novello songs and operettas).

It was a seven-month deployment to Australia. We were due to spend Christmas and New Year in Adelaide. Our first port, Lisbon, we always enjoyed. Then we went to Gibraltar. Bernie and I went ashore for drinks, ending up in the Gibraltar Arms in Main Street, where a bunch of UK matelots and marines were drinking. We bought a pint, sitting nearby. Bernie couldn't wait to join them. Sure enough, we got chatting and they asked us to join them. Madam was doing her Butlins best camp entertaining, flirting loudly and outrageously, asking me to get in more pints. The charming barmaid with a face like a smacked arse said, "I ain't serving you. We don't want *your sort* in 'ere!" I went back and told Bernie we weren't getting served. He said to the guys, "Come on, boys. They won't serve us. Let's go somewhere else." We all trooped out to another pub, leaving the barmaid open-mouthed and gobsmacked.

*Tidepool* sailed on through the Suez Canal (the 'sewerage canal', as we called it), stopping in Aqaba, Jordan. I don't recall going ashore, although I remember waving to the King of Jordan flying past in a helicopter. Don't know what he thought about Madam Bernie sunbathing in just a pink thong! Next stop was the port of Bandar Abbas in Iran. I'd never visited Iran, the place something of a mystery to me. I knew its ruler, the shah of Iran, was married to Farah Diba, reputedly the most beautiful woman in the world. I felt intrigued.

Bernie really loved birds (mainly the feathered kind). Finding a crested quail at sea resting on deck, he made a nest box for it, with food and water. Next day at anchor he tried to get the bird to fly ashore. Ms Quail was having none of it; it was much too far to fly. Bernie told me, "We'll have to take it ashore ourselves, dear." Later boarding a liberty boat (ship's lifeboat) we chugged a great distance to shore, along with a mad jock greaser wearing a kilt, and strangely a marine who must have been part of the military crew. Once ashore, we let the quail go. Walking in the heat looking for a bar, Jock and Marine tagged along with us. It seemed a usual sort of port, although we couldn't find anywhere to get a drink, and asked a taxi driver to take us to a bar. He took us some distance to Rosa's Bar, "the best bar in Iran." I suspect one of the *few* in Iran. We signed something strange, like a declaration of alcoholism, and gave it to a cashier, plus money. He gave us beer tokens. After a few beers and laughs, we managed to get a taxi back to the ship.

Just before Christmas we docked in Adelaide, to spend Christmas and New Year R&R (rest and relaxation). It was a strange Christmas, with weather gloriously hot and sunny. As we were to be alongside for some time, Bernie and I decided to rent televisions. to stay in and watch them. Mine arrived one afternoon while I was resting on my bunk. It was delivered by a gorgeous young Aussie, dressed for hot weather. Extremely friendly, he said, "Your bed looks cosy, mate." Half joking, I said, "Like to try it?" He leapt into bed. I thought, *Whoopee, so good to be back in Aussie!* People told us we'd hate Adelaide, a dreary, religious place, a church on every corner. However, we loved it, enjoying a wonderful time. (Who said you can't believe and have fun?) We made many friends and went to many barbies. (Aussies loved barbecues.) Visiting a beer and wine festival and barbie on Boxing Day, the weather was so hot I guzzled too many pints, got totally legless and had to be put to bed very early. Bernie had a ball, with a supposedly straight guy.

Bernie told me later the guy said in bed, "I want you to blow in my mouth." Bernie, thinking he was kinky, said, "Open wide," actually blowing in his mouth. "No," the guy said, "with your cock." We had a good laugh about that later, both thoroughly enjoying Adelaide. I had fun there with a very fit, handsome male ballet dancer. He sent me a rude and graphic post card. Purser Mike B handed it to me, having a good chuckle. I often worried about picking up infections like the clap. Previously, as hospital attendant, part of my job was to issue crew condoms. Crew came to see the baby doc (junior crew doctor) with gonorrhoea, which became apparent because of the discomfort and discharge. It was dealt with by a course of antibiotics, and the sufferer was advised not to drink (so that they didn't pass it on drunkenly)! If something worse was suspected, like syphilis, this needed tests ashore. In every case seafarers were advised to visit a sexual health clinic on leave. I was extremely lucky; I only ever caught gonorrhoea, which is easily dealt with.

Despite enjoying myself, I missed Dominic so much. I'd pray that things would work out between us. Perhaps I would become more sensible and devoted. Maybe he could be less controlling and jealous. We wrote loving letters constantly, and were both overjoyed to learn my ship was overnight with his ship, *QE2*, in Singapore. We booked a hotel for the night. Meeting that afternoon, we had a wonderful, loving time together, then enjoyed a romantic dinner, then spent a wonderful, romantic night in the hotel. It was marvellous. We promised each other we'd get together again very soon.

Although it was a long voyage (seven months), the *Tidepools* trip home was good fun. Bernie organised a Crossing the Line ceremony. He was Queen Neptune, and made me go as nurse instead of doctor. Concocting revolting coloured mixtures of flour and water, then taking leftover food, raw kidneys and so on, we did unspeakable things to those who'd never crossed the line before. Some of the officers and petty officers' wives were initiated. We were gentle with them and it was all good fun, but when we'd finished, the crew swimming pool was a revolting mess. Our captain was brilliant, great fun, with a wonderful sense of humour. Bernie organised a Gash Bag Ball. Everyone, including even the master, made an outfit from trash bags.

While helicopter crews were training, the Old Man asked us one day if we'd like a jolly (a quick flight in the helicopter). Bernie, myself and the two Michaels took up his offer. We boarded, strapped in and were given flying helmets, with built-in radios, earphones and throat microphones, so we could hear what was going on. It soon became apparent everybody heard each other when the pilot asked us to kindly refrain from idle chatter. Crew drilled us what to do if the chopper ditched (went down in the water), i.e., stay in your seat until the cab fills with water, release safety harness, open door and swim out. (If you left before it submerged, revolving rotor blades could decapitate or injure you.) We heard the pilot announce we were ready to take off, then heard our captain announce, "Queen's flight cleared for take-off," which set us all giggling. The chopper flew around our naval deployment and as we passed low over one of them, posh Michael said, "Varder at all those bona matelots, dear." That was heard by all. Next we heard someone on the navy ship's bridge say, "Who the hell have you got up there with you?" We all had a good laugh and our patient pilot took us safely back to the ship.

*Tidepool* returned to Portsmouth 19th April 1978. I'd accrued two months leave. First I went home to see Mum and Dad. I knew Dominic was paying off *QE2* on April 22nd and travelled back to Southampton, to meet him when he left the ship. We went to stay at Lee's guest house, having a fraught time again, as I wanted to spend most of my time with Dominic. Lee had other ideas. Poor Dominic was rather intimidated. It led to a bad atmosphere. I can't really remember exactly what happened, except I returned home. I don't recall if Dominic went to Belfast. I think he stayed with Terry and Jim, two gay friends, who owned the Amsterdam. There was a *QE2* queen, Tommy/Tara, staying there, who Dom was friendly with. I think they may have had a romantic dabble too. Who could blame him? I wasn't around.

Eventually, I received orders to rejoin *Tidepool* on the Tyne June 19th, 1978. Dom and I had long talks. He decided to join me aboard *Tidepool*, still on the Tyne, July 7th, 1978. Life went on much as before. Again, sadly, we had our ups and downs. In a moment of madness and after a few drinks, the lovely Morag talked me into us both getting Afro hairdos. (The TV show *The Professionals* was all the rage, and Martin Shaw, 'Doyle', had an Afro hairstyle.) We eventually arrived back on the ship well-trashed with these demented hair styles. The Old Man thought it was absolutely hilarious. Dominic was not impressed and absolutely furious! To him it was another sign I was happier having a laugh and entertaining my gay friends. He almost frightened me at times; he couldn't seem to handle someone like me (which, looking back, is no surprise). Eventually I 'got the hump' and handed in my notice, paying off in Portland September 29th, 1978. Dominic stayed on, as the ship was going on a deployment to the USA and he wanted to see his sister Veronica living there; they were extremely close. He saw her, as I did later. We didn't know it then, but this would be the last time either of us would sail separately by choice. Things finally worked out for us. For the rest of our time at sea we only sailed separately when it was completely unavoidable. (Such as in later years when we were contracted with P&O/Princess, being allocated separate ships.)

He stayed on *Tidepool*. I was sent to join one of the newest largest stores/ammunition replenishment vessels, RFA *Fort Grange*, 24,000 grt, completed 1976. It was a happy time. Dear old Alfie Kendal was the senior purser and there were a few camp queens on board. The ship was mainly rock dodging (sailing round the UK coast), spending a lot of time anchored out in Plymouth, which was great fun. We'd go to the Lockyer Tavern, then to jumping Union Street and end up in Mr Harry's Club, a gay/mixed club which stayed open extremely late. Sometimes we nearly missed the last liberty boat back to the ship. I became friends with a lovely queen, Geoff Saint, one of the STON (stores) guys aboard. He's one of the funniest, kindest and nicest people I've ever met. He lived in a house in Royal Navy Avenue, Plymouth. He told me there were so many queens living in his house and in the street that neighbours called it Royal Nancy Avenue!

Dolly Potter (Ronnie) and Flo were aboard too, along with quite a few other queens. We took over running the crew bar. We'd wonderful nights. The Pig was jumping every night. Nerve gas flowed. We'd play Andrews Sisters numbers like 'Hold Tight, Hold Tight' and 'Boogie Woogie Bugle Boy', dancing and singing along to the music. At this time the big hit musical was *Grease*, starring John Travolta and Olivia Newton-John. We'd play music from the movie: hits like 'You're the One That I Want' and 'Summer Nights'. One of the STON crew fancied himself a dancer, grooving along to these songs. We queens nicknamed him Olivia Newton-Faggot, which amused everyone. Even he heard and was actually proud of it!

Even in the dining room we'd a few laughs. One gay guy, Alice, was another violent queen, who wouldn't hesitate to batter anyone who upset him. I found him extremely amusing. Often minced beef appeared on the lunch menu. When Alice asked an officer what he'd like as a main course, if the answer was "mince," Alice would do an exaggerated mince all the way to the serving hatch, which would get me tittering.

I was captain's steward again, serving another delightful Old Man. One day a Navy admiral visited the ship, arriving by helicopter (a Royal Navy squadron aboard). A Navy rating escorted the admiral to the captain's cabin, where I 'stood by'. Approaching, he asked the RN guy, "I understand there are bars aboard this vessel. Operated by whom?" "Well, sir," he replied, "a bar steward in the officers' bar. The POs run the POs' bar. And the crew bar is run by queers." "Quairs? Quairs? Good grief," said the admiral. I couldn't help laughing to myself. Naval officers lived in a completely different world to Merchant Navy officers. Navy discipline was very strict. Openly homosexual men not tolerated and were liable to be dismissed with a bad discharge. In the MN it was much more relaxed. Gay stewards were usually good workers. Anyway, if they were sacked, companies found it difficult to get good catering crew.

*Fort Grange*, as an ammunition ship, visited many interesting ports, mostly in Scotland. It was a place I'd never visited before and found it enchanting, especially some of the lochs we visited, like Loch Long and Glen Douglas. These I assumed were the location of stores/munitions we loaded and delivered. (I'm not revealing any state secrets here, these details can be easily found online.) The scenery was green and lush like Scandinavia, the lochs' seawater crystal clear. When tied alongside, ships' Chinese laundrymen dived into the cold, clear water, swimming down to collect the shellfish and mussels we could see clearly growing on the piers, pontoons and rocks. They'd take these back to the laundry, preparing a fresh seafood feast.

Dominic and I wrote long letters, which were lovely, laughing at some of the things happening aboard his ship. We missed each other terribly. We also sent each other romantic, inspirational cards. I remember sending him one saying something like, "If you love someone, and they're unsure, set them free. If they return, they're yours. If they don't, they never were yours." I think it struck a chord with him, as he kept the card. I'd say prayers too, for our relationship to sort itself out. While Dominic was in America seeing his sister Veronica, he had a great time and took a driving test for an American driving licence. As his voyage came to an end, he docked back in the UK in February. I docked shortly after, in March. We agreed to meet, maybe both visit America. Dom could visit Veronica. We'd heard that Freddie Laker was running the Skytrain, a no-frills airline service from UK to New York, at a third the usual fare.

# 23

# Domestic Bliss at Last

I'd written to Dominic telling him I'd be paying off *Fort Grange* March 23rd, 1979. I sent a telegram too, just in case the letter didn't reach him. (He's kept the telegram to this day, so romantic, bless him.) The ship anchored off Plymouth March 22nd. I was due to hand over to the new captain's steward next day and pay off. Unbeknown to me, Dominic hired a car, a Ford Capri, drove to Plymouth and came aboard that night, waking me. What a lovely surprise. I wept with happiness. We spent the night cuddled in each other's arms. It was so good to be together again. Things finally settled down for us. Next day we took a liberty boat ashore, driving to my home to make plans for our leave. My folks were used to seeing Dominic by now and all was good, although we were still just 'mates'.

We checked out Laker's Skytrain jet airline service: just £59 each way. After seeing his sister in the US, Dom wanted to return there with me, to meet her and do a trip round America on the fairly new American Amtrak trains. It sounded great. So, armed with a book, *See America for $9 a Day*, we took Skytrain to New York and embarked on a grand tour of the US. The first nights in New York, we stayed at the YMCA, as it was so cheap. The hit song *YMCA* hadn't been released then and I'd no idea these places were like the *tubs* (steam baths), packed with randy young men having an enormous amount of fun with each other. We heard doors banging open and closed all night long.

After a couple of enjoyable days in New York, we took the Amtrak train to Newport News, Virginia, to be met by Dom's sister Veronica and her husband Keith. They now lived in Hampton, Virginia. I worried, in case they guessed I was gay and, being Catholic, would hate me. My fears were unfounded. They both welcomed me with open arms. I took them to heart immediately too. They'd met while Veronica worked in Germany; Keith was stationed there in the US Army. Now they were married with two children, Nova and Dominic. Nova is what we'd call mixed race and extremely beautiful. Dominic is handsome and black like his father. The family were good company, extremely kind, and we spent a most agreeable time with them. One day Veronica asked me if I wanted to drive the car. When I told her I didn't, she took me to the local Virginia Motorists' Licence Center. I whizzed through the US Highway Code, answered a few questions, then drove round a circuit with sensors. Passing the test, I became the proud owner of a Virginia driver's license.

Departing Hampton, we purchased a thirty-day USA Rail Pass for £240 (about £100 then), taking the Amtrak train to Miami to continue our tour of America. We spent a wonderful few days in glorious sun in Miami. In those days people from the cold north would fly to Florida to spend the winter. Being a long drive, they'd get agencies to drive their cars down, which needed to be driven back. We'd seen adverts for a car delivery agency wanting drivers. They didn't pay you, but it was handy for free travel between north and south, although delivery time was limited. We thought it might be fun seeing America by road, and approached the agency with our US driving licences. We ended up driving a splendid Chevrolet to Chicago, with a two-day deadline.

I won't bore you with all the details of our American trip. However, after a couple of splendid days in town, we departed Chicago by train and travelled all around America: San Francisco, Los Angeles, New Orleans, Washington, and finally back to New York. Although we didn't have much money, I truly loved our journey. We were only able to afford coach class reclining train seats, though sometimes kindly guards, hearing our accents, gave us a free sleeper. Americans are such kind people, though. We always tipped them well. In the various cities we usually stayed in the YMCA or a cheap hotel. Sometimes, unable to afford a meal, we'd buy sandwiches, cheese and a bottle of wine, for dinner in our room. We really enjoyed this – *so* romantic. Although these days we have ample money, we sometimes still like to do the same thing, after all these years, for old time's sake. Thankfully, things finally settled in our relationship. I'm not sure whether it was getting away from the distraction of Lee, Roy, and the other queens, but we were truly happy. At the end of our US trip, following a few days in wonderful New York, New York, we returned to the UK on Skytrain.

Staying at my parents' for a few days, a letter was waiting from Dominic's sister Veronica. She'd taken to me immediately and was extremely fond of me. She also wanted to ask a question, saying whatever the answer was, it absolutely wouldn't make any difference to our friendship. She asked, was I gay? Were Dominic and I lovers? In those days I was shocked at her openness. I asked Dominic what he thought about a reply. We both agreed that honesty's always the best policy. I wrote, including, "Yes, indeed, Veronica. We are a couple and truly love each other." Happily it was the beginning of a beautiful, enduring lifelong friendship to this day with Dominic's dear sister. Leave finished, we headed back to Southampton, planning our next move.

We'd kept in touch with Pearl, who'd moved into a two-bedroom house in Firgrove Road, Freemantle, Southampton. We'd planned to stay in the seamen's mission, however Pearl kindly invited us to stay with him. His delightful terraced Victorian house, full of antiques, was near busy Shirley High Street, with frequent buses to town. There was a cosy, friendly little corner pub, the Duchess of Wellington, a hundred metres from his front door. We loved living in Southampton by this time and really liked the Shirley area. We thought we'd probably settle down there, which is exactly what happened. I'd previously opened a Building Society account with the Woolwich, setting up a monthly standing order, to save a deposit for our own home. After a while at Pearl's, I was offered RFA *Olna*, sister ship to *Olmeda*. I think we called the Mad House, securing Dominic a job too. We received orders to join the ship on the River Tyne in Wallsend dry dock June 7th, 1979.

# 24

# Flying Sauce Bottles!

We caught a train via London to Newcastle, then a local service to Wallsend, North Tyneside, joining RFA *Olna* in dry dock. With no accommodation or meals aboard, we were given excellent subsistence money again, booking into a nearby guest house. *Olna* was a 36,000 grt fast fleet tanker, with eighty-eight RFA crew and up to forty Royal Navy personnel, to operate a maximum of three helicopters. First day aboard, June 7th, 1979, I was given Old Man's steward job again. When I first met Captain Rutterworth, he made a big impression: a smart man, extremely dapper. We had a pleasant chat about how he liked things done. He was charming, highly intelligent, a straightforward, no-nonsense type of person. I sensed we'd get along extremely well.

Next morning Dominic and I were waiting with crew to catch a bus to the ship when the Old Man drove past in a large Opel car. It was very posh then. He was dressed immaculately, wearing leather driving gloves. He stopped and, to my embarrassment, asked if I wanted a lift. I told him, "No, thank you. I'm waiting with my mate Dominic." He replied, "Hop in. I'll give you both a lift." We climbed in and couldn't miss the surprised looks from the crew. It was most unusual for a master to offer a lift to lowly crew members.

Work aboard was easy: catering side storing and cleaning. Dominic and the deck department were busy rigging the replenishment gear. At lunchtime we'd go to the Wallsend docks Ship Inn, run by a lovely couple. We enjoyed bottles of Newcastle Brown ale and delicious baps filled with ham, mushy peas and mustard, all layered inside the bap.

Prior to sailing, the captain spoke to the carpenter about alterations to his bathroom, extra towel rails and the like. He asked me, "As your mate Dominic's a deckhand, would he paint the bathroom deck swimming pool blue?" Of course he did. To complement the blue deck, I was sent ashore to buy blue fluffy toilet and bath mats, plus a stock of blue toilet paper. (Loo rolls in RFA were NAFFI issue, more like greaseproof paper.) The bathroom ended up comfortable though truly 1970s. When the Old Man actually embarked to live on the ship, a huge trunk was delivered. It took two deckhands to manhandle it to his cabin. I noticed all his uniform was adorned with captain's stripes, including his personalised flying outfit. He even had a beautiful black cape, plus an ebony walking cane with a solid silver top. I thought, *That's a bit camp*, but knew he was happily married; I guess he was a bit of a poser. He brought an amazing assortment of beautiful crystal decanters, which he filled with various spirits and liqueurs for entertaining when exercises finished and the ship was alongside, for R&R. Officers would often join him after lunch on a Sunday for glasses of port, cognac, or stickies (liqueurs).

There were a few queens among the crew: Geordie Stan (Lana), and lovely Morag. Also a young catering rating, David. We named him Tina Tits, due to his moobs (man boobs). He spoke with humorous eloquence. Lana referred to the Scottish crew mess man as that "sweaty sock" (rhyming slang). Tina

Tits wouldn't lower himself to use such vulgar parlance and amusingly referred to him as that "odorous footwear"! (This was not meant as insulting. We all got along just fine.)

We sailed to Portland, Dorset, for a usual work up: fire, boat, NBCD (nuclear radiation, biological and chemical defence) drills, and flying/refuelling exercises. The Cold War was still a threat then. Even Russian submarines secretly followed us. They allegedly picked up our ditched gash to see if there were any classified documents within. Of course they were shredded secretly and disposed of.

My safety muster duty was a stretcher party, with a junior purser as team leader. One fire drill we practised rescuing a casualty from an enclosed space. They used beautiful Morag as a casualty, complete with fake blood and gore. He wasn't a pretty sight at the best of times, but as a casualty he was horrific. When our stretcher party arrived on the scene, the team leader/junior purser saw the blood, turned pale and fainted. A RN chap overseeing the drill asked, "I say chaps, who's in charge heaire?" Struggling to conceal our mirth, we pointed to the prone young purser, chortling. "Him." They hastily arranged a new stretcher party leader.

Following work up, exercises and such, we headed off towards the Med, with a small deployment of Royal Navy ships for further exercises, replenishments alongside and astern, and vertical replenishment by helicopter, called VERTREP. Apart from replenishing our own helicopters, we replenished choppers from other ships. We replenished NATO vessels, as well as replenishing our own frigates, destroyers and aircraft carriers. It took great precision, and was extremely clever and interesting to watch. Dominic, being deck crew, was actively involved, whereas I had a ringside seat watching this piece of amazing theatre.

Royal Fleet Auxiliary masters' cabins were extremely spacious. A large day room with seating plus a desk for meetings, a large double bedroom, a bathroom, plus a private dining room he used a lot between exercises to entertain captains and commanders of other vessels. The Old Man ate the same breakfast in his dining room every day, grilled bacon and tomato with Worcestershire sauce. One day, serving his breakfast, I returned to the pantry and heard him almost screaming loudly for me. I rushed back, thinking something was terribly wrong. "What's this?" He said, pointing at the sauce. "A bottle of Worcester sauce," I answered. "Yes, but it's not Lea & Perrins, is it!" he replied. I explained the ship's stock of Lea & Perrins had run out; the new supply included another brand. He was having none of that, deciding to sort it out before his next breakfast. We were near Gibraltar. Sometime later, crew were summoned to flying stations and a helicopter landed with cases of Lea & Perrins sauce. I thought, *Flying sauce bottles. Is that camp or what?* Only a captain with real style would go that far. It sounds a little over the top. Actually it was a good opportunity for pilots to accumulate extra flying hours, plus exercise crews.

*Olna* sailed down the Med, with more exercises and drills on the way, including night-time 'darkened ship' drill exercises. During these the Old Man would sleep in a cabin on the ship's bridge. I believe it was the pilot's and captain's bridge cabin, handy for the bridge if required. He'd give me a list, to duplicate all the things he needed for his stay up there. The toiletry items included his special Captain Molyneux cologne. During these exercises, which sometimes lasted a week or more, I served 'flying suppers' on the bridge in pitch darkness, except for extremely dull red lights. Delivery was quite a feat after a few of pints of nerve gas in the crew bar! It was rather exciting, exercising, with all the other RN ships, watching choppers landing and taking off. I thought it was almost like war training, which of course it was.

When the exercises finished, most Royal Navy ships returned to Gibraltar for R&R. As Captain Rutterworth knew a good restaurant in Cyprus, we anchored off for a week. Dominic and I loved to sample local drink and cuisine, going for a wander. After a couple of beers we strolled to the harbour front with its countless bars and restaurants. The Old Man was there, calling us to join him. We approached, trying to make excuses, as we'd feel uncomfortable actually joining the captain and some crew might resent us for it. He was having none of it, making us sit down and join him. I squirmed with embarrassment, not used to socialising with gold braid. However, he was so relaxed, friendly and informal, he soon put us at ease. We had an interesting meal with him and his guests. It made me realise what a great, fair man he was. At work we're there to do our respective jobs. Socially, we were equal.

On our return to the UK, *Olna* docked in Rosyth, Scotland. Even though Captain Rutterworth was English, he was married to a Scots lady and they lived in Invergordon. In the evening Dominic and I went for a walk and a drink. As we made our way along the jetty, a liberty boat from an anchored RFA ammunition ship arrived. We stopped to see if we knew anyone. To my delight, who should get off but dear Patsy, ex-*QE2*. After a joyful reunion, he accompanied us for drinks and a few laughs in the nearby pubs. When we walked back to the docks to see Patsy onto a return liberty boat, to his dismay the weather became stormy and boats were cancelled. We told him, "Never mind. You can come back and stay on our ship." I told him, "I can share with Dominic and you can get your head down in my cabin." After more drinks in the bar we turned in. The next day we heard Patsy had caused absolute mayhem overnight, apparently having an outrageous time in the crew bar. During the night he went to the bathroom, got the cabin mixed up, and leapt into the wrong bunk on top of an unsuspecting old quartermaster! Oh dear.

Word must have got around, for when I turned to the chief officer asked was a friend of mine on board? Confirming this, I explained the cancellation of his liberty boat due to bad weather. The old quartermaster obviously reported the incident to the chief officer. I was instructed to ask my guest to get off the ship immediately! Patsy duly returned to his ship. Happily, we heard no more about it. This was the last time I ever saw him. Sadly, three years later, after returning from the Falklands, Patsy took his own life. I don't know whether it was because of the thought of getting older, which he especially hated, or due to some of the dreadful sights he saw down there during the 1982 conflict. Innocent, good-looking young men being killed or badly injured in a war that was – he felt – unnecessary. Whatever his state of mind, it was extremely sad: a young life lost. I'd been so fond of him.

It was a happy ten months aboard *Olna*. Time flew by and we had great fun in the crew bar, with plenty of parties. I started making cocktails. Everyone loved them, especially my gin martinis, which were basically neat gin with a splash of vermouth. Very more-ish and extremely potent! Tina Tits and I even did a little drag number to entertain the boys: 'Money, Money', from the musical *Cabaret*. At this time I owned a plastic pineapple ice bucket, which I'd fill with ice and take to the crew bar. One day, a deckhand (we'll call him Dick, he was, and I suspect homophobic) came round my cabin shouting I'd stolen the crew ice bucket. I told him, "It actually belongs to me, so bugger off." He punched me in the eye, so I smashed the ice bucket over his head. It all got very ugly. Dominic, hearing the commotion, got involved. Dick challenged him to a fight on the flight deck. A short time later Dick reappeared in the bar saying he'd really sorted Dominic out. However, Dick's face was a grazed, bloody mess. Dominic reappeared without a scratch on him and everyone laughed, much to Dick's embarrassment. Apparently Dominic got the better of him, rubbing his face on the flight deck (which was painted with sharp grit to stop the helicopters sliding when the ship was rolling).

Next morning before work, I covered the black eye with slap. I always travelled with some Max Factor. You never know when you'll need it! I don't know how but the Old Man knew all about it. When he questioned me, I explained it was all just a silly misunderstanding. Later he told me, "I've spoken to the man involved. If he ever lays a finger on you or anyone else on my ship, he'll be off in the next port. I will not tolerate fighting and that sort of behaviour under any circumstances." It was amazing. He knew all that was going on *and* whether anything else was amiss.

He owned about a hundred pairs of different coloured socks. One day, he told me a pair were missing, describing them to me. I visited the laundry to see the laundrymen. In those days all RFA laundries were staffed by Chinese from Hong Kong, who had the contract. Either they didn't understand or couldn't be arsed about the socks, and I had no luck. When I told the Old Man, he went down himself and reappeared with the missing socks. A truly amazing man in every respect and extremely kind. Most Old Men showed their appreciation. He went even further. Every month I'd receive a cash envelope. An incredible, intelligent, judicious and generous man.

After ten months, our time on *Olna* came to an end. Captain Rutterworth took leave in Rosyth, Scotland. Dominic and I also paid off April 8th, 1980. We'd a few days alongside before leaving. As it was such a long train journey, we decided to buy our first car. The second-hand Ford Escort cost about £450 out of our wages of roughly £120 a week. We drove all the way home to my parents' house first, then on to Southampton, which felt like home, to stay with Pearl. He was good fun and kind, but always complaining about life in general, as well as being a dreadful hypochondriac. He'd consult ancient medical books, where some of the cures were frankly medieval, like blue unction, leeches and so on!

When our leave finished, we telephoned the Mad House, asking for any ships sailing to the US (to visit Veronica). We were in luck. The sister ship to *Fort Grange*, *Fort Austin*, was leaving on a US deployment. We asked to sail on her. Following the usual formalities with the Pool, Union and so on, we were given rail warrants, and joined *Fort Austin* in Rosyth, June 30th, 1980, leaving the car parked at Pearl's.

I was given the officers' barman job. The Old Man was Captain Lagan, who I'd sailed with on *Tidepool*. There were a few queens on board too, including the delightful funny man, Geoff Saint. I guessed we were in for a good trip. The ship lurked around the UK coast for some weeks, exercising and so forth, then sailed to Plymouth to pick up a mystery cargo. Next we sailed to Scotland, calling into various ports including Loch Long and Glen Douglas, which are set among truly beautiful highland scenery. I believe it was in Glen Douglas that a rumour went round that we were loading or unloading more mysterious cargo. It must have been something extremely important. They had running water cannons standing by on the jetty, guarded by Royal Marines with automatic weapons. We were sternly warned *not* to watch or take photographs. Finally we sailed, bound for a mystery destination in the US, escorted by a Royal Navy vessel. There was much speculation and gossip among the crew. Most thought the cargo must be some kind of secret nuclear weapon, missiles, or warheads.

*Fort Austin* finally docked in Port Canaveral, Florida, where the mysterious cargo was discharged. Once the task was accomplished we were allowed ashore. We made a beeline to the nearest town. I do remember it was summer and incredibly hot. Disembarking the ship, we were eaten alive by mosquitoes. I thought, *Wow, this is where all the space explorations and moon landing rockets were launched from when I was a boy.*

We were alongside about a week, hiring cars from Ugly Duckling Car Rental. They were second-hand, enormous gas-guzzling monsters. We didn't care. Gas (as Americans call it) was extremely cheap, as were rental charges. We had enormous fun. We then sailed to Fort Lauderdale. To us it was a more interesting place, as there were gay bars, restaurants and such.

Time off abroad was quite difficult to organise for crew on board. To our delight, Veronica, Keith and Nova drove south for two days from Virginia to visit us for a few days.

While in Florida, one Sunday Dominic and I went to see a live show, starring the world-famous camp pianist, Liberace. He was known as 'Mr Showman'. I didn't think much about him before the show. To me he was just a camp piano-playing queen. However, by the end of the show, we were all spellbound; he had the audience positively eating out of his hands. Not just blue rinsed matrons, even the young girls and boys were spellbound by the spectacle of his performance. The show was truly clever and extremely entertaining. No wonder he was known as Mr Showman. That night in bed I'd an extremely strange, vivid dream. I was floating, looking around his fabulous mansion (which I'd never visited?) when a beautiful demitasse coffee set caught my attention. Strangely, I was to see this actual coffee set many years later!

One day after lunch I drove in to town shopping. Tina Tits asked if I would take him with me. As we arrived in town, I saw an extremely long American train slowly approaching a traffic crossing. The warning bells sounded, lights flashed. (Most small US towns have unmanned crossings with no barriers/gates, just approaching train warnings.) As the train was slow, the road quiet, just for a joke I stopped the car on the crossing, saying "Oh dear, the engine's conked out." The poor boy let out an ear-piecing scream. I told him, "Only joking," pressing the accelerator. He was so shocked, his throat was hoarse for days. He did see the funny side of it later and forgave me. After some time on the US coast, we departed and headed back to Blighty, Plymouth.

## 25

# A Skin Boat, and Lee

The Royal Fleet Auxiliary at that time was an excellent company and offered interesting work. However, after five years Dominic and I had got itchy feet, fancying a change. We both gave notice. I terminated my contract. (I still received a small, welcome pension at sixty.) We signed off October 14th, 1980, in Plymouth and went home to my parents. Mum and Dad were accustomed to Dominic by this time. However, sadly, we could never reveal the fact we were a couple, especially to my father. They laughed watching John Inman camp it up as Mr Humphries in the TV sitcom *Are You Being Served?* Mum thought he was a lovely man, even though Dad laughed. He still referred to Inman as a big *poof*. Dom and I slept in separate beds at home, even when we bought our first home. Our flat needed two bedrooms, with beds, in case Dad suspected we slept together. It was still like that then. After leaving my folks we went to stay with dear Pearl, in Freemantle, Southampton, which by then was becoming something of the norm.

Leave ran out. We visited the Pool to make ourselves available. Eventually they offered us both a Fyffes banana boat sailing to the Caribbean, mv *Manistee*, 6,613 grt, built 1972. We joined December 1st, 1980, in Jarrow, on the Tyne. I looked after the Old Man and senior deck officers. Firstly we sailed to Hamburg, picking up a small cargo of fertiliser. Then we sailed an almost empty ship, transatlantic, to Panama 'for orders'. Crossing the Atlantic in December, the weather is often horrendous. It was. Massive waves made the ship roll and pitch dreadfully. At night we'd jam ourselves in our bunks using a lifejacket as packing, to avoid being tossed out of bed. Everything else moved around. Even drawers slid out, falling on the deck. Strangely, in those days it didn't bother me at all. Now I'd be uncomfortable, plus a little nervous.

Sadly Captain Roberts was obnoxious. The crew called him Cobby Robby. Shortly after sailing he sent for me, saying I hadn't cleaned behind his toilet properly. The toilet was flushed using sea water (now banned). The flush handle leaked. It was obvious salty sea water had leaked, dripping behind the toilet *after* I'd cleaned it. Rather than argue, I filled a bucket with soapy water, then 'soogied' behind the toilet again. I never warmed to him after this; that's how things panned out for the trip. *Manistee* was a good ship and the food fine, but not the crew bar. It was run by regular Fyffes men. For whatever reason, they disliked us 'Pool men'. One guy, Richard, was hostile toward us being a gay couple. It caused bad atmosphere. We never made a secret of the fact, nor threw it in people's faces. But they guessed, being the only ones aboard. I figured there was a secret reason for Richard's hostility; later I was proved correct. Eventually, after a week or more at sea, we neared the Panama Canal and anchored off Turbo, on the Colombian coast. A barge was brought alongside and the bags of fertiliser discharged onto the barge, to be taken by small boats. We all wanted to go ashore but the Old Man refused. Dominic knew the rules, saying if we weren't allowed ashore we must be paid captive time. The bridge hastily organised a liberty boat.

To get ashore, we climbed down a rope ladder onto the barge alongside. A large dug-out canoe with an outboard motor was to take us to land. Before departing for the shore, the helmsman made us pull a tarpaulin over our heads. I thought it didn't look like rain. However, when we departed, ploughing through huge waves, sea water sloshed all over us. Eventually we sailed up a narrow estuary and finally up a large river through jungle. We stopped in a clearing, at a settlement of wood, tin, and mud huts. It was a most bizarre experience, almost like a scene from *Indiana Jones*. Among these huts was a bar and we piled in for a drink. Seemingly it was also a kind of brothel. Local ladies wearing what looked like small bowler hats were drinking beer and – can you believe – cherry brandy, as chasers. We joined in and after our spell at sea we thoroughly enjoyed ourselves. In fact I don't remember going back to the ship, or how I climbed the rope ladder. Next day I'd a ghastly hangover. A lad I worked with, a Fyffes regular, said, "You were brave to go ashore, mate. If you'd have fallen in the river… it's full of piranhas!"

We sailed on to various banana ports: Puerto Armuelles, Panama, one in Honduras, and our favourite, Golfito, Costa Rica. Our ship's run was from the banana ports through the Panama Canal, taking bananas to the US East Coast ports like Baltimore, Savannah, and Charleston. Seamen refer to banana ports as "a good run ashore," especially Golfito: cheap drink, beautiful warm weather, local girls or lads who are very amiable and good-looking. This was in the days before tourism. It wasn't uncommon for regular Fyffes men to have concubines (second wives). Accordingly, they preferred not to work nights. By law ships in port are required to have a night watchman (someone to keep an eye on mooring ropes and gangways). Dominic wasn't interested going ashore drinking, so he volunteered for this job. The first night, due to tides, Dominic was told to keep a close watch on the gangway. In the early hours before going for his night supper, he pulled the gangway higher, thinking the tide was going out (ebbing). Unfortunately the tide was rising, bringing the gangway even higher. While he was eating in the mess, the bosun and a few others returned to the ship, but were unable to get aboard. When Dominic finally returned to the gangway, he was confronted by an angry crowd who had obviously been drinking. He quickly lowered the gangway. The bosun, who didn't like Pool men, threatened to report Dom. Dominic wasn't happy about this. When it was time to call the crew, he reported the bosun to the chief officer for threatening behaviour. The relationship between the bosun and Dominic didn't get any better after this incident.

Held up by the need to spend a few days loading the bananas, catering staff had plenty of time for fun. Strangely, it rained every evening around 6:00p.m. for about half an hour. You could set your clock by it. There was an island off Golfito called Tom's Island. It was a great day out. Occasionally the ship sailed early. If this was during the night, the crew were called and cabins checked for visitors who needed to get off. Sure enough, they found a good-looking young local man in Richard's cabin. Obviously he'd been smuggled aboard while things were quiet in the late evening. I'd already guessed he was closeted: it was always those guys that bad-mouthed you. They weren't man enough to admit what they were, and hated you for having the balls to be honest.

One day an amusing incident happened. Dominic and I were enjoying a few beers when news broke that US President Ronald Reagan had been shot in an attempted assassination. In an emotional moment, exacerbated by the beers, I decided to send him a telegram to wish him a speedy recovery. I weaved my way to the radio room and did just that, addressing our telegram to Ronald Reagan, The White House and so on, signing it, "Best wishes, Michael and Dominic." Much to our amusement, amazed word went round the ship: "You'll never guess what? Those two know the president of the United States!"

*Manistee* was a GP (general purpose) ship, and although stewards stayed in catering, deck and engine GPs had to take turns on deck and in the engine room. The bosun arranged for the regular Fyffes crew to work in the engine room in cold weather and on deck in the warm weather. This pissed off Dom and the other ABs who'd come from the Pool. It backfired on the Fyffes crew; they'd spent most of their time in the engine room. They weren't good at tying knots and other seaman-like tasks, especially when it came to transiting the Canal. Going through the locks, one of them fainted on the helm, causing the ship to veer starboard, hitting the lock side. They nearly lost a marine pilot because they'd hadn't fixed the ladder properly. When the pilot stepped off the launch onto the ladder to climb aboard, it gave way and had to be rigged again properly. Stepping aboard, the pilot remarked, "You've got a problem on this ship." These episodes didn't go down well with the Panama Canal. This was also an embarrassment for the ship. The Old Man needed to take swift action; he wanted fully qualified and experienced deckhands like Dominic to take us through the canal *every* time. But there was a problem: Dominic and other proper ABs were stuck in the engine room for their two-week stint. They would only agree to help if they could stay on deck *all* the time, so the other regular crew ended up working permanently in the engine room. This too caused some resentment.

One day at sea I remember clearly. It was the same time that Beatles singer John Lennon was shot and killed in New York. The captain sent for me after I'd already cleaned his cabin. Thinking, *Here we go again, more trouble*, I rapped on his door. He called me in, saying he was sorry but he'd received a telegram addressed to me: "It may contain bad news." As he handed it to me I saw it had been sent by dear Debbie (David Boaz) and I read, "Regret to inform you after a short illness dear Lee passed away. Funeral March 4th. Regards Debs." I was upset and shaken, though not surprised the way Lee drank and smoked. Unusually, the Old Man kindly said, "I can see you're upset, Michael. Don't turn to for lunch. The other steward can see to all that." (In other words, "Go and have a drink; drown your sorrows.") Which, of course, I did, with Dominic. We were remembering good times and fun I'd had with dear Lee. I was still extremely fond of him, although after meeting Dominic, things could never be the same. It really broke my heart I wouldn't be able to go to his funeral. He wasn't family, so I couldn't ask to be flown home. Following drinks and a bite of lunch, I got my head down, drifting off to sleep.

Then the strangest thing happened. I felt someone touch my shoulder. I looked round and Lee was standing next to my bunk, looking young, beautiful and absolutely radiant. I thought, *Oh my God, Lee, you're dead!* Lee seemed to know what I was thinking. He replied, "I know what you're thinking, darling. I've just come to say goodbye and don't worry about me. I'm fine and so happy. I shall see you again one day." With this he faded and I drifted back to sleep. When I woke up, I couldn't work out if it was real, or had I dreamt the whole thing? To this day I'm still not sure, though Lee was a really great believer in spiritual matters. I truly believe it was him saying farewell.

*Manistee* spent months sailing up and down the East Coast of America delivering bananas. One of the ports was Charleston, South Carolina. Because of its name, I thought it would be really exciting. But, typical of Southern states, being a Sunday all the bars were shut. It was impossible to get a drink. With the help of a cab driver we managed to get a drink in the American Legion, which is equivalent to the British Legion.

An interesting experience happened one day drinking in a Baltimore bar. One of the local ex-seamen told us we wouldn't have dared to show our faces there in the 1950s. He told us, "You

Brits stole our jobs, as you were cheaper labour." United Brands, an American Company, owned Fyffes and formerly employed American seafarers, until they were replaced by cheaper UK seamen. History repeated itself when us Brits all finally lost *our* jobs at sea because of cheaper labour from the Orient. At the end of March, ships articles ran out and we were given the choice to stay or go. We chose to go, flying home from Baltimore on April 1st, 1981. Back in Southampton, we stayed a while with Pearl. It seemed strange I couldn't pop in and see dear Lee, or ever enjoy his outrageous, hilarious company again. Later we both went home. Dom flew to Belfast.

While at home I decided to change the car. I bought a little yellow Honda Civic. Just before leave ended, Dominic asked me to take a car ferry to Ireland, pick him up and meet his family. This filled me with foreboding. I thought, being Catholics, they'd probably dislike me. He said they'd be fine. I wasn't to meet Dominic's father, as he had his own flat and probably wouldn't have understood. It took him years to forgive Veronica for marrying a black man.

I was due to sail overnight Liverpool to Belfast. However, I missed the ferry. Luckily I managed to get aboard the Irish car ferry overnight, arriving in Dublin May 5th, 1981. Dom met me and we drove slowly to Belfast, hearing tragic news on the radio: the sad death of Irish Republican Army MP and hunger striker Bobby Sands. He was actually a cousin of Dominic's. The news of fierce rioting in Belfast made me extremely nervous and apprehensive. Dominic calmly taught me how to say the prayer Hail Mary (which I still remember, and say) in case we were stopped by Catholics. Reaching Belfast, I saw what looked like bonfires in the middle of the road. As we drew closer I saw they were cars set alight by Catholics protesting about the death of Bobby Sands. Having never seen anything like this before, I was a nervous wreck.

We safely reached Dominic's home in Andersonstown, west Belfast. His Catholic family turned out to be friendly and agreeable, putting me at ease immediately. Dominic's mother, Colette, was delightful. To my surprise she allowed us to sleep in her double bed. But she forbade alcohol in the house; we'd have to go out for a drink. In the past her brother had a drink problem and she didn't want it repeated. Next day Dominic showed me around the city centre. I was astonished: security barriers everywhere, all the people and their bags searched. This was the reality of the Troubles; the evidence was everywhere. Before I'd only seen it on the TV. Dominic and his brothers took me to a Republican club one evening for a few lovely pints of Guinness. I was incredibly nervous. I needn't have worried; because I was with Dominic's family, everyone was welcoming and friendly. The only awkward moment was when they played the southern Irish national anthem. Everyone stood up and sang. Naturally, because of where I was, I joined in.

We even went for drinks in the newly opened Europa Hotel, which became the 'most bombed hotel in history'. The IRA saw it as one of the largest landmarks to target in the city and a symbol of all that was wrong. Because of the Troubles, tourism to Belfast had all but dried up. Most of the guests were from the media, anxious to get the latest news regarding the situation. Having said that, most people in England had no idea what was *really* going on, or what really started it: our government's censoring press made sure of that. Northern Ireland at this time was also a gay-hating and extremely homophobic place. One of the reasons we visited the Europa was because the bar was known to be gay-friendly. The hotel only managed to keep going through the Troubles because of press patronage and the gay community. I recently watched a TV documentary regarding this period. The Europa actually gave ties to journalists, embroidered with the number of times they'd stayed when the hotel was bombed! I enjoyed our days in Belfast. They were an eye-opener, furnishing me a better understanding of what was really going on. Prior to leaving, I was surprised when Dom's mum said to me, "I'm so pleased our Dominic's met a good man like you, Michael." This from a devout Catholic lady who attended Mass every day, at a time when the Catholic Church was perceived as homophobic. Sadly, you wouldn't have heard that from my parents in a million years, especially Dad.

We took the ferry back to England. On the way back to Pearl's, Dominic told me he'd big plans. Jobs on cargo ships and tankers were few and far between, especially for an AB and steward wanting to sail together. The only solution was a return to cruise ships. Dominic heard about Princess Cruises, who operated three cruise ships on the West Coast of America sailing to Alaska, Mexico and the Caribbean. We could also see more of Dominic's sister Veronica and family, who had moved to California. The first step was to get a job with P&O, the owners of Princess Cruises.

He first needed a job as a leading hand, as Princess Cruises deck crew were Asian; only the leading hands were from the UK. By contrast, Princess cabin and bar stewards were British. So I just needed a permanent cabin steward's job, then a transfer. We visited the Pool, both seeking jobs with P&O. I was settled first, as relief BRS (bedroom steward) on *Canberra*, May 15th, 1981. It seemed strange to be back on her and in a new job. Last time I was a drinks waiter in 1971. There were a few old faces on board – queens – which made me feel at home. On May 29th Dominic landed a leading seaman's job on P&Os *Oriana*. The position put him one step closer toward a job on the West Coast. As holiday relief on *Canberra*, I was paid off June 8th when the permanent BRS rejoined. Dom carried on sailing aboard *Oriana*.

I frequently visited the Pool, hoping for a job on *Oriana* with Dominic. Luckily I soon got a job as BRS, on June 12th. It was great to be on a ship together, although, as Dom was a leading hand, we ate and drank in separate mess rooms and bars. Luckily he had a single cabin. *Oriana* was mainly UK cruising, plus a Caribbean cruise. I immediately noticed the ship had changed. Maybe it was because I was now older: thirty. Some deck crew and many others aboard weren't as friendly as usual. They also seemed shot away most of the time. Also I didn't know many of the queens on board. They weren't as friendly as past colleagues. Maybe the old crowd were all on the West Coast? (They were.)

On *Oriana*'s Caribbean cruise the ship docked in Barbados until late evening. We went ashore for a walk and a few drinks. Strangely, although prostitution is *legal* in Barbados, running a brothel or soliciting is prohibited. Nevertheless, there's plenty of it going on, especially around The Garrison and the notorious Nelson Street. Many of the bar girls took tricks home nearby and some bar owners had upstairs rooms to rent by the hour. Queens on board told me there was beach bar known as Piles Hilton where you could pick up rent boys and men. Rooms to rent were upstairs and the kinky owner liked to watch guys having sex, through two-way mirrors.

That evening Dominic and I visited notorious Nelson Street, joining some of Dom's mates. Booze flowed. One of the bar girls made eyes at Dominic, sitting on his lap. She got her tits out and he was playing with them and she was playing with him, much to his and the lads' delight. I felt a little uncomfortable that he was doing this in front of me and obviously enjoying it, although I knew he was bisexual. I thought, *Who am I to object, with my free and easy attitude?* I was secretly pleased too, that although bisexual, he chose me to love. I knew my relationship was with a real man and Dominic was *all* man.

Being a relief steward, I paid off at the end of the cruise, returning to Pearl's. He had no time for religion whatsoever, so I never discussed it with him, or let him know I believed. One day while Dominic was out, or away, Pearl said to me, "Your Dominic goes over to *Bona Ekes* (St Boniface's Catholic Church) every day praying for promotion, to get a job on Princess Cruises. For *all* the good it'll do him, dear. A complete waste of time." I had to bite my tongue, as Dominic's prayers are indeed often answered. Sure enough, August 1st, 1981, Dominic was promoted to coxswain, a petty officer's position. A few weeks later he was informed that he'd be joining Princess Cruises, paying off August 20th. After just over a week's leave, he flew to Vancouver August 29th, 1981, joining the *Sun Princess*.

After weeks of visiting the Pool, calling P&O, and working as a relief, I landed a permanent BRS job on *Canberra*, joining September 24th, 1981. It was great to be back. Many of my old mates were aboard too, including my old mate Bernie/Flo. I asked him why he'd left RFA. Apparently, he'd been working on *Fort Austin*, an ammunition ship. During the deployment they tied up for a weekend with a Royal Navy ship. As usual, matelots came aboard and partied in the crew bar. Bernie became friendly with one of the sailors and invited him to his cabin for a drink. As a result the unfortunate boy was late back for duty on his RN ship, a disciplinary offence. Officers advised the lad if he confessed exactly why he was late, they'd look at the matter sympathetically…

When Bernie's ship finally docked in Plymouth, two MOD Plods (Ministry of Defence Police) boarded. They sent for Bernie, questioned him in a private room and asked if he knew Mathew Parks (not his real name), an RN seaman, who told them he went aboard an RFA *Fort* ship and met Bernie. "Yes, I remember Matthew," Bernie replied.

The plods told him, "We have a statement from Matthew here, alleging you both met in your crew bar. Later inviting him to your cabin, where you unzipped his trousers, placing his penis in your mouth."

"That's a lie." said Bernie.

"You deny putting his penis in your mouth?" they asked.

"Yes, it was too big, dear!" said Bernie. "I couldn't get it in!" Struggling to keep a straight face and suppress laughter, the MODP advised Bernie an official report had been made. He wouldn't be allowed to sail on top security ammunition ships in future, only on lower security tankers or stores ships. Bernie wasn't bothered by this. Being laid back like me, he decided it was time for a change anyway. We always kept in touch and he knew I was back with P&O. That's how he came to be on *Canberra*.

Bernie told me a delightful story about while he was working aboard RFA *Fort Austin*. Her Majesty the Queen and Prince Phillip visited the ship in Portland on June 26th, 1981, to honour the Commodore with their presence at luncheon. Bernie said all the crew were extremely nervous when the Queen and Philip entered the officers' dining room. However, when Her Majesty sat down, she kicked off her high heels, took out a powder compact, checked her lipstick in the mirror and powdered her nose. Everyone, immediately, relaxed!

We had a lovely bunch of queens on board *Canberra*, especially Sophie. Welsh, a little plump, she was so funny and wonderful company. Thus began a happy period on *Canberra*, Medi cruising before the ship sailed on its world cruise. In 1974 the ship had been converted to one-class cruising, retaining UK cabin stewards in the old first-class sections. The old second class cabin stewards were all Asians and Goanese. Our passengers were delightful, well-heeled people paying more for the former first-class cabins. One queen on board, Mick Jay, Miss J, was always down on his luck and when ashore lived in the seamen's mission I felt sorry for him, and Pearl suggested he come and stay with us. It turned out a disaster. He was incredibly clumsy, washing up like he was on board ship, under running hot water. Pearl was having kittens about the energy bills.

## Anything Goes at Sea

One day while both home, Miss Jay was up, with Pearl and I still in our beds. The gas man knocked on the door asking to speak to the owner. Madam Jay shouted loudly up the stairs, "Pearl, girl, the gas man's here to see you." Looking like the wreck of the *Hesperus*, Pearl staggered downstairs to see the gas man, saying, "Hello. As you've heard, I'm Pearl." The poor man nearly fainted! It was the last straw. Miss Jay was banned from the house and made to live in a caravan at the end of the garden. It had an electricity supply and its own chemical toilet, which Pearl instructed Madam to empty in the sewer drain hole or house toilet. We walked into the garden one morning and to our disbelief saw pieces of blue toilet paper with blue *chocolate logs* in the flower beds! When questioned, the daft queen said she thought it'd do the plants good! This really was the last straw; Madam was evicted, although we laughed about it.

In the various ports that summer we'd go ashore for lunch, sometimes enjoying rather too much wine. Even Flo, who *never* lost control from excess drink, was found asleep with his head in a pantry sink. We'd all check and cover for each other. One day dear Sophie went missing. Word went around, so we all went to his section to do his turn downs (prepare passenger beds for sleep). When finished we took a passenger elevator and there, to our horror, was Sophie, sat in the corner of the lift snoring his tits off! We took him to his cabin, thinking he'd be in big trouble. However, no one actually made an official complaint; passengers were more tolerant and jolly then. It wasn't quite so 'them' versus 'us'. Even management were more tolerant then.

P&O were an extremely good company to work for. One of the lads advised me if I signed a company contract, the company would pay towards our mortgage. It was also a way of keeping crew at a time of certain labour shortages. I duly applied for and signed a P&O company contract. We'd already saved a deposit with the Woolwich Building Society, and been home hunting.

We'd thought, as we were at sea, having our own secure flat was a sensible option. After weeks of looking, I found a beautiful art deco flat not far from Pearl in Archers Road, Southampton: 'The Archers'. (Dominic was away when I found it but, hearing the details, he approved.) We'd actually walked past these flats while staying with Lee and thought we'd love to live there. Dear Pearl wasn't at all happy we'd got our own place. I think he liked us living with him, helping with bills, shopping, visiting the pub, taking the dogs for a walk and so on.

Our flat had been professionally refurbished, new kitchen, re-carpeted, and the like. Sadly, the lovely parquet floors were carpeted over to deaden the noise for the flat below (a lease condition). Even central heating was included. It was on the second floor, facing south, with a thick strong door in a metal frame, and a Chubb lock. I had the back balcony door replaced with a secure double-glazed door. It was the perfect place to lock up and leave when you went to sea. The old Scots janitor, Jock, kept an eye on it for us too. On our first leave we gave him a bottle of Scotch whisky and he went missing for a few days. Rumour had it he was poorly. In reality he'd a drink problem, falling into an alcohol-induced stupor! We never gave him another bottle.

When I contacted P&O, regarding help with the mortgage, they actually paid towards our home. This was when P&O really was P&O and UK-owned. Now its owned by the giant US Carnival Corporation. By this time things between Dom and I had settled down completely. He wasn't so controlling, I wasn't so flighty. Our relationship became extremely close, and this was shown through mutual patience, affection, tenderness and devotion. When Pearl saw our finished flat he was extremely critical, saying *he* wouldn't have allowed them to refurbish it, covering the beautiful parquet floor and such. However Dominic and I loved our cosy little home. It faced south, with an abundance of windows; it was extremely bright and cheerful.

We gave Pearl a set of keys to check the flat if he was passing, as he always did with his place.

About this time, Bernie also bought an apartment, a compact one-bedroom flat with a balcony, in Whithewood Mansions, Shirley Road. It was really handy, with a bus stop right outside. On leave I'd meet up with Bernie in our latest favourite gay pub, the Smugglers Inn, near the docks and on the corner of Bernard Street and Threefield Lane. It was owned by a gay couple, Terry and Jim. Terry had previously been a top-notch TV executive, directing *This Is Your Life*, including the hour-long specials on Lord Mountbatten and their good friend Danny La Rue, one of the world's most famous female impersonators. In later years, when we left the sea, we too became friends with Danny, a delightful, charming man. He would have dinner with us occasionally and we visited his exquisite home in Bassett. He had a beautiful baby grand piano, and told us about all the people who'd played and sung at the piano when he ran his own nightclub. Danny La Rue's, in Hanover Square, London, was the nightclub to be seen in. People like Noël Coward, Judy Garland, Princess Margret, Burt Bacharach, Marlene Dietrich and many others went. He owned some beautiful pieces of porcelain and china. I noticed an exquisite demitasse coffee set, which looked exactly like the one in my Liberace dream. I mentioned it and to my astonishment Danny confirmed his friend Lee (as Liberace was known to friends) had indeed gifted it to him. Spooky or what?

Bernie wore outrageous clothes going out for a drink: skin-tight shirts, sometimes see-though trousers, lace underwear and occasionally a pink jacket. Being such a large, imposing man, he kind of got away with it. One evening we were having a drink in the Smugglers, full of gay men, when in walked a bunch of obvious straight guys. They bought drinks, looking around, and one of them in a loud voice said to his mates, "I'll give you a fiver (£5) if you can spot a woman."

"I'll give you ten pounds (£10) if you can spot a *man*, dear!" remarked Bernie loudly. It was a tricky moment; however, they all laughed, joining us for a drink.

A gay Irish man, Pat, took over the Smugglers from Terry and Jim. He was helped part-time by his partner Norman, one of the very first male UK midwives ever. Norman actually featured in the *Sun*. A woman wrote she was in hospital to give birth, when in walked the midwife, a beefy butch man! I'm not sure what drugs she was on. You could hardly describe blonde, slender, camp Norman as butch and beefy!

An amusing incident happened at the Smugglers one day. Dominic was on Union business in Southampton and I dropped him at the office. Later, as arranged, he telephoned from the Smugglers, asking me to collect him. His voice sounded slurred, unusual for him. I parked in the pub car park, nipping in for a quick drink. Dominic was talking to fellow Irishman Pat, the landlord. Both were obviously extremely drunk, slurring their words. After my drink, I convinced Dominic he'd had enough, and helped him make his unsteady way to the car. Pat, helped by his partner Norman, came to say goodbye. Opposite the pub was a fishing tackle shop, with some old geezers outside taking a great interest in the proceedings. As Dominic sat in the car, Pat gave him a big slobbering goodbye kiss, full on the lips! You should have seen the shocked faces on the old geezers. It was priceless and hilarious! I was particularly amused, as Dominic has a thing about germs, never kissing anyone on the lips except me. He was mortified when I told him later, though he laughs about it now.

I'd informed the P&O crew office of my interest in joining *Sun Princess*. Meanwhile, I remained on *Canberra* for the 1981 Christmas cruise. My passengers were friendly, kind people. Some even bought me Christmas presents, bless them. They all guessed I was gay. It went unspoken; it was a wonderful time for people like me then. I moved section for the 1982 world cruise, to a veranda suite section near Bernie. Again, we had really brilliant passengers. It was a good trip and with so many queens on board, great fun. We enjoyed watching classic camp old movies starring our heroines, like Bette Davis and Joan Crawford. Movies like *What Ever Happened to Baby Jane?*, *All About Eve*, as well as the new *Mommie Dearest*. A harrowing biopic about Joan Crawford, it was based on the shocking biography by her adopted daughter Christina. Joan *forced* her children to call her *Mommie Dearest* always. If they didn't eat their 'din-dins', she'd repeatedly serve the food cold, until they did. Catching Christina using a wire – not padded wooden – coat hanger, she punished her by beating her with a hanger. While watching, I commented loudly, "Who does she remind me of?" Much to everyone's amusement, someone said loudly, "Bernie." He liked that and thereafter he was known as Mommie Dearest. Many, though not all gay guys, sometimes love to emulate their screen heroines.

In *Beyond the Forest* Bette Davis dramatically enters a room downstairs, looks around, saying loudly, "What a dump." We queens *really* took this on board: *everything* was a dump. One morning cleaning a cabin, Bernie told me he was making us some coffee. "I'll be along, soon I've finished hoovering this *dump*," I said. Behind me, I heard a female passenger voice say, "Really, Michael; I paid an awful lot of money for this dump." I was totally mortified, explaining we'd watched *Beyond the Forest* and were just copying a line from the movie. Thankfully she had a wonderful sense of humour and was fine about it. I think my obvious mortified embarrassment really amused her. If she'd reported me, I could have been sacked. These days every little remark or comment is taken *so* seriously. Even amusing jokes are misconstrued and made out to be bad. In fact it's almost gone too far the other way.

I'm sure around this time we made friends with a dancer on board, a gay girl, Sandra. She's sure it was another time, but I really can't recall. She went on to have an enduring relationship with Anita, who founded the Anita Priest Whispering Angels Scholarship Foundation in Florida. They were also great friends with Danny La Rue. He would spend time with them in Florida. We're still in touch with Sandra, catching up with her when dear Danny passed.

# 26

# Sun Princess, and a Strange New Disease

*Canberra* sailed westerly round the world, calling at Fort Lauderdale, the Caribbean, through Panama, and up the US coast and so on. Prior to San Francisco, I received a message from P&O Head Office advising me I was transferring to the West Coast. Yippee! I flew home from San Francisco January 29th, 1982, then flew to San Juan, Puerto Rico, to join *Sun Princess* February 13th, 1982. She was 17,000 gt, 760 passengers, built 1972 for P&O as *Spirit of London* to break into the lucrative American market. When P&O bought Princess Cruises in 1974, she was renamed *Sun Princess*.

On arrival in San Juan, the usual formalities, work section, boat station, cabin allocation and sign on. As I signed, a young purser said, "I see you haven't sailed *Princess* before. Welcome aboard." That's never happened at a ship's sign on before; I thought it a good omen. I didn't tell Dominic I was joining, wanting to give him a surprise, and went looking for him. When we caught up with each other, we were absolutely delighted. Clinging to each other, he told me he'd had a strange premonition I'd be arriving that day.

My work section was on a lower C deck, working in teams of three, two men and a female. My team were Steve and Maureen (Mo). Cabins were presented in a slick, professional US manner: paper bands sealed cleaned toilets, bearing the words, "Sanitised for your protection." Even clean glasses were wrapped in sterile bags. It was very much aimed at Americans. Plenty of towels, including face cloths. All cabins had private facilities, mainly outboards, plus inboards with a few double beds, some top bunks/upper berths. We even had wonderful 'maids' trolleys'. A first time for me, wheeling them along, stocked with towels, ice, soap and so on. They made cabin servicing professional and easier.

As mentioned, in 1974 P&O acquired US Princess Cruises, continuing to operate the ships in a slick professional American style, with wonderful food and fabulous service. However, when the tiny 17,000-gt *Spirit of London* joined the fleet as *Sun Princess*, they had some issues with the vessel. Cabins were not as large or luxurious as other ships, like the *Island Princess* (former *Island Venture*). Plus we had three- and four-berth family cabins. They also had issues with the tiny laundry on board. Due to space restrictions, there were no automated sheet-pressing machines. Instead they used wash and dry 'wrinkle-free' sheets. The Chinese laundrymen would tip the hot sheets out the dryer into bins, folding them when they'd cooled. Sadly this left baked-in wrinkles when we made up the beds with fresh sheets. Despite being stretch-fit, they were still a little wrinkled. We had to really stretch them as tight as possible. Even then some guests thought we hadn't changed the beds! What was even funnier, when we changed them again after a couple of days, the weight of the passengers had ironed them beautifully. Yet we had to send them back down the laundry! Nevertheless passengers adored the ship. It had a wonderful atmosphere and was what we seafarers call a happy ship.

I was made up to see lots of familiar faces onboard too: Fanny Brace, Dusty, and others such as Rainbow, who was so called because he regularly changed the colour of his hair. I shared a cabin with a Yorkshire queen, Harvey, who – can you believe – had been a former Grenadier Guardsman. Strangely he drank very little, spending his leisure time knitting, rug-making, and doing macramé and other handicrafts. He even talked me into making a rug. It took weeks and weeks, me sweating my tits off in the hot pantry; it nearly killed me. Harvey dated a rather plump Puerto Rican lad, telling me he loved fat guys. He was a 'chubby chaser'. It's the first time I'd heard this expression, and it made me chuckle. There was a delightful gay couple on board, John and Jeff, who were as camp as a row of tents. They got the amusing nickname the Climax Sisters, though I can't remember why. There was another delightful gay couple on board, David and Ian. They'd met many years earlier on the old *Oronsay*. We became friends and visited them when they later opened a B&B on the seafront in beautiful Dawlish.

Another queen, Yorkshire Ruby, was a real character. About six foot six and slim, he had bleached blonde riah, backcombed gutless. It was reminiscent of Bet Lynch, the blowsy bar maid in *Coronation Street*. Dominic told me some female staff actually fancied Ruby. They figured that being over six foot he'd be well hung. He loved his drink, vodka and whatever, any time of day. Was he camp or what! So much so, not long after he joined, the purser sent a message to the accommodation officer, asking Ruby to "tone things down," or "de-camp," as he put it. When Ruby was informed, he blew his top (rather like the in-denial gay Derek in the *Catherine Tate Show*). "How very dare you!" Ruby went completely *on the screaming piss*, ranting and raving, until he received an apology.

*Sun Princess* was a fantastic, happy little ship. Dominic occupied a single cabin as one of six chief petty officers aboard. Three were watch-keeping. Three were maintaining safety equipment and driving tenders ashore. All were part of the ship's fire team. They were a lovely bunch. Big Arthur was a larger-than-life character who drank hard and loved to sing. Bungee looked an old sea salt with his beard and pipe. Brian married a shop girl from Seattle. He later settled there and became a deep-sea tug captain. We still keep in touch. To be fair, Princess captains and officers were a great bunch, completely different from some of the stuffy ones on *Canberra*, *Oriana* and *QE2*.

The crew mess was aft on one side of the ship. On the other side was a fantastic crew bar, the SunDowner, which sold everything: beer, spirits and even cocktails. Outside this was a crew sun deck complete with sun loungers. I've never known a ship to provide sun loungers for the crew! The ship was sailing weekly Caribbean cruises to Barbados, Curaçao, Martinique, Saint Martin, St Thomas, and so on. Our turnaround port was San Juan. On every cruise the *Sun* visited a beautiful private island, with golden sands, Palm Island. It was practically uninhabited, but set up to cater for visiting cruise ships. Anchoring off, the ship ferried food and drink ashore in the lifeboats. Passengers were taken ashore for a day of swimming, sunbathing, guzzling piña coladas, stuffing their faces and partying. It was delightful for passengers and crew. At the end of the day everyone's feet carried large amounts of sand back to the ship. That caused a big mess to clean up, especially in cabin showers. The ship usually listed, so cabin stewards used witches' brooms to swish the wretched sand down the scuppers.

Dominic had a few dramas driving the wretched old tenders ashore. They were old, basic, single propellor and difficult to manoeuvre. On one call in Barbados a new exhaust had been fitted to a lifeboat. Dominic took it out for a trial run around

Barbados harbour. On the other side of the harbour he spotted an interesting old tug, taking the boat across a stretch of water. He failed to notice some navigation marks and sailed close to some rocks, which ripped off one of the propellor blades. The poor boat bunny bounced up and down on the return trip. He reported the matter to the chief officer, who was more concerned about passengers seeing the broken propeller. (Boats were housed on the promenade deck, in full view of the dining room windows.) The chief officer even toyed with the idea of making a temporary replacement blade of cardboard and tin foil, so no one would notice the defect. Later the deputy captain joked, "You'd better tell us where that rock is, as we're about to take the ship out!"

Dominic had another drama one day, driving a boat ashore in Saint Martin, a half-Dutch, half-French island. The ship anchored a good bit off, about a fifteen-minute run to the shore. On a hot day you can get extremely bored, ploughing back and forth. The main concern was a large mooring buoy. It was hard to see if you had a boat heavily laden with large Americans in the stern. A seaman stationed in the bow would look out for obstructions. The guy on this occasion had a most annoying whining voice. While sailing between anchored yachts Dom noticed that one had a nude young lady aboard, with boobs and nipples you could see a mile away. Nor did she seem bothered about passing tenders. Being a man attracted to boobs, he took the boat in nearer for a closer look. The seaman up front started whining, "Dominic, Dominic," but didn't say exactly what was about to happen. Dominic thought, *What now?* Suddenly there was an extremely loud bang, like an explosion, as the tender hit the mooring buoy. Sea water shot up in the air, drenching passengers. Everyone screamed as the boat scraped past. Realising that there was no real damage or harm done and feeling fed up, Dom just carried on as if nothing had happened!

An American gentleman gave Dominic a strange look and shook his head, saying, "You need help, boy." Returning to the ship, passengers, even the disabled ones, leapt back on board, reporting the incident to the purser's office. At the next day's chief officers meeting, the coxswains were asked, "Which one of you hit the buoy?" Dominic admitted it was him and got a bollocking. Exiting the office, big Arthur whispered, "That'll teach you to go looking at boobs." "Yes, Arthur. But it was worth it. She had lovely nipples," Dominic replied.

Dominic was the only coxswain with a gay partner. However, they were extremely kind to me. I'd sit drinking with them in the crew bar. I think they found it all highly amusing. We had plenty of laughs. Every week the cruise director broadcast a crew radio show. One week he sang the Cole Porter song, 'Let's Do It, Let's Fall in Love', inserting the words, "Even coxswains and their mates do it!" I went ashore one day in Skagway, Alaska, with big Arthur. After rather too many beers in the Red Dog Saloon, he suddenly burst loudly into song; he actually had a good voice. I'd had a 'few' and joined in with his singing. After a while we were both thrown out the pub! I was most indignant; it was the first time in my life I'd been thrown out a pub. (Apart from Gibraltar, where Mommie and I were asked to leave.)

They were happy days, with plenty of tips. The purser's office recommended passengers pay two dollars per person per day, which meant $28 per cabin each week. We had ten to thirteen cabins, so our tips gave us about $280-plus or £180-plus a week. That was the monthly equivalent of $900 or £700. Such tips doubled our wages, which were about £90 a week. This was a great help when we had a mortgage to pay. No wonder everyone wanted to work on West Coast ships.

Catering on board was provided by an Italian franchise, which was excellent. The cooks and waiters were all Italian. Female passengers adored the good-looking young waiters, who were more than happy to oblige. They were great fun too. The food aboard was delicious, very Italian. The caterers laid on hot and cold deck buffet parties for crew too, serving exceptional food. Dominic told me when the Italians first took over the catering franchise, they asked what sort of food the British crew liked to eat. One of these was steak and kidney pie. Their first version of this was a pie filled with kidney, and *whole* steaks! Crew had a good laugh about this, explaining exactly how it's actually prepared in the UK. Dominic later told me a story of when he worked a stint on *Island Princess*. They were at anchor in Acapulco with the *QE2* and the crew club managed to get some good old English bangers off the *QE2* for a forthcoming pub deck lunch. However, when the Italian chefs cooked the sausages, they couldn't resist smothering them in garlic!

Dominic was heavily involved with the crew club. Most passenger ships had such clubs. The members were elected by other crew to organise social events and outings. These were usually paid for by one-armed bandits and other gaming machines in the crew bar. Dom organised free drinks at deck parties and everyone had a great time. *Sun*'s itinerary was great too. We spent winter months in the Caribbean during their hot, dry season. Then trans-Canal, and we spent the summer months, June, July and August, in Alaska (which wasn't hot). Between times we sailed on Mexican cruises from Los Angeles to Acapulco and back.

There were many gay men and queens aboard, mostly cabin stewards. Lots were my old mates: Dusty, Fanny, and others from Shaw Savill and P&O. Roy Emery from the *Oriana* worked further along on A deck. He'd worked on Orient Line many years ago and a queen told me in those days Roy was known as 'Rosie both ways', which tickled me. He loved a drop of gin. Any empty cabin became a temporary gin palace. Fire drill and boat drill stations were our section. If we didn't need to go to the abandon ship drill we'd have a gin with Roy. During one drill we were slurping gin in one of his empty cabins when a lifeboat lowered past the cabin's large square porthole. To our horror the chief officer was in the lifeboat! We quickly scattered, while Roy cleared away the evidence. Later the chief officer had a quiet word with Roy, with a smile on his face: "Next time, Roy, *draw the curtains, please*."

The majority of our passengers were truly delightful although, as usual, there were the odd one or two complete horrors. I tended to 'take the good with the bad' and look after the vile ones just the same. However, some cabin stewards took it really personally if a passenger got nasty. Woe betide them. If they weren't careful their toothbrushes could have been used to clean the toilet! If they left clothes strewn all over the deck, 'tidying up' meant these were kicked under the bed. Some items were left when guests departed: it was the birth of the 'kick-under'. If some of us noticed an excellent piece of clothing, it would be kicked under, in the hopes it would be left behind! In those days the only cleaning cloths issued to us were J-cloths. They were useless, so most of us used soiled towels to clean the cabin and bathrooms. The tiny size of the ship's laundry presented issues; sometimes there was even a shortage of towels. I dreaded going down the laundry to collect fresh towels because the laundrymen were most uncooperative. We had no choice but to fold and re-hang used towels in the bathroom, hoping nobody noticed it!

It was around this time news broke of a mysterious and frightening disease. Authorities thought it appeared to be sexually transmitted. It was mostly found in gay men and seemed to be fatal. Waves of fear went all across the world, including in Great Britain and especially America. Little did anyone know how awful this was to become. Nor did we imagine the fear, hostility and bigotry the 'plague' would produce. You can get a measure of what it was like by watching the 2021 television series *It's a Sin*. Set in London from 1981 to 1991, the drama depicts the lives of a group of gay men and their friends during the HIV/AIDS crisis. I actually cried when I watched it. The way some of those poor boys were treated, even by their own parents, was dreadful. I empathised strongly. I'm lucky I found Dominic, otherwise I too may have caught this awful disease.

The 1970s were increasingly a golden time of acceptance for gay people. But in the 1980s AIDS would change people's attitudes towards homosexuality for a long time. It still has, as it's stupidly referred to as a 'gay plague'. I never heard of anyone on the ship actually catching AIDS, although if you visited the doctor it caused concern. People were worried about the disease. But being at sea felt safe, so we weren't particularly scared about getting infected. At this time the disease was seen mainly as an American disease, and their problem. As far as I could make out, only a limited amount of casual gay sex went on aboard the ship; it certainly wasn't like the good old days on *Oriana* and the *Star*! There were an abundance of female crew and passengers for the heterosexual lads, and many people like us were safely boxed off.

We carried on partying. St Thomas in the Virgin Islands was most crew members' favourite island. The port included a shopping mall, marina and, nearby, a delightful bar and restaurant, The Virgins' Oar House. One afternoon when I was enjoying a piña colada there, I telephoned Mum. She asked me where I was calling from. When I told her the name of the place, she said, "It sounds rather unsavoury." I had to laugh and explain it.

My favourite beach was Morningstar Beach in St Thomas. Dominic didn't like it much, as he said there was more cigarette butts than sand. One afternoon while sunbathing, a familiar voice said, "Hello, girl." Looking up, I could hardly believe my eyes. There was my old mate Barbra (John) from *Canberra* with another guy. It turned out he'd left the sea and met Geordie Ken, now his lover, and they'd decided to return to the sea. They were aboard *Cunard Countess*, also in St Thomas, working as concessionaire waiters; it was the only way they could both get to sea. We had a moving reunion, promising to keep in touch afterwards. And we did.

The whole *Sun Princess* crowd were fun. Everybody visited the SunDowner Pig, including us gay boys camping it up, and telling amusing stories. There were no shows as such, or dragging up, although we had fancy dress nights and bingo. The female BRSs and PRSs were great fun too – Lisa, Valerie, Mary, Carmen, and Anita, to name a few. Angie was camper than most gay men! I worked with Carmen, who was an old-school Spanish matriarch. She was always perfectly made up and coiffured. She used the expression "Wan-nee" for wasn't it, isn't it, or doesn't it, which amused me. One day cleaning a cabin, there was a hot water bottle–type douche hanging in the bathroom. I cheekily asked Carmen, "What's that thing for?" "For the fanny, wan-nee," she replied. We worked with a straight guy, Jimmy, who Carmen wasn't fond of. I asked her one day if she could fancy him? "I'd rather do it myself, wan-nee," she replied, which I got, and found amusing. I keep in contact with these girls and boys now.

One stewardess, however, Margie, was a frightful woman. She was miserable, morbidly obese, and always moaning. One lad thought she just needed a bit of dick, so he fixed her up with an Italian waiter. Next day she was *still* moaning "I never slept a wink. He wanted to do it *all* night!" You just can't please some people. She gets a nice bit of cock and is still moaning! Most of the time aboard, Mary, a delightful, hard-working, no-nonsense Scots lady, formed part of our work team and was therefore part of the small dramas that were always happening aboard. One day flowers were delivered and left outside one of our passenger cabins. As I passed, to my horror a large scorpion ran out the bouquet. I ran screaming to Mary. "There's a deadly scorpion in the alley." She matter of factly took off her shoe and splatted it, killing it outright!

When passengers called room service, they were put through to a large pantry on A deck. There the bellboys answered the call and relayed requirements to the cabin stewards. However, one day a dozy bedroom steward queen, Chicken, was topping up fruit bowls in the pantry from boxes of fruit. As he was taking out some bananas, he picked up a huge, hairy tarantula! He screamed his tits off, dropping it on the deck. Everyone in the pantry, including the bellboys, saw the hairy monster scuttle underneath the pantry cupboards. That was it! *Everyone* screamed their tits off, fleeing for their lives. Of course passenger calls were still coming through but no one was brave enough to go in and answer them. It was hilarious. Eventually help was summoned to get rid of the monster. Normal service resumed.

Dom and I made friends with a really charming older cabin stewardess, Marje (Marjorie). She looked a bit of an old boot but she was actually a sweetie, with a wonderful mischievous sense of humour. She'd worked on the old Cunard Queen ships when things were truly first class and strict. She told us that every morning the chief steward would inspect their starched white uniforms to make sure they were up to muster. Even young bellboys were inspected. Marje loved a glass of sherry after work, before we ate. I'm not sure how it came about but we'd get together in each other's cabins for sherry, scandal and scurrilous stories. She loved scandal, especially if a little risqué.

One Christmas there was a party going on on our ship. The mad Eastern European doctor asked her for a dance, saying, "Would you like a drink, you old trout?" "Old trout?" she replied, throwing her drink in his face! He was indeed mad. I developed two painful ingrowing big toe nails and couldn't get my shoes on. I went to see the Doc and he told me to go for a drink and lunch, he'd see me after. I later went to the surgery and lay on the operating table. He gave me a painkilling injection in my toes and was fiddling around with them. When he finished he told me they'd be a little sore when the painkillers worked off, and when I went on the open deck to take the dressings off, to let the air at them. They later became extremely painful. When I removed the dressings, I nearly fainted. He'd pulled the big toe nails *out by the roots*, leaving two bits of raw meat where the nails had been! I thought, *Oh well, at least they're sorted.* Can you believe, they regrew and in-grew again. Eventually I visited a professional chiropodist who sorted them out for me.

Every Friday *Sun Princess* docked in St Thomas alongside *Cunard Countess*, and again Saturdays in San Juan. As we'd sailed on the *Countess* when it was new in 1975, doing a *run job* from the Copenhagen builders to Italy to be fitted out, I went aboard to see the finished ship. The colour scheme, especially carpets, were extremely gaudy: bright blues, yellow and orange. Nevertheless, the ship had a good atmosphere. It became extremely popular, with a long and successful career. In the crew bar I was delighted to see guys I knew, straight and gay. Among them Slippery Sid, ex-*QE2*, who was thrilled to see me and still wheeler-dealing. One cruise, knowing I was flying home the following trip, he asked me if I'd any room in my suitcase for a parcel of unframed paintings? He'd give me a painting as a reward for transporting them. He *said* he'd obtained the pictures when he bought house contents in St Lucia. I knew Sid had a friend there, Frank Delmonte, from a fabulously wealthy family. As I had room in my suitcase, next time we docked in San Juan, I collected the bag of paintings and Sid gifted me an attractive little watercolour of Douglas, Isle of Man. The collection arrangement in the UK went as follows. The Sunday after I arrived home, at midday I was to wait outside The Crown pub in Shirley, where they'd be collected. That's exactly what happened. A shifty-looking man pulled up in a car, asked if I was Michael, and I gave him the parcel of paintings.

Sadly the watercolour Sid gave us had rust-like marks on it and was framed with a poor quality type of antique cardboard. We showed it to Jewish Amber, who was knowledgeable regarding antiques/paintings, to see if anything could be done. Amber explained the effect was known as 'foxing', and it needed to be treated by a professional art restorer. Luckily, he knew one in Eastleigh, near Southampton. After Amber had a chat with him on the phone, we drove to this man's studio. He gave us his card and we left the painting with him. When we telephoned some days later, to our alarm he claimed he couldn't find where he'd put it! We had strong words, warning him he'd better find it or we'd go to the police. Eventually it turned up and he returned it to us; it *appeared* to be the same picture.

Years later Sid telephoned, asking if he could have the painting back, as he thought it might be a Turner. We made an excuse that we'd sold it. I thought it was a colossal bleeding cheek to ask for a gift to be returned. By then even *I* knew that paintings by William Turner were worth a fortune. When the *Antiques Roadshow* appeared at Osborne House, Isle of Wight, I took the picture to be valued. After queuing for hours in the hot sun, the expert advised me it was probably painted by a student of Turner's. She peeled back the cardboard-type frame and managed to find a signature – not Turner's. She thought it was only worth a couple of thousand pounds. A real Turner would have been millions. We don't know to this day whether the art restorer ripped us off, or if Amber or Sid also had a hand in it. Nevertheless, we stayed good friends. They were both extremely kind, good fun and we were truly fond of them.

# 27

# The Falklands Conflict

Shortly after joining *Sun Princess* in early March 1982 we'd heard rumours of a possible Argentinian invasion of the Falkland Islands. There was talk of government plans to use UK cruise ships to convey British troops and supplies down there to the South Atlantic. Dominic and I agreed that if our little ship was sent down, we would indeed volunteer. On April 2nd, 1982, Argentina invaded the Falklands. Plans were afoot to take the islands back, using a task force of Navy, RFA and merchant ships. *Sun Princess* wasn't requisitioned, possibly due to insufficient endurance or capacity. However, a hundred or so Navy, RFAs, merchant cruise ships and large ferries were used during the conflict, including *QE2*, *Norland*, and *Uganda*. My old *Canberra* was hurriedly refitted in Southampton, sailing on April 9th with 3 Commando Brigade and a task force to the Falklands.

Most non-UK crew were removed from UK ships. *Canberra*'s deck and engine room ratings, for example, were Asian and replaced by British volunteers. All jobs aboard ships were covered by these brave volunteer crew – men and women.

They included many of our friends, such as Vera/Brian, sailing on an RFA ship, Mommie Dearest/Bernie, on *Canberra*, and the legendary Roy 'Wendy' Gibson on the ferry *Norland*, taking 2nd and 3rd Battalion parachute regiments to and from the islands.

Della (Derek) and Wendy (Roy) both worked aboard North Sea Ferries. We'd met Wendy a couple of times when he came down from Hull and visited Della in Southampton. Wendy was around my age; he was a delightful, kind, humorous man and a talented pianist. He was well known in local Hull pubs and clubs for his entertaining, Liberace-style piano playing and cheerful banter. Inheriting his grandmother's piano, he had painted it bright tarty pink and took it on board *Norland* to entertain crew and passengers. By the time the Falklands' conflict started, his Joanna was knackered. So when Wendy volunteered to go to war he managed to talk the Mission to Seafarers port chaplain into letting him take their piano with him to entertain the boys. The chaplain asked Wendy not to let the piano fall into Argentinian hands. Wendy assured him the *Norland* was only going as far as the Ascension Islands. Little did they know!

During this conflict *Canberra* was an extremely large target, which put our brave (straight and gay) volunteer friends at serious risk. In all, 120 military and civilian medical staff, also voluntary, were embarked, as she was to be used as a hospital ship. However, as she carried troops (Royal Marines, and three Para) and was lightly armed, she wasn't protected by the Geneva Convention/Red Cross. Therefore the ship was a 'legitimate target'. There was little on board in way of protection either, only fifty-calibre machine guns lashed to the rails. She was sent all the way to the Falklands and was away for three months. In the process she gained the affectionate nickname of the Great White Whale. Similarly, *Norland* also carried troops and was therefore a legitimate target. *Norland* crew were initially informed they were taking troops to Ascension Island. On arrival, the crew were told there was a change of plan. They'd be taking troops all the way to the Falklands. P&O gave them the opportunity to fly home; of course, few did. Being gay or camp doesn't mean you're a coward or a wimp. Seafarers are usually loyal to their shipmates, to their ship and to duty.

Thankfully, by some miracle, both these ships survived the conflict. Gay friends told me initially there was a certain amount of tension on board: military versus merchant navy. Each 'side' didn't know quite what to expect: hostility, maybe queer bashing? It didn't take long for all to get along fine. Merchant Navy crew teamed up with the military, defending the islands and each other. Wendy went one step further aboard *Norland*, dragging his piano to the forces' mess halls, to play morale-boosting tunes. He continued to entertain all the way down to the islands many times, and all the way back to the UK.

His endless cheer, kindness, humorous banter and bravery led to troops taking him to their hearts. They named him Our Wendy, and woe betide anyone who upset or disrespected their Wendy. During the trip Paras expressed their esteem by giving him a red beret and making him an honorary paratrooper. When he passed away in 2021 he was given a full military send-off on June 29th. My friend, author Dr Jo Stanley, knew him too, attending his funeral. She told me his coffin was draped with a Union Jack and buried with full military honours. Uniformed men bearing Official Standards marked his funeral, with not just one, but *five* flags. Further to this, at their Aldershot headquarters, Paras showed appreciation by putting up a memorial plaque on the 'Goose Green bench'. It read as follows:

Roy "Wendy" Gibson
mv Norland 1982
1/5/1954-2/6/2021
OUR WENDY

## Anything Goes at Sea

On June 14th, 1982, the Argentinians surrendered: it was a great British victory. I could relate many stories regarding the Falklands conflict, but don't wish to bore you. There are a plethora of publications about the war offering the Navy point of view, but only a few with the Merchant Navy perspective. One of them is *They Couldn't Have Done It Without Us*, by John Johnson-Allen. Another is the extraordinary *All in the Same Boat*, by Warren Fitzgerald. He wrote it assisted by the crew, including Wendy, who'd actually served aboard *Norland*. The book relates the volunteers' incredible experiences in a war that turned out to be far more dangerous than expected. These bizarre voyages demonstrated that amazing, lasting bonds can be formed between the most unlikely people.

Following the war, crews came home as heroes. I watched *Canberra* return to Southampton July 11th, 1982, to a rapturous welcome. So much for heroes. Things soon returned to normal. I understand, for example, that all *Canberra*'s brave UK voluntary deck and engine room ratings were immediately replaced with (cheaper) foreign crew. If Britain entered another war today, there are extremely few UK-owned and no UK-manned cruise ships or large ferries to use as troop ships or hospital ships. As of 2024, there were just two UK-registered Saga cruise ships with foreign crew. Britain's primary casualty receiving ship is RFA *Argus*. Even P&O and Cunard, which masquerade as British shipping companies, belong to the ubiquitous American Carnival Corporation, along with many others, including Princess Cruises, Holland America Line, and Costa. P&O have ships registered in UK. However, they are foreign-owned and foreign-crewed.

Following his leave after the Falklands Conflict, my old mate Mommie Dearest, Bernie, was offered a West Coast voyage. I was delighted of course, and eventually shared a cabin with him. Later in 1982, *Sun Princess* repositioned from the Caribbean, making a trans-Canal cruise to Los Angeles, and was based there for Mexican cruises. These called at Mazatlán, Puerto Vallarta, and Cabo San Lucas. After that, we repositioned in Vancouver for a summer season of weekly Alaskan cruises. This was my first visit after my brother Peter and his wife Linda emigrated there in 1971. I enjoyed a brief emotional reunion with them, meeting their two children, David and Louise. The weekly Alaska cruises sailed along the famous North American Fjordland Inside Passage, calling at Ketchikan, Juneau, and Skagway, and visiting Glacier Bay. The scenery was breathtaking. We seemingly sailed extremely close to massive glaciers, witnessing massive pieces of ice breaking off into the sea. It wasn't possible to drive to most places we visited. The only way in was by ship or air, which made seaplanes very popular. When we first visited, some of the towns hadn't changed much since the 1890s Klondike Gold Rush; old buildings and unmade roads remained. It was an interesting place, although it never stopped raining. Indeed Ketchikan boasted it was the Rain Capital of the World. It was!

Work patterns were wonderful: four months on, with four weeks off. I flew home from Vancouver June 12th, 1982. After a month's leave we flew back to Vancouver, rejoining *Sun Princess*. It was a happy little ship. Our hotel bosses were amiable, and occasionally all gay. There was accommodation officer John, who wasn't effeminate; assistant accommodation officer Jeff/Judy Garland, and accommodation supervisor Steve/Stella Bags: he'd previously been a baggage steward. Stella has a lifelong relationship with one of the other coxswains, Frank, a delightful big bear of a man.

The accommodation office was close to the ship's shops. Passing by one day, the Old Man said out loud, "Morning, girls!" The accommodation office answered, "Morning, Captain." He laughingly told them he'd meant the shop girls, not them! Such a laid back ship. Once, during Captain's crew inspection, they found the printer (who must have had a hard night) fast asleep *underneath* his bed. On any other ship it would have been a drama. However, the rounds report amusingly stated, "Printer to be removed from beneath bunk."

There were many characters on board too, even some of the entertainers. One section I worked in housed a ship's comedian, Bobby, in one of our single cabins. He was an extremely funny guy with curly Afro hair. One day as I crashed a vacuum cleaner under his bunk it jammed. On inspection I discovered a curly wig stuck in the hoover and realised Bobby was bald! Looking beneath his bed, I discovered several wigs of different lengths. He obviously changed into a shorter wig to make it appear he'd been for a haircut. It certainly fooled me. Dominic even told me on the gangway Bobby would say he was going for a haircut, taking a shorter wig with him, which he donned for his return, reinforcing the illusion of real hair. On other occasions he put talcum powder on his shoulder to look like dandruff!

Another of my cabins housed the ship's pianist, a youngish, good-looking chap, who was camp as a row of tents. He was a typical American gay, and we nicknamed him Liberace. During Alaskan cruising the ship carried a park ranger, who'd broadcast commentary from the bridge. He'd explain the wildlife and scenery we were passing. One day we caught one of the hunky handsome regular park rangers leaving Liberace's cabin. As he passed guests, he said in a deep butch, wholesome voice, "Howdy, folks." It tickled me. If only they'd known where he'd just been. Apparently the ranger would visit a lounge where Liberace was playing and sit near the piano listening to him play. With a beaming white smile, the pianist altered some lyrics of songs to flatter the Park ranger.

When summer ended we repositioned to the Caribbean, again operating Mexican cruises from Los Angeles on the way. Passengers cruised down the Mexican coast to Acapulco, spent a week there, then flew home. Others would fly to Acapulco, enjoy a week there, and cruise back to LA. Mexican food played havoc with some guests' bowels: we called it Montezuma's revenge. On one cruise departing Acapulco we were unable to service a cabin. A "Do not disturb sign" constantly hung on the door handle. Finally, knocking, I explained to the gentleman we truly needed to clean his cabin. He revealed his wife was extremely embarrassed, as she'd suffered a dreadful accident in bed. I assured him it was no problem; we were used to this sort of thing. When they finally vacated, we found madam had indeed suffered a dreadful accident. It was so bad that we called the catering office for a replacement mattress. However, the ship had none, as so many guests suffered the same problem. I asked, "How do we resolve this?" The office told us to sanitise best we could, turn it over and make up with fresh bedding. They'd make a note that cabin A13 required a new mattress. Not long afterwards I flew home on leave from LA, forgetting all about it.

While home on leave in our cheerful, cosy flat, I found that if we left a window open a dear little affectionate cat, Boots, would climb through and spend time with us. We were happy with that, both being animal lovers. In fact, we'd liked to have owned cats or dogs but, being away for long periods at sea, this was impossible. One night I was walking though the apartment and saw Boots crouched over the plug hole in the bath. I could hear the splashing of liquid and realised the clever cat was peeing right down the waste pipe. He even peed in the toilet (which was better than on the carpet). This arrangement continued until we moved, where at our next house another cat adopted us, obviously sensing we were cat-friendly.

Rejoining *Sun Princess*, I returned to work in my old A deck section, Caribbean cruising. One morning an American guest approached, saying, "Hi, Michael, I think we have bed bugs in our cabin."

"Bed bugs!" I said. "This is a British ship, sir. We don't have such things as bed bugs. What's your cabin number? We'll check it out." When he said A13, I thought, *That number rings a bell.* Later, on servicing the cabin, we turned the mattresses. To our horror, one of them had a vile stain underneath. Obviously the note we'd left for the office, weeks ago, had been missed. We called the catering office for a new mattress, thoroughly sanitising the cabin and making it up with fresh linen. Although it was a shocking cock up, we did find it incredibly amusing.

A rather amusing, slightly alarming, incident happened one evening in Barbados. The ship was sailing late at night this visit. A large US Navy ship also docked. Everywhere was busy. Dom and I went ashore with another crew member. We visited Nelson Street for beers and fun, watching guys enjoying themselves. About 9:00p.m. we wandered through the capital, Bridgetown, on our way back to the ship, feeling the warm glow of a few drinks. As we passed the main bus station, three local young men pulled knives on us, holding them to our throats, and demanded money. I think they thought we were rich drunken Yanks off the US carrier. I felt humorous and perfectly calm, laughing and saying to my guy, "Put the knife down *please*, I'll write you a cheque!" He moved the knife away from my throat and I gave him my cash. Dominic tickled me, saying to his guy, "Here's my money. Now give me some dollars back to get a beer." Strangely, he did, and they ran off. We were fine, putting it down to experience. I think hearing our "limey" accents, they knew we wouldn't have much money anyway.

A new P&O/Princess super cruise liner was being built for Princess Cruises. It was set to be one of the most luxurious afloat. Well-appointed, every cabin and suite was outboard, with windows or large portholes, some with balconies. There were no windowless inboards. Every stateroom had a bath as well as a shower, unusual at this time. Prince Charles's recent marriage to Diana made Princess Diana everyone's darling, so the ship's name just had to be *Royal Princess*. The new ship was to be built in Finland, launched early 1984 and enter service later that year. We saw the brochures, all the TV and hype about it and thought…?

An American TV show, *The Love Boat*, was based on Princess Cruises. Parts of it were filmed aboard *Sun Princess*, also on *Island/Pacific Princess*. The show was rather corny, though amusing. People loved it and so our little ships became extremely popular, with a happy atmosphere. On every sailing the *Love Boat* theme song played over the ship's loudspeakers. Indeed it still is. But no, people weren't really having stupid affairs and mad sex all the time as in the series. Dominic, as crew club chairman, organised plenty of crew deck parties. In Alaska we'd have hot toddy parties on deck while cruising around Glacier Bay. The ship even sent a lifeboat to collect some glacier ice for drinks. Not surprisingly, this non-ecological practice has now ceased.

June 1984 I rejoined the ship in Los Angeles, where it laid over two days before repositioning to Alaska. While there *Princess* replaced Asian crew with Mexicans. Little did I know this would be my last time working on the *Sun Princess*, or that she almost would be destroyed by fire. Los Angeles wouldn't permit rubbish to be disposed of alongside, or even taken off. All garbage was stored in the working alleyway, along with drums of highly inflammable oil, paint, acetylene gas and such. On sailing day a considerable amount of gash was stored, ready to be jettisoned later when we were out in deep water. At the time no one realised how bad this was for the oceans and our planet. Thankfully, this practice was banned in 1988.

After work I'd have a few beers and gins in the crew bar, then toddle off to bed. Around midnight we were awakened by the ship's general alarm signal. Because we had regular drills, we knew exactly what to do. Bernie and I dressed quickly, going to our work stations, rousing passengers and getting them to put on life jackets and warm clothing, ready to abandon ship. Then they went to their muster station, usually a public room, where they could be assembled in safety and accounted for. In my section, I found thick, acrid, choking smoke filled the alleyway. Donning a wet face covering, I crawled along the alley with my work mates, calling passengers, getting them prepared and directed to muster stations. Meanwhile, fire parties got into fire suits, attached BA (breathing apparatus) sets, and tackled the blazing working alley. Dominic's fire party were one of the first at the scene, working at the front line of the fire. He and the third officer really worked hard, skilfully using fire hoses. Eventually they managed to get the fire under control. When it was extinguished and all passengers accounted for, everyone 'stood down' from emergency stations. The crew bar was reopened, allowing the brave firefighters to celebrate with a much-needed drink.

Next day the captain held a meeting with senior officers, coxswains, leading hands and anyone involved in tackling the fire. Discussions revealed the crew member who'd initially discovered the fire pressed a fire alarm. When he didn't hear any response he walked to the next fire alarm, pressing it. Again not hearing an alarm, he walked to the next one. He should have known that pressing a fire alarm button only alerts the bridge with a light on a fire panel. Rather than ringing a bell, the silent light shows the fire's location, which is rapidly investigated. Pressing so many fire alarms made it appear there were multiple fires. Consequently, the fire had time to become really nasty. It would have been a lot worse if the highly inflammable oil drums and gas cylinders had caught fire. Dominic and the third officer were picked out for saving the ship and highly praised for the heroic way they tackled the blaze. The cause of the fire remained a mystery; we heard it was probably spontaneous combustion. It also came to light unofficially that a tough guy in a fire party actually *hid* during the fire. He was scared. This was a man whose hostility towards Dominic and I for being gay was not helped by the AIDS scare. I think he thought gay men weren't real men, yet he was too scared to fight the fire. Dominic was not.

*Sun Princess* sailed to Vancouver for a summer season of Alaska cruises. On June 29th, 1984, we were alongside in Skagway. While cleaning a room, I listened to the BBC World Service as usual on the cabin radio. I heard about the sinking of the cruise ship *Sundancer* in Alaska. A passing lady passenger heard this, saying to me, "Gee, honey! Have we sunk?" I couldn't resist it: "No, madam, the unfortunate vessel that sank is the *Sundancer*. This is *Sun* Princess, a *British* ship, and we rarely sink." Looking relieved, she toddled off. Apparently *Sundancer* struck rocks off Maud Island while transiting the Inside Passage. She limped to a flour mill dock, tied up and sank, pulling fifty metres of the dock down with her. Fortunately, all 787 passengers and crew were saved. Strangely enough, we didn't know it at the time, but one of our friends was working as a contractor in the engine room. His nickname is Dangerous Dave. He always seemed to end up in alarming situations.

Weather in Alaska is usually inclement with poor visibility. As our cabins were near the water line, alleyways between crew compartments were divided by watertight doors. In poor visibility these doors were closed from the bridge. Part of Dominic's job was to demonstrate how to pass safely through them. These hydraulic doors were very dangerous and had been known to cut a person in half. One evening a fancy dress party was held in the crew mess, where I went as Boy George. After a few drinks the party began to swing, and Bernie realised he'd left his camera down the cabin and rushed down to collect it. To get through watertight doors, you pulled the rather stiff watertight door handle on one side of the door. When it clanked open, you then reached through, grabbed the handle on the other side, stepped though, and released the handle, letting the door close.

On this occasion, when Mommie was passing through the door his hand slipped off the handle and the door began to close on him, leaving him dangerously trapped. He couldn't quite reach the handle on the other side of the door. Feeling the door begin to painfully crush him, and genuinely thinking his fate was to be crushed to death, he began to lose consciousness. Miraculously, he told me, an invisible hand grabbed his hand, pulling hard on the handle. The door opened and he fell through, gasping, and collapsed on the deck. He was extremely grateful he was still alive. When he returned to the bar I could see he was agitated. He recounted the incredible story. Even to this day he still doesn't understand what actually happened. Although a nonbeliever, he thinks he felt an unseen force like an angel coming to his rescue. As far as I was concerned, God moves in mysterious ways. It wasn't his time to go. This was another little incident confirming my belief in our loving Father. In the next port, Bernie/Mommie went ashore and bought a solid-gold crucifix.

# 28

# Two Royal Princesses

In summer 1984 various crew received notification of transfer to the new ship. The people affected included me, Dominic, Mommie Dearest and many friends working on *Sun Princess*. I felt quite honoured. Rumour had it only the *top* workers had been hand-picked. Dominic and I flew home from Vancouver August 22nd, settling into our cosy Shirley flat, awaiting orders. Meanwhile P&O sent everyone joining *Royal Princess* on firefighting and sea survival courses at the nearby Warsash Maritime Academy. In a *Southampton Daily Echo* article about the new ship, we were actually pictured fighting fire at Warsash. Under the photo was the caption, "Royal Firefighters," which amused us. If they only knew how many of us were indeed queens! After two months' Southampton leave, we were excited when P&O announced we'd be flying to Helsinki October 30th, 1984, to prepare *Royal Princess* for her maiden voyage.

With so many of us living in Southampton, P&O chartered a coach to take us to Heathrow to catch the short flight to

Helsinki. This is when I first met an adorable married couple, John and Marion Griffiths. When we arrived at the shipyard, we were amazed at the sheer size of *Royal Princess*, the first new ship of that size to be built for many years. She was built and ready; she just needed finishing touches. Some of those touches were down to us. The ship wasn't yet ready for us to live on board. No catering or accommodation facilities were in place. Instead, we were berthed on a nearby chartered ferry, staying a few days in single cabins and eating onboard the ferry too. First evening in Helsinki I told Mommie we were going to have a wander to town for a beer. He came with us, grumbling, "I bet it's freezing cold, probably expensive, dreary, anti-gay, dear." Wrong. The first bar we visited sold delicious draught beer and was not expensive. Then, in the city centre, we saw a large sign blatantly stating in bright lights, "Gay Bar. All Welcome." Wow! It was fantastic. People were friendly, again. It was not too costly. I looked at Mommie. He couldn't help smiling. Next morning, he even brought a gorgeous Finnish hunk into breakfast.

We began the work of distributing all the finishing items round the ship. Things like mattresses, toilet brush holders, cleaning gear, small bins, bedding and towels. Meanwhile Dominic and the other CPOs were familiarising themselves with the ship's safety equipment. When we toured the ship, we were immensely impressed: this was the first new ship that I myself, and most of us, had ever been on, however long we'd been at sea. It was a rare treat and a privilege. She was beautiful and the suites were fabulous. The two top suites, the Royal and Princess suites, were huge, with marble bathrooms, Jacuzzis and their own dining room. We were informed the ship was equipped with a revolutionary new vacuum toilet system. When the flush bottom was pressed, a small amount of water was released and the vacuum system sucked the effluent into large holding tanks. There it was treated by waste-eating bugs and chemicals, then by ultraviolet light. It was rendered almost like water and could be safely discharged into the ocean, or pumped out alongside. This was the forerunner to all modern sewage systems aboard cruise ships. No more salt water flush, dripping flush handles and dumping effluent into the sea.

The next few days were spent getting ready for sailing, preparing crew and passenger cabins, cleaning, and making up beds. Finally all crew boarded. We departed for sea trials before finally heading towards Southampton and the naming ceremony on November 15th. There was much excitement about this. The ship was to be christened by Her Royal Highness Princess Diana. Between cabin stewards, there was much speculation about who would be assigned the royal suites. *Island Princess* and *Pacific Princess* (previously *Island Venture/Sea Venture*) were larger and more luxurious than *Sun Princess*. Cabin stewards from those ships considered they'd be given the top jobs. That was especially true of Daisy, a kind but bold queen from *Pacific Princess*, who kept telling anyone who'd listen that he had been hand-picked for the royal suites. The accommodation office was staffed by the same men off the *Sun Princess*: Chris, Judy and Stella. On sailing, by law all emergency station cards (which are your work stations) are handed out. I was taken completely by surprise when given an emergency card for the Royal suite plus adjoining suites. Mommie D was given the Princess suite and adjoining suites. It put a few noses out of joint! Daisy was especially upset and, after a visit to his doctor ashore, signed off.

Cabin stewards on the new ship had many more cabins in their sections than usual. P&O employed Mexican assistant cabin stewards to help. They turned out to be delightful young men. On the *Sun*, we'd cover approximately thirty-six cabins, twelve for each steward. Aboard *Royal Princess* it increased to forty-eight cabins, sixteen for each steward. The suite sections covered one royal suite, and seventeen further suites, working in teams of two: nine each. Arrival at Southampton brought a mad flurry of activity getting the ship ready for the royal naming ceremony on November 15th.

The maiden voyage was November 19th. I thought it really exciting. Little did I know! Looking around the ship, I loved the clever interior design: modern, attractive, practical and comfortable. Most bulkhead coverings were a neutral beige, emphasising the beauty and texture of furniture, artwork, plants and decorative items. In the plaza, an atrium went vertically through two decks. In front of the guest services desk was a large weeping fig tree and a tall, beautiful sculpture, entitled Spindrift. A fountain had metal seagulls seemingly flying around it. I thought, "If we hit rough weather that water is going to slosh everywhere." Another thing surprised me: the handrails on the stairs appeared to be real untreated brass. I knew they'd take constant polishing. If the Brasso polish wasn't completely buffed off, it would rub off on guests' clothes, especially discolouring men's white tuxedos. (It did! In later years the handrails were covered with teak.)

My stewardess, Mary, was someone I'd worked with on the *Sun Princess*. She was a delightful, down-to-earth Scots lady. Mommie's workmate, also off the *Sun Princess*, was Norma Jean, nicknamed Goddess. She looked like an elderly Marilyn Monroe, as well as sharing Monroe's original name. One of the ship's Scandinavian designers visited us in the Royal suite while we were getting it ready. "What do you think of my lovely ship?" he asked us. I told him it was truly beautiful, though there were a few problems. "What do you mean?" he asked. I told him about the brass handrails and fountain. Dismissing our misgivings, he asked how we liked the artwork? I told him most of it was also beautiful but some, like a painting in the Royal suite, was awful. I pointed it out: "What is it supposed to be?" "What do you think it is?" he replied. I told him honestly, "It looks like some kind of lighthouse, above which appeared to be someone's bum sticking through clouds, with flies buzzing around the arsehole." He was furious, saying boldly, "Do not criticise that what you do not understand," and flouncing off. The picture remained on the bulkhead.

The ship's crew bar opened while we were in Southampton. Again, following a crew club meeting, Dominic was elected chairman. The bar was a good size, comfortably furnished, with a dimmer switch for evenings. However, there was no jukebox, music, nor any decorations or pictures as on *Sun Princess*. Dominic decided to buy a jukebox and some decorations with his own money, which would be repaid by the jukebox. We bought some framed pictures and prints in Southampton. However, as currency aboard Princess Cruises was US dollars, we needed a jukebox that would accept quarters (twenty-five-cent coins). Luckily, Pearl was in the industry, so he knew exactly where to purchase such a thing: Germany. Dominic ordered one, which cost over £1,000.

Before the naming ceremony, a list of names was drawn up for representatives from various departments to be presented to Princess Diana. Unbelievably, both my name and Dominic's were on the list. We were both absolutely thrilled. We were advised how to address her: no touching, no picture taking, and only speak when spoken to. You said, "your Royal Highness" first, then, "Yes, ma'am" (rhymes with marm) and so on.

The encounter took place November 15th in a wide passageway between Princess Court and the Riviera Club. To my surprise, champagne was served and we formed a line. Princess Diana approached, appearing absolutely stunning. She spoke to everyone and even shook hands. Reaching me, she looked directly at me with those beautiful blue eyes, asking, "And what is your job, Michael?" "Cabin steward, your Royal Highness," I replied. "And how often do you change the sheets?" she asked. I smiled, saying "Once a month, whether they need it or not, ma'am." Giggling, she carried on down the line. It was my little joke: we changed sheets every other day in suites, or every day if requested. While Princess Diana continued her ship's tour, we all rushed to the forward open deck to watch the actual launch ceremony. It was the usual, "I name this ship *Royal Princess*, may God bless her and all those who sail on her." Then a bottle of bubbly was smashed against the bow, to the sound of loud cheering. We all watched from the siderail and were pictured. It was all extremely moving.

We'd become firm friends with a lovely couple aboard *Royal Princess*, John and Marion Griffiths. John was educated and extremely clever, making things like jewellery, clothing and such like. He had a very outrageous, camp sense of humour. On board was a regular ship's cabaret star, Beryl Davis. She'd been discovered by Glen Miller in WWII, singing to the troops. Postwar she'd sung with big bands, plus stars like Frank Sinatra. Still singing in her eighties, John wickedly referred to her as *Burial* Davis.

Extremely glamorous, Marion looked like Joan Collins from *Dynasty*. When they first met on the *Pacific Princess* Marion was a public room steward (drinks waiter) and John was a cabin steward. He wanted her to change jobs to work with him, but she didn't fancy cleaning toilets, part of a cabin steward's job. With his excellent tips, John bought her beautiful diamond earrings. He told her that while cleaning toilets she could look in the bathroom mirror, see the beautiful diamonds and remember *why* she was working in cabins (loadsa money). It *had* to be earrings though; BRS wore rubber gloves while cleaning, so she wouldn't be able to see it if she was wearing a diamond *ring*! His gift of the gab worked. He won her heart. I had to chuckle when I heard when Marion introduce herself to passengers, because she was *so* gorgeous that some of them said, "Gee, honey. You're so beautiful we should be looking after you!" They were one of the first couples to occupy *married quarters*, sharing a cabin. Usually two people of the same sex shared a cabin. I believe that at one time married couples and siblings were not allowed to sail together. This is thought to have been a precaution after the *Titanic* sinking, which left many Southampton families decimated and destitute because such a large number of close relatives were aboard (they'd arranged for jobs for each other).

During the ship's building a competition was organised to name the new ship, also to create a design for the ship's crest and motto. The winning ship's crest was a princess tiara, with a princess trade mark: 'sea witch' hair. Our new friend John won the prize for the ship's motto: *Persequere Excellentiam*: Pursue Excellence. (I told you he was well educated.) Later, aboard *Royal Princess*, Marion enquired why John hadn't received a prize. He was eventually given a ship's plate with the winning designs on, which we'd all received anyway!

Dominic's crew jukebox arrived, the ship was made ready, and passengers embarked November 19th, 1984, for our maiden voyage to Miami. We cabin stewards introduced ourselves to the guests. Unlike *Canberra*, where we took orders for morning trays, with *Princess* it was American-style service: guests telephoned the pantry with their requirements. Next morning we turned to at 6:30a.m. for a 7:00a.m. start. A lady in one of my suites was waiting outside the pantry, demanding China tea. When I checked, I found there was no China tea in the pantry. Our ABR went to the stores, only to discover no China tea had been loaded aboard, only Indian. When I told madam, she made a terrible fuss, grumbling it was available on every other ship. I explained this *was* the maiden voyage, and it must have been overlooked. She grudgingly settled for Indian tea. Very soon everyone was ringing for tea trays. To our horror, we ran out of tea pots. We managed to get more from the stores, but not enough. The shortage was a nightmare, with much moaning and complaining; worse was to come.

Heading towards America across the Atlantic, the weather deteriorated badly. We found ourselves in extremely stormy seas, the ship heaving and rolling violently. The captain made safety announcements and headed 'south about' to Miami. Nevertheless, the seas were mountainous and some passengers extremely nervous. Going for drinks in the Pig that evening, we noticed, to our consternation, that the £1,000-plus jukebox was sliding around with the ship's movement; there'd been no time to make it fast. This really concerned Dominic. Before leaving that evening he paid the Asian deckhands to keep an eye on the situation all night long and keep hold of the jukebox, until the chippy could secure it next day. The ship also had a problem with the engine's computer system. The supposedly advanced technology malfunctioned and actually stopped the engines running, even extinguishing the lights. They went into an emergency mode and lighting, until restarted. This too made passengers feel rather concerned.

The violent movement of the ship made life aboard very difficult. Shipyard workmen had omitted to fit magnetic locks on pantry fire screen doors, which meant we struggled getting in and out with trays. In the end, the carpenter made wooden wedges to hold the doors back. One afternoon watch, someone in a suite ordered a daiquiri cocktail. The only bar open was the Riviera Bar aft. As the suites were forward, I went down aft to collect the cocktail, holding onto the handrail to cope with the ship's movement. Daiquiris are served in stemmed coupé glasses, and by the time I'd returned to the suite, most of the cocktail had slopped onto my silver tray. I had no choice but to tip it back into the glass! I also noticed on my walks that the fountain in the foyer was indeed, as I'd predicted, slopping all over the carpet. It needed to be drained. The huge, beautiful weeping fig tree, towering through two decks, didn't like the atmosphere of the ship either; it shed all its foliage. On arrival in Miami it was quickly 're-foliaged' with silk leaves.

Madam, from day one, continued to be difficult. One morning she told me she'd spoken with the head chef, ordering a cabin lunch for 1:30p.m. I enquired what she'd ordered, so I could check prior to delivery. She told me, "Chef knows all about it." At 1:00p.m. I visited the galley, giving the Italian head chef her cabin number. He cried, "Oh that dreadful woman!" The galley was aft, so you can imagine the ship's movement made it extremely difficult to carry a large tray of food to Madam's suite. While serving lunch, Madam mentioned I'd forgotten the peeled tomatoes she'd ordered. I politely pointed out she'd omitted to inform me *exactly* what she'd ordered, and asked if there was anything else. Then I went all the bumpy way back to get the peeled tomatoes. On my eventual return, she then told me they'd missed grapes for her cheese. I returned to the galley for the grapes. By now I was seething and drank a large glug of gin. Bernie knew what was going on: "I wouldn't put up with it, dear," he said. I delivered the grapes, fuming, saying to Madam, "Next time you order a meal, would you kindly inform me exactly what you've ordered." Her husband jumped up, saying, "How dare you speak to my wife in such a manner."

That was it. I completely lost it, telling him, "I haven't finished yet!" I was sick and tired of her giving me a hard time. "I've spent over an hour getting your lunch and I have sixteen other suites to attend to. If this continues we will refuse to service your cabin!" Bernie, hearing all this, put his head in the door, saying, "Neither will we, dear." Before leaving, I calmed down a little and felt awful. I apologised, saying, "I've never answered back or been rude to guests in my life and I am extremely sorry, but you drove me to it." Later that day I told the accommodation office about my 'run in' with the guests. I said they'd probably complain. The way I felt, if I was sacked and flown home, that was fine with me. I dreaded facing them again in the evening. However, while folding towels on the maid's trolley, they left their suite, walking towards me. She said, "I'm so sorry about all that, Michael. Can we please be friends?" "Of course we can," I answered. She smiled, slipping $100 in my hand. The rest of the voyage, we got along fine. They wanted nothing special. No complaint ever received regarding my behaviour.

Prior to arrival in Miami, we were informed that during the two-week trans–Panama Canal cruise, taking in Mexico en route to Los Angeles, American Broadcasting Corporation were to film a special episode of *The Love Boat* aboard. (A lot of this popular US sitcom was shot in LA studios, but some was filmed aboard ship to add realism.) TV and movie stars would be boarding. They included Lana Turner, Anne Baxter, Stewart Granger, Hayley Mills, Elizabeth Ashley, Stella Stevens and Andrew Stevens, her son. He starred as Charles Bronson's sidekick in the movie *10 to Midnight* and was a 'doll', so handsome. Also aboard were the Puerto Rican boy band Menudo, featuring the now extremely famous (and well hung) Ricky Martin.

Having just read Lana Turner's autobiography, *Lana: The Lady, the Legend, the Truth*, I was excited she'd be aboard. She had a prestigious career and an even more astonishing private life. It included a long, passionate, turbulent relationship with a reputed gangster, Johnny Stompanato. He was stabbed to death in her Beverly Hills apartment in 1958, allegedly by her fourteen-year-old daughter, Cheryl. However, there were rumours that Lana herself actually stabbed him. She got her daughter, a minor, to take the rap. Reaching court, the daughter said he'd "come on to her." The verdict on Cheryl was 'justifiable homicide'. Rumours continued, hence the book, and title. It also stated in the book that Miss Turner had given up drinking alcohol completely…

# 29

# Celebrity Maiden Trans-Canal Cruise

Due to the bad weather, instead of spending three days alongside in Miami we turned around there in just one day; it was chaos. The US Coast Guard boarded to inspect the ship. I think the captain and co thought it would be easy: give them lunch and a few free drinks. Instead, the coastguards were an eager young bunch who drank only cola, and got on with examining all the ship's safety equipment, watching us perform our fire and boat drills. We were called to emergency stations mid-morning. As a result, we were unable to make much progress preparing cabins for new guests. The drills dragged on for hours. Finally, when finished, there was a mad rush to get the rooms ready. Boarding was delayed until late afternoon. Lana Turner was in one of Mommie's suites. Her Spanish maid boarded to get her room ready, telling Bernie the maid alone would be taking care of Miss Turner. A case of diet cranberry juice plus a case of spring water arrived in the pantry. The maid collected this, informing us that that's all Lana ever drinks...

Gavin MacLeod, the TV *Love Boat* captain, occupied our Royal suite, Stella Stevens the Princess suite. The rest of the suites were occupied with a mixture of stars, camera crew and fare- paying passengers. Mary and I looked after the *Love Boat* doctor and barman. Mommie took care of Stewart Granger, Andrew Stevens, and Lana Turner, in his section. As usual, we stood by with a passenger list, introducing ourselves to guests. A woman who looked like a bag lady opened the door to one of my suites. I politely introduced myself, asking her name. She replied "Elizabeth Ashley, darling." Not recognising who she was, I checked the passenger list; indeed it was her cabin. (She'd been married to the much younger actor George Peppard.)

That evening we sailed to a massive send-off, for an inaugural *Love Boat* trans-Canal to Los Angeles. The first morning, a beautiful woman emerged from Elizabeth Ashley's cabin. I said, "Good morning, ma'am. Are you sharing with Miss Ashley?" "It's me, darling; Elizabeth," she replied. "I've been to make-up." I didn't recognise her, and jokingly said, "Where's this make-up place? I need to go there too!" We both giggled. Preparing the pantry ready for breakfast service, we heard a voice: "Hello, anybody there?" Before Bernie could say, "Passengers are not permitted in here," in walked a vision of sexiness. It was the truly gorgeous Andrew Stevens, wearing only a pair of skimpy underpants. Both our tongues were hanging out. Mommie soon changed his tone. "Oh *good* morning, sir. How can I help you?" His eyes were popping out his head.

There was plenty of fun and games with the celebrities on board. Stewart Granger loved practical jokes. To order breakfast, guests filled out breakfast cards to hang on their door handles the previous night. One morning, Mommie showed me a card hung on Andrew Stevens's door. "Look what this prat's ordered for breakfast, dear," he said. Nearly everything on the list was ticked. When he plonked this grossly overladen tray in Andrew's cabin, the poor boy hadn't ordered anything! One of Stewart Granger's little practical jokes.

Later, Lana's maid came to the pantry to empty the cabin trash can. As she tipped it in our large pantry bin, there was a loud clonk. When I looked, it was an empty one-litre vodka bottle. So much for Miss Turner not drinking! That evening on the way to dinner, she was so smashed that Mommie had to help her to the dining room. During the cruise they became extremely friendly; women always loved Bernie. She'd order breakfast the previous night. In the morning he'd take in the tray, sitting at the end of her bed, talking to her. She was delightful, charming and extremely amusing, he told me.

One of the *Love Boat* stars wore a *syrup* (wig). As we were cleaning the Royal suite one day he walked in, supposedly looking for the *Love Boat* captain. He sneezed violently and his wig flew off, startling Mary. Thinking it was a spider, she screamed her tits off. Killing himself laughing, he picked up the toupee, saying, "I'd better not leave this here, or you'll start dusting the cabin with it." Mary and I were in stitches.

Stewart Granger and Lana Turner were supposed to be a love item in the script, but in reality they actually hated each other's guts. She annoyingly kept him and the cast standing around for a long time, waiting for her to make an appearance and shoot a scene. One of the old Hollywood film crew maintained Lana told him, "As a starlet on the way up the ladder, they all f—ed me. Now it's my turn to f—k them."

Arriving in Panama for the Canal transit, one of our delightful rich passengers approached the maid's trolley, saying to Mary, "We're halfway now, so here's your halfway tip. Thank you, guys," and handing her $500 cash. She was surprised, saying, "That's far too much, sir." I quickly jumped in, saying, "That's really kind of you, sir. Thank you so much," prising the money from her mitts. True to his word, he gave us another

$500 tip when he disembarked. In fact, everyone was extremely generous. The TV company gave us $200 for each suite and the stars themselves gave us generous tips. We did extremely well.

All the *Love Boat* hype meant that when we docked in Los Angeles, the whole city apparently turned out to welcome us. Princess Cruises, ABC TV, along with Aaron Spelling Productions, heavily publicised the arrival of the new *Super Love Boat*. Proudly, the public relations people announced the ship had just been christened by royalty: HRH Princess Diana. Much media interest was generated. Travel agents were invited aboard for tours. It was exciting, but we crew were kept very much in the background. We were alongside for a few days. One evening a gala event was held aboard, complete with entertainment. Diahann Carroll, one of the stars of *Dynasty*, would be headlining, singing for the guests and assembled celebrities. On the pier were red carpets, potted palm trees and grand pianos all along the route.

During the day, the captain brought celebrities to see the Royal suite, occupied by Princess Cruises' chairman, Joe Watters, a charming man. The Old Man brought Joan Collins up to see it, asking me if it was unoccupied. As it was, I unlocked the door. Miss Collins looked absolutely fabulous, even though she was in her fifties and established as a gay icon. She handed me her champagne glass, murmuring, "Get shot of this for me, darling." I rushed to the pantry, where queens were hoping to get a glimpse of celebrities. They all passed the glass around, slurping the remains of the champagne from the glass that'd touched the famous lips of Alexa in *Dynasty*. Diahann Carol occupied the Princess suite.

That night, in front of the gathered stars and celebrities, Miss Carroll was the star of the show, singing for them. When she began singing, the engine computer malfunctioned, plunging the lounge into silent darkness. They managed to restart it and she began singing again. Sadly it malfunctioned, again. I didn't watch the act, but heard on the third occasion she 'threw her toys out the pram' and stormed off the grand stage.

Meanwhile, Mary and I were turning down the beds in our section as usual. While in the Royal suite, I don't know why, but Mary and I laid on the bed to see how comfortable it was. To our absolute horror, in walked Joe Watters. We jumped up, embarrassed, apologising. This delightful man just laughed, saying "Don't worry, guys, just as long as you are out of here by 11:00p.m. tonight!" In 2002, he went on to join Bob Binder and Frank Del Rio to form the Miami-based Oceania Cruises. It was an upmarket cruise company operating fabulous luxury cruise ships, and is still expanding to this day.

While in Los Angeles, Dominic was approached by some rather shady gentlemen who, after seeing the jukebox in the crew bar, told him they represented a firm that could install fruit machines and other gaming machines for free. The deal was, for every two machines they would keep the profit from one. The crew club would keep the profit from the other. I think their firm was possibly the *Costa Nostra*! The deal was agreed and two $1,000-jackpot one-armed bandits, as well as other gaming machines, were installed. This was to support the activities of the crew club. Departing Los Angeles winter 1984, we began a season of trans-Canal cruises and, after Christmas, Caribbean cruises from San Juan. Life on board was fun, but gruelling, though tolerable, work. Social life was good. We still enjoyed bingo nights, deck, fancy dress parties and such, though drag was a thing of the past.

In 1985 movie and television stars sailed aboard, giving talks about their lives and careers. Among them were Cary Grant, Fred MacMurray and Rosemary Clooney. She was a singer and a movie star, appearing in the classic film *White Christmas,* and was an aunt of heartthrob George Clooney. Cary Grant let it be known he'd be by the main swimming pool every day between 11:00a.m. and 12p.m., for photographs and autographs. He was so charming. Mary and I met him and had photos taken with him. As crew club chairman, Dominic invited Fred MacMurray, his famous actress wife June Haver, and Rosemary Clooney to the crew bar. On the evening Rosemary visited, she and I hit it off. She was truly delightful, great fun, and by this time, as big as a house. I've got a photo of me practically sitting on her lap. We had a long chat. Guessing I was gay, she asked if I'd heard about this new disease. I said, "Yes, it's dreadful." She told me, "Poor Rock has it too," meaning her friend Rock Hudson. He was appearing in the TV show *Dynasty* at the time; Rosemary said, after his diagnosis, he now called the show "*Die Nasty*!" Rock Hudson was such a handsome macho hunk that nobody ever suspected he was gay. The studio even made sure he married.

This terrible, whispered-about disease was better known in the US than in the UK. Little did I know it would also claim the lives of some of my dear friends. On July 25th, 1985, Rock Hudson publicly announced he was suffering from AIDS. Sadly he passed away that December, aged just fifty-nine. His death raised public awareness of how fatal HIV/AIDS could be. His good friend, actress Elizabeth Taylor, impelled by compassion and moral courage, became one of the first global celebrity HIV/AIDS activists. She urged empathy and dignity for sufferers. Miss Taylor was some lady!

Life aboard the ship carried on much the same as before, as most people saw it as a gay disease, meaning it would not affect them. Some crew were a little concerned and more cautious. AIDS, as it was publicly misunderstood, also seemed to make ill-informed people less friendly towards gay men. This was to get slightly worse, and to continue for some time.

We held parties in various places around the ship, the bar and cabins. I remember one party was held in the Burma Road, near the morgue. This refrigerated morgue was handy if it was empty, because we could store perfectly chilled cases of beer in there. It could be a little alarming when you opened the door for a beer and saw two feet looking at you! Parties could have after effects on bodies, though I never heard of any killing a crew member. My friend Stella was always up for a party and could be extremely amusing. I remember one day he had heaving diarrhoea, which is a nasty ailment (not to mention difficult to spell). He said he was going to see the crew doctor about it. Later, when I caught up with him, I asked him how he'd got on. It made me chuckle when he started singing the 1984 hit song 'Solid' by Ashford & Simpson.

As crew club chairman, Dominic and the committee organised crew discos, deck parties and fancy dress, all paid for by the gaming machines. Fancy dress parties were an opportunity to see some people's secret fantasies, although most did it just for fun – which it always was. Marion, John, Mommie and I decided to go as the movie characters from *The Wizard of Oz*. I wanted to be Dorothy, as played by Judy Garland. However, John organised the whole thing, and wanted Marion as Dorothy. I was a bit miffed, but as they'd already made the costume, I agreed. John hand-made his scarecrow outfit, and it was brilliant. Marion made her Dorothy outfit out of a 'mislaid' gingham tablecloth and a sheet.

She plaited three pairs of tights, for pig tails, and bought the brightest, highest "f—k-off" red high heels she could find in Acapulco, as her ruby slippers. I just had to try them on! Mommie went as the cowardly lion, sewing his outfit by hand using 'mislaid' ship's brown blankets. He was very talented like that. He helped me with my Tin Man outfit, insisting I couldn't be the Tin Man. I *had* to be a Tin *Woman*! We made my costume from cardboard boxes and tubes, plus aluminium foil, complete with tin foil eyelashes! Camp or what! For my metallic eke, we 'borrowed' Marion's silver eyeshadow, slathering it all over my face and neck. She only knew about it when she saw me made up. Checking her make-up case, she found the silver eyeshadow container empty; as usual, she saw the funny side to it. Dominic arranged a bar set up on the aft deck under the stars. We had the campest, most hilarious night. The only problem was, the cardboard restricted my movements so much that I could barely bend my arms. I got into the most bizarre positions trying to guzzle gins and fell flat on my face a few times, much to everyone's amusement.

# 30

# Approaching Demise of British Seafarers

In the 1980s, rumours circulated regarding more shipping lines getting rid of UK seafarers, to replace with them cheap foreign labour. I'd heard this happened with *Cunard Countess* in 1980 and *Cunard Princess* 1981. Both cruise ships staged good-natured sit-ins and strikes while in Barbados. I assume a compromise was agreed, as all the cabin stewards and drink waiters currently aboard were still from the UK. However, the restaurants were staffed by concessionaire labour, mainly from Caribbean islands.

Princess/P&O similarly decided to get rid of British seafarers to increase profits. In early 1986, crew were asked to vote on a redundancy package. It would allow us to carry on working on board, with lower-paid and much longer contracts. This only applied to lowly ratings like me. It excluded leading hands, petty officers like Dominic, and officers. For some, I believe their turn came later, when leadings hands and petty officers were made redundant. Strangely, some companies struggled to find qualified replacements and were forced to re-employ these LHs and POs.

The lead-up to the Princess/P&O 1986 vote caused much bad feeling. Selfish people wanted to take the money and run. One tight-as-a-duck's-arse stewardess, who never visited the bar or spent any money, told me she'd been there years, made her money and wanted off. I thought, *Charming! How about people like me who've only been here a few years? We need the job and the money!* I understood where she was coming from but, nevertheless, she angered me. Others said, "It will happen eventually, anyway. Say no the first time, to get a better offer later." Some, like me, thought we should say absolutely no in this vote. We should fight to keep British seafarers' jobs, as many thousands of livelihoods would be affected. The first time it was put to the vote, the crew went on strike in Vancouver. They rejected the deal, until the company improved its offer. Princess/P&O backed down and we were allowed to carry on under our original pay and conditions.

However, the writing was on the wall. Many companies, like Royal Caribbean/Holland America Line, already employed cheap labour. They had done so for years. Princess/P&O returned with an improved redundancy package, and put it to the vote again. This time most crew realised the company were *determined* to get rid of us. *Plus*, greed and selfishness ruled some people's heads. The deal was accepted. I personally voted no. Nor did I sign up for a lower-paid contract. It seemed to me we were selling our jobs and eventually there'd be no more British seafarers left. Nevertheless, the companies would probably have forced us out anyway. It's inevitable with big businesses. Even though they're making money, they have to make even *more* to keep the shareholders happy. That's the way of this modern world. Meanwhile, Dominic, being a vociferous spokesman for the seamen's union, had been transferred to *Canberra* in March 1986.

While Dominic was serving on *Canberra* in April 1986, as a chief petty officer coxswain, the cruise director asked him to take part in an evening's entertainment for the passengers. It was The Generation Game. Dom was asked to demonstrate how to tie certain knots. Contestants had to replicate them in a fixed time. He did so. When the demonstration was complete, he stood by the lounge door to get a better idea of what was going on. He was approached by the chief purser, a Mr Davis, known to crew as Danger Man. He shouted in a rude, aggressive and obnoxious way, "What's this, the crew show?" Dominic explained why he was in passenger accommodation. However, he was offered no apology or sentiment of regret for being spoken to in this manner. As a result of this incident, Dom wrote an official report, complaining about the events of that evening to the chief officer. He ended with the words, "As a result of this incident, I find this man nothing better than a School Yard Bully with Stripes. The same notion held about him by the majority of the crew." The shit really hit the fan, because bullying and harassment weren't seen as so incorrect at that time. The chief officer asked Dom to withdraw the words "school yard bully." He refused, unless he received a personal apology from the purser. It never came, which demonstrated the sort of person Danger Man really was, and the state of official policy and practice about rights for non-elite people at that time.

Dom was working aboard *Canberra* when she went to Bremerhaven for dry dock, hull cleaning, refit, painting and refurbishment. *QE2* was there too. Between October 1986 and April 1987, *QE2* was converted from steam to diesel/electric. During this time Cunard did exactly the same thing about employment rights as Princess/P&O. In early 1987, most UK ratings serving aboard *QE2* received redundancy notices. Some signed the new lower-paid contracts, others left and were replaced with less skilled, cheaper labour.

Flying home from San Francisco for the last time, in July 1986, was a very sad day for me indeed. Although every rating aboard received a redundancy payment, it wasn't enough to pay off our mortgages. I didn't pay off any of ours. I saved it as an investment. After a month's leave, I spent another month looking for a ship. Eventually, Mr Tinkler at the Pool telephoned, saying he'd a second steward's job, requiring someone experienced but "not too long in the tooth." Would I visit him? I wasn't sure what that expression meant until he explained it to me ("not too old"). He asked would I like to take a look at the ship, which was nearby in dry dock? It was the RRS *Challenger*, a 938-grt Royal Research vessel operated by the National Environmental Research Council (NERC). At that time their headquarters were in Barry, but they were moving to Southampton in 1994. It was a tiny ship, so I asked Mr Tinkler where was it going; I wouldn't fancy a transatlantic run on that! He said it was sailing down the Mediterranean. He added that he'd worked a transatlantic crossing aboard the infamous Lady Docker's yacht, *Shemara*, which was the same size. I'd be fine.

I signed on September 23rd, 1986. The *Challenger*'s catering department comprised just one steward, one cook/chief steward, and me. I found the vessel was extremely dirty. We worked by in Southampton for a few days, cleaning and preparing for sea. Lunchtime I'd go to the nearby Smugglers gay pub for a pint. The cook asked to join me and when I explained it was a gay pub, he was fine with that. We went a few times and he thoroughly enjoyed it.

After sailing, the steward and I got down on all fours to scrub the oily alleyways. By the time we docked in Barry my knees were sore and swollen. The first night I went to a gay/mixed pub in Cardiff, the Quebec Pub in Bute Street. Cookie asked to join me again. At closing time we visited the Showbiz Club in Custom House Street. We had a fantastic night and he met a handsome young man. They went home together, falling madly in love. Next day Cookie didn't turn to, so yours truly had to cook the breakfasts. Luckily I knew what to do.

Later that morning the captain arranged a doctor's visit regarding my knees. Doc prescribed tablets, telling me to rest and giving me a sick note. I paid off later that day. Oh dear! Two crew down. The captain and crew weren't happy. They blamed me, thinking I'd led Cookie astray. Now we were *both* gone. I took a taxi to Barry station and a train back to Southampton, where an Irish lady, my mate Mad Betty, collected me. I'd only been on the ship nine days and caused pandemonium. Betty thought this was absolutely hilarious.

My next ship was a Townsend Thoresen car ferry, the *Pride of Cherbourg*. We were sailing between Portsmouth and Cherbourg. I signed on as a waiter November 3rd, 1986. It was a ghastly job. Starting 6:00a.m., working until 23:00 or later, I was serving meals, cleaning, storing and so on, with few breaks. I started in the freight drivers' restaurant, which I thought would be fun. It wasn't. My Torquay friend Barry tells me he was working alongside ex-*QE2* Jane in the truck drivers' eatery. Jane was wearing the usual, blue eyeshadow, and had blonde hair in kiss curls. Jane remarked to him, "That truck driver over there can't keep his eyes off me." *No wonder*, Barry thought! Next, I worked in the restaurant and so on, lasting until November 24th – three weeks! It was vile, though I met a mix of delightful, amusing ferry crews, especially the girls. I'd meet a lot more in the coming years. We'd dash to the terminal for a quick beer between sailings, where I met Jackie C, an amusing stewardess off another ship. We got chatting, just clicked, and remain friends to this day.

At this time property prices were going through the roof. We put our beautiful flat on the market. It sold fast for £45,000 (it had cost us just £17,000). Then we bought a three-bedroom detached house in Freemantle for only £49,000. The previous owner had hung himself in the house, so it went cheap. However, we'd no qualms about things like that. Soon after we moved in a pretty little cat started hanging around the back patio doors. Naturally we let it in, bought some cat food, and it adopted us. His name was Leo and he became a regular visitor. What an affectionate, clever little soul he was. He'd climb on Dominic's shoulders and walk around with him!

We renovated the house ourselves. Dominic worked his socks off, decorating, refitting the kitchen, clearing the garden, laying a lawn and patio. When it was finished we had a delightful home and were near Pearl, which we thought he'd like. As usual, we gave him a set of keys to keep an eye on our home. One evening when we were visiting the Smugglers with Pearl, I was talking to the landlord, Pat. He said he'd heard Dominic and I'd moved: I must give him our new address. I replied light-heartedly, "Yes, darling. We've gone detached." Pearl's demeanour suddenly changed. He gave me a strange look. He later told me, "You must never tell people you live detached." "Why ever not?" I asked. He said, "They'll *hate* you for it." I thought this was a load of unbelievable balls and wondered if he was jealous that we'd bought a detached house?

Meanwhile, Mommie (Bernie) obtained a provisional licence and I taught him to drive in our little automatic Volvo. It was really a DAF in drag. (Volvo had just bought out the DAF company.) It had an automatic variomatic gearbox full of pulleys and elastic bands, which later we'd have dreadful trouble with. Mommie thought driving was easy-peasy and rushed out to buy a huge second-hand Jaguar. (Trust her to be flash!) I took him for driving lessons in the Jag. One day we pulled in to a Shirley petrol station and while manoeuvring he hit a fuel tank ventilation pipe. One of the staff saw what happened, and angrily approached Bernie, saying, "Fancy learning to drive in bleeding great Jag." Mommie furiously replied, "I'll learn to drive in whatever I *like*, dear." They had a massive row; it was hilarious.

Once he'd got a full licence, Mommie went looking to buy or lease a pub with his redundancy money. He found details of one in the Black Country, West Midlands. Thinking we might like to run it with him, he drove us there in his latest car, a huge Daimler Double Six five-litre. It went like a rocket. The pub was absolutely hideous in every respect. Closed down for some time, extremely cheaply renovated and decorated, and sadly next to a run-down housing estate. Dominic and I hated it. He wanted us to take on the pub with him. "You can be chef, Mish. I'll tend the bar. And Dominic can be the handyman." Dominic wasn't impressed. "So I'll be Benny" (the thick handyman on the much-disparaged TV soap opera *Crossroads*). "I don't think so." We also thought there would not be enough income for three people. Nonetheless, Mommie was determined to take it on. He sold his flat and became the new landlord. Sadly, as we predicted, it was a disaster. He ended up abandoning it, threw the till in the boot, locked up and drove home to his folks in Plymouth. At this time we heard from friends working aboard P&O there was labour trouble brewing, as you will hear later.

In 1984 the Thatcher government sold British Rail/Sealink, including thirty-seven ships and ten harbours, to the Virgin Islands–based Sea Containers, for the knock down price of £66 million. The harbours alone were worth more than that! The new Sealink British Ferries attempted to run a 'posh' service to the Channel Islands, using the ferries *Earl Granville* and *Earl William*. The company sent the ships to Denmark, where passenger accommodation was stripped out and rebuilt. The ships came back with classy restaurants, cafe and passenger en suite cabins with TVs and tea/coffee facilities. They were billed as *Star Liner* and *Bateaux de Luxe*. The service began in 1985, and expensive ticket prices reflected the new luxury. Unfortunately this coincided with the loss of the Sealink traditional monopoly of island services. Newcomer Channel Island Ferries took advantage of the new high fares to steal most of the business. Despite reducing prices, the new Sealink British Ferries service was a failure. Both ships were laid up in the River Fal in Falmouth.

March 6th, 1987, on the now infamous Townsend Thoresen ferry, *Herald of Free Enterprise*, disaster occurred. Departing Zeebrugge, the bow doors were not closed properly. The ship took on sea water and sank, with 193 people dying. It was very unusual for such a major loss of life at sea in peacetime, especially in European waters. It was the worst disaster since 1919. Evidently the assistant bosun had the responsibility to close the bow doors; he was asleep in his cabin. However, an official inquiry revealed many shortcomings and failures in the whole operation. No one had been designated to double-check that the doors were actually closed. There was no 'doors open' indicator light on the bridge. Furthermore, crew members were revealed to have fallen asleep due to fatigue caused by excessively long shifts. There was a lack of internal bulkheads to restrict the ingress of water. Matters were made worse by the top-heavy design of the vessel. To deflect criticism from the company, blame was shifted to the crew. As a consequence, most ferry companies banned the sale of alcohol to crew. However, deck crews I've worked with never drank prior to starting a watch. They acted in a professional, responsible manner at all times. This was a time when UK crew reputations were being clobbered from every side.

Meanwhile, in March 1987 Dominic left P&O/Princess Cruises. Early in 1987 two former Sealink bosses started a restricted daily ferry service to Cherbourg. In April Dominic took a job with Sealink British Ferries, travelling to Weymouth to join *Earl Granville* to inaugurate the service from Portsmouth. I'd been ashore from November 1986 until June 1987, and then joined Dominic aboard *Earl Granville* as a catering assistant. I worked everywhere: cabins, restaurant and cafes. The ship was what seafarers call "chatty (dirty) but happy." Crew accommodation was extremely chatty. It was near the waterline, by watertight doors. The alleyway carpets were dirty and oily. Bathrooms were horrendous: peeling paint, wobbly toilet seats and mould everywhere. While showering, I touched a mouldy bulkhead and actually caught 'athlete's arse hole', a fungal infection like athlete's foot, can you believe? The itching was unbearable. Finally I remedied it with an ointment from my doctor, though it put a temporary end to our much-reduced sex life.

The *Earl Granville* operated a daytime service to Cherbourg, Monday to Saturday. We sailed 8:00a.m., and were back in Portsmouth about 5:30p.m., with nothing to do until the next day. Some went home for the night; Southampton was just a twenty-five-minute drive away. Others stayed aboard for a few drinks. This could be most amusing. One night two ABs were so drunk they flaked out on a bunk together. The other lads wrapped the sleeping Tim and Dave's arms around each other, and took photos. Shortly after, a picture was posted on the crew notice board, with the caption, "Thanks for a good shag, Tim." Everyone had a good laugh about it, including Tim and Dave. It was just seaman's banter. The two ABs were straight. It was OK, just a bit of fun.

There were friends from other ships aboard, like Lisa, Lulu, and Della. Lloyd, a handsome, delightful young man just off *QE2*, joined. We fast became firm friends. He had a boyfriend at home, Bernie, so at first Lloyd was reserved and quiet. Because he socialised with me, the Scouse financial controller Annie asked me, "Is he a shirt-lifter too?" I told Lloyd, who by this time had settled in. He thought it hilarious, saying he didn't care if she knew. I told her, adding, "Though I think he'd prefer gentlemen to lift *his* shirt." "What a waste," she said. I assured her he definitely *wasn't* wasting it. Lloyd started work in a bar, asking an experienced hand how to fiddle *tizzy* (money). He told Lloyd to over-ring the till a couple of quid now and then, slipping it down his knicker legs. At the end of shift, Lloyd's pockets bulged with pound coins. We were highly amused. You're supposed to change it into notes!

The season finished September 28th and we were paid off. We survived the winter on Pool money, odd bar jobs and our savings. Luckily we'd bought our first home cheap and sold it for a lot more money, so our mortgage wasn't too bad. We'd saved nearly all our redundancy money. We thought it'd be a great idea to buy or start our own business, and looked at guest houses, pubs, car hire businesses and the like. Nothing seemed feasible or profitable enough. Dominic noticed an empty garage near us in Shirley and thought "it'd make a wonderful US-style automatic car wash." Maybe one day we might even site them in supermarket car parks. We made enquires, did our homework, sought prices and then approached the bank for a loan. They declined, telling us, "It'll never take off." They actually laughed at us about the supermarket idea. Nevertheless, a few years later this garage became an extremely busy, profitable US-style carwash. Plus, ironically, nearly every major supermarket now features carwashes. At this time, Dominic also had a vision of starting and operating our own coach and minibus company. I thought it was crazy, but didn't discourage him. He began diligently studying for a Passenger Transport Certificate of Professional Competence. Little did I know this would indeed happen, and we'd own a successful business.

March 1988 we returned to *Earl Granville*. I was unhappy, and signed off 10 April. Dominic stayed on; it was week on/

week off. I think he didn't want to spoil his transport studies. We were both fine sailing apart when necessary by now. We'd a loving, monogamous relationship. After I left in April, P&O in Dover sacked all their ferry crew ratings in an attempt to de-recognise the NUS (National Union of Seamen). The crew formed picket lines, stopping trucks from boarding, and asking Sealink crew for their support. Portsmouth P&O Ferry crew struck to support Dover, as did Sealink crew. All manned picket lines. P&O unkindly refused any food for their striking seafarers in an attempt to demoralise and remove them. In Portsmouth, Sealink donated sandwiches to the grateful P&O crew. On one ferry in Falmouth dry dock, the ever-wicked P&O even cut off the supply of electricity and water to toilets and bathrooms. They also refused crew any food aboard.

Lloyd later told me a funny story when he was on the picket line in Portsmouth. Dan McCauliffe, the general manager of Sealink South Coast services, approached. He was extremely dapper, with his coat over his shoulders (his arms not in the sleeves), clutching two bottles of champagne. A seaman, who didn't recognise him, asked, "Are you a merchant seaman, and are you aware of the strike?" Dan replied, "My dear chap, do I *really* look like a merchant seaman?" and minced off to the ship moored nearby.

Through the Pool and P&O on April 14th, 1988, I was delighted to secure a bedroom steward's job on dear old *Canberra*, Mediterranean cruising. It was like going back in time, although the passenger accommodation had been upgraded. The Crow's Nest, unlike in 1971, was now beautifully furnished, with a bar in the centre, a small stage, a grand piano and elegant seating. Sadly the atmosphere among crew had changed distinctly; it was almost slightly homophobic. I'm sure this hostility was down to the AIDS epidemic, which had generated fears of contamination. UK newspapers fuelled this, with lurid headlines like, "Vicar said he'd shoot his son if he caught AIDS." Despite lack of enthusiasm from Prime Minister Thatcher, a TV health campaign was launched, with terrifying adverts showing tombstones and headlines like, "Don't die of ignorance." It was a bad time. Fear-filled stupidity really bought out the worst in people. And aboard ship we lived close together, so the tension was felt. Even the few queens didn't seem as friendly as previously, so I was delighted that dear old Slippery Sid was on board. Life remained fun. I'd go ashore for lunch in various ports with Sid. Evenings we'd visit the Pig for drinks. On closing, we'd go to his cabin for more drinks and music on his tape player. We shared fun with invited chosen guests – the friendly ones, who were mainly all straight. Life on ships now had become nothing like it used to be. Before we'd have real fun, rich high camp and laughs. This was more or less a thing of the past, though we still had amusing moments.

We'd slotted into a leave pattern. After just over a month aboard, Sid and I were given a short leave. We signed off, disembarking from the ship together. On our way through customs a female officer stopped us to check our bags. She asked me to put my main suitcase on a table and checked it. Then she asked Sid to put his suitcase on the inspection bench. His case was large and heavy. He struggled and swung it violently to lift in onto the table. Instead it hit the poor customs officer hard between the legs. The poor woman let out a piercing scream, holding her hands to her crotch. It was dreadful, but as usual I saw the funny side of it, and desperately tried to suppress giggles. She just waved us on. Was it a genuine accident, or did Sid have something he didn't want anyone to see? I went home to our lovely little house in Freemantle and Sid went off to London and his usual nefarious adventures.

We rejoined *Canberra* on June 4th, my dear mum's birthday. Some shipmates on board knew I'd worked on the West Coast, had been made redundant and received a lump sum. Word got around and it caused some resentment. A few asked outright: "How come you got redundancy from P&O and are now working for them again?" I explained honestly that this job was from the Pool. They'd sent me to P&O Personnel, who appointed me to this ship. Shipmates' usual comment was, "You must be loaded." I was tempted to say, "I am." Instead I explained I'd only worked there four years, so the redundancy money wasn't much. However, some were extremely resentful, especially Willy, a cabin steward. I told him, "Your time will come." Sure enough, a year later, in 1989, the majority of UK ratings aboard *all* P&O ships and UK catering crew were also made redundant.

Everyone thought Willy was a great guy. He talked endlessly about sport, girls and fishing. He gave Sid and I bad vibes. We were friendly and polite, as we'd heard he had a violent temper. He liked to think of himself as a hard case, though usually picked on young or vulnerable people. Apparently on a previous trip he'd attacked and beaten up a boy rating. The poor lad had been too terrified to report it. Sometime after we rejoined, one evening when the Pig closed, Sid and I went to Sid's cabin for drinks. Invited, mainly straight, guests followed. Sid was very personable, getting along well with the guy he shared with. Cabins were comfortable, with curtains and day settees. Sid added touches, like a table lamp, music and ice bucket, although the days of Clarence House were well gone!

We were having a great time, when shortly after guests arrived, Willy pushed open the door. He demanded a drink from Sid, who informed him he hadn't been invited. Willy, who'd obviously been drinking heavily, became nasty, saying to Sid, "Pour me a large brandy, you f—ing old poof, or else." I stood up saying, "How dare you speak to my friend like that." Willy punched me hard in the face, also punching Sid in the face. The crowd jumped up, restraining Willy. With blood pouring down our faces we made our way to the ship's hospital. On arrival, the nurse was horrified, saying, "Goodness, what happened to you?" Sid and I'd had a few drinks, and, giggling, one of us said, "We've been to the house of whacks!" She was not amused. Nevertheless she cleaned us up, stitching cuts above our eyes, and reported the incident to the bridge.

Next day we both had black eyes and a stitched gash on our eyebrows. Later we were sent for by the captain, who wanted to know the details. The guys who were in Sid's cabin that evening didn't want to get involved. They said, "You don't *grass up* a mate." I understood loyalty of ratings against officials; however, I felt disappointed. I could have put it down to experience, but Willy had also attacked a young vulnerable boy rating. I thought he needed to be held to account.

When called to the bridge, I explained to the Old Man exactly what occurred. To our astonishment, he told us all the time Willy had been on board, he'd never been in any trouble. As we'd just joined, *we* must be the troublemakers. Furious, I told the captain that Willy had actually attacked a boy rating previously, who was too terrified to report the matter; we were *not*. However, the Old Man wouldn't believe us, nor act on it. The next call in Southampton, I contacted a solicitor and took out a civil action against Willy. Seeking criminal injuries compensation, I furnished photos taken by Sid of my black eye and stitched eyebrow. I understood Sid didn't want to make a fuss; he was getting on in years, liked the job and at his age would struggle to find another. Nor did he want to rile Bonkers Willy.

Sometime later we docked in Southampton and Willy received a letter from my solicitor. He came looking for me. Apologising, he said he really liked me, deeply regretted what happened and was extremely sorry. Would I think it over, maybe drop the case? I told him, "Willy, in reality you don't *like* me;

you *are like* me. I won't drop the case, because you could end up killing or maiming someone." He wasn't happy, and asked would I meet him after work to discuss the matter. I foolishly agreed. He arranged to meet on an aft promenade deck that evening.

I arrived at the meeting place, a deserted strip of outside deck. It felt eerie. He arrived and asked me to go to the ship's side rail with him for a private talk. My blood ran cold, thinking this deranged lunatic is thinking of throwing me over the ship's side! I quickly stepped back inside. He followed me, asking what was wrong. "You must think I'm stupid! Go to the ship's rail where you could chuck me over the side," I said. (I wasn't being paranoid. People have been chucking nuisances over ships' sides for centuries and there's evidence to prove it!)

"Don't be ridiculous," he said. "I'd be the number one suspect if anything happened to you." "Exactly," I replied. "As you'd be the number one suspect, they'd think it *couldn't* possibly be you." I hastily left, visiting the crew bar for a drink, quite shaken. Whether he was planning to throw me over the side, or whether that was just a product of my fertile imagination, I'm not sure. But it has and does happen. Feeling lonely, and rather unhappy about Willy being on board, I paid off 16th July 1988.

At home Dominic saw my injuries. He became extremely angry towards Willy. He tried to find out his address (he lived in Boshom, near Chichester). However, the one person Dominic knew who could provide him with Willy's address wouldn't give it to him. He knew if Dominic confronted Willy, Dom would have beat Willy within an inch of his life! Later we heard that on *Canberra* some of the more mature stewards, apparently fed up with Willy picking on junior ratings, confronted him. "How about picking on us?" they challenged him. As usual, like most bullies, he hurriedly left the ship.

With Dominic's help I quickly landed an assistant steward's job (another name for a dogsbody) on *Earl Granville*, joining

July 17th. Later I received a heathy compensation cheque from the Criminal Injuries Compensation Scheme, for the Willy incident, without having to fork out a penny. I was happy to be back on *Granville* with Dominic, and eventually acquired jobs that enabled small cash fiddles, or tizzy, as crew called it. I didn't really like doing it, but didn't want to expose others by not going along with it. It was a happy, though chatty, little ship with a great crowd. Friends from the West Coast were aboard, including lovely Lisa, Lulu, and appalling Margie. She was worse than ever, even more rotund and given the rather unkind crew nickname of 'Keg on legs'. She worked as ladies' lavatory attendant, which meant cleaning the main ladies' bathroom and toilet block, plus a small disabled toilet next to it. She wanted to spend time in Pompey guzzling vodka, so before docking she'd clean the lavatories and put brooms across the main toilet entrance. She'd man the door with a trout face, telling passengers, "Use the disabled toilet, please." "But I'm not disabled," one lady said. "You bleeding will be if you walk on my wet floor!" Margie replied. The lady complained. When hauled in front of the purser, she said she only meant to warn Madam about the dangers of slipping on a wet deck.

Most people on board were given camp nicknames. Lloyd was good at this. Lisa Goodchild became Lisa Bona Feelie, and her straight boyfriend was Emma, because his surname was Peel. (Emma Peel was the spy heroine in *The Avengers* TV series; she wore kinky black leather and boots.) The second steward's surname was Smith. He was rather elderly, so Lloyd gave him the nickname Granny Smith. Lloyd too received a nickname: Lolly lick a lot. The officers' steward on my watch was a delightful, extremely amusing older queen, Rodney/Pepsi. Pepsi was friends with Debbie and I'd met him a few times when visiting his previous ship, the *Reina del Mar*. He got his nickname because in the early days he only drank Pepsi-Cola.

By now he drank anything *but* Pepsi-Cola. The Old Man and officers adored him. He was a charming, kind and hilarious funny man.

Lloyd was truly outrageous and loved a bit of camp. Between us we decided to drag up, to 'do a number'. I was up for that and purser Ken thought it would be a good laugh too. We borrowed a couple of stewardesses' uniform frocks. They organised our wigs and made us up. We staged our number in a passenger bar one evening. The DJ played the song from *Cabaret*, the musical: 'Money, Money'. We performed a dance routine, with a couple of ship's plastic cash bags. Everyone laughed, knowing it was all about "tizzy, tizzy, tizzy." They enjoyed it and was great fun. Docking next morning, serving in the cafe, I had one hell of a hangover. Passengers recognised me and asked, "Was that you performing in the bar last night?" "No," I groaned, "that was my twin brother."

That season on *Earl Granville* Dominic was convener for the National Union of Seamen again. It was a difficult time, as certain companies like P&O were trying to finish off the Union. The battle certainly led to NUS funds being sequestered. The Union folded in 1990 and amalgamated with the National Union of Railwaymen, becoming the RMT. Dominic was still enduring trying times with Margie, the lavatory attendant who was never happy in any job. She tried to get him, via the purser, to get people like Pepsi's job. But Dominic put a stop to it, as Pepsi was happy in the job and had done nothing wrong. Every position Dominic got Margie didn't suit her, especially if she couldn't go and smoke her tits off every five minutes. One job she took was in a small motorist's lounge, selling microwaved pizzas and burgers. The more food was in the ovens, the longer time they took to cook. When a passenger asked Margie when would her pizza be ready, she threw it in the poor woman's face. Up for a disciplinary before the purser, Margie claimed, "It slipped off

## Anything Goes at Sea

the plate, honest." Sometimes Dominic felt he was defending the indefensible.

The winter of 1988–9, the company were awarded a contract to run a freight-only service to Jersey and Guernsey using the *Granville* and *Earl Godwin*. Pepsi and I, along with other crew, started the service on the 31st of December 1988, on the *Earl Godwin*. Built in 1966, 4,106 gt, she was a quirky little ship, with passenger cabins below the car deck. The gents' toilet had enormous urinals, which no matter how hard we cleaned them, or what you poured down them, smelt like somebody had died in them!

It made a change to work during the winter and we occupied single passenger cabins. We'd great fun working together, popping ashore for a few bevvies on the islands, though there were few gay-friendly bars. Happily, the chef from *Granville*, 'Dot' Cotton was aboard. (His surname was Cotton.) On the 21st of January we all transferred back to the *Granville* to continue the service. Dot was a delightful man, an excellent chef, with a wonderful sense of humour. Although straight, he loved a bit of camp. One trip at sea Pepsi and I were walking along the main alleyway, when we bumped into Dot and his mate, the chippy, who also had a wicked sense of humour. (He needed it, he fixed the plumbing and toilets.) As they passed, the chippy said to Pepsi, "Ere, Rodney, I was fixing a bog the other day, when one of your turds floated past." "Don't be so disgusting," said Rodney, then thought for a minute, asking, "How did you know it was one of mine?" Chippy said, "Because it had a countersunk end!" We couldn't help laughing. Rodney took it as good fun too.

The following season, in March 1989, due to the restaurants not making a profit, the company were looking for new head waiters for *Earl Granville*. Dominic, bless him, as conveyor saw the fleet general manager, Dan McCauliffe, who previously worked aboard the Royal Yacht *Britannia*. Dom told Dan I'd be perfect for the job, and trustworthy too. Dan interviewed me at length and appointed me restaurant manager. I had a posh uniform, stripes, plus a single (though still rather grotty) cabin. The restaurant was forward with good views. It was elegant for a ferry, with an acceptable wine list. We served an upmarket self-service carvery lunch and dinner, and buffet breakfast. I was pleased that Dot Cotton was chef; I knew the food would be excellent. I was expected to organise a small tizzy for all restaurant staff, including cooks. Being an extremely honest person, I truly disliked fiddling money. However, as it was expected by colleagues, I did. I was sensible about it, though. I think the company suspected it went on. But the restaurant on my watch made a good profit, so they were happy with me.

Truck drivers ate in the restaurant. Their meal vouchers were rung through as money. When passengers paid cash, I simply rang through the occasional driver's voucher, keeping the cash to distribute. Everyone was happy. However, the restaurant manager on the opposite watch kept *all* the cash, only paying in cheques or credit card slips. Then he wondered why he was sacked.

One of my waiters was Tina Tits. I'd sailed with him on RFA *Olna*. He had a wicked sense of humour. As meals were buffet service with a set price for adults and children, we simply wrote on the bill, 2 x A, 2 x Ch. Tina would write in gay Polari: 1 x Homie, 1 x Palone, 2 x Cod Feelies. I was usually at the till when they paid. If they queried the Polari I told them, "One of the waiters isn't from around here!" With Lolly and other mates on board, it would be a great fun season (and it was).

# 31

# Mona's Queen and Others

Life continued happily until 31 August 1989. While I was on leave, *Earl Granville* struck rocks outside Cherbourg. She limped into port, discharged passengers, and struggled to a naval dry dock, partially sinking. Sadly the Thames pleasure boat *Marchioness* sank the same day, taking all the press limelight. Our ferry was hardly mentioned.

Ken, our purser, later telephoned me to say the company had found a replacement for the *Granville*. I was to join a chartered Isle of Man Ferry, the *Mona's Queen*, in Portsmouth 5 September. I met Ken in Portsmouth docks, watching this imposing black ship dock, and waited for the bow doors to open. They didn't. Instead, a massive gangway was hooked on the ship's side. This vessel was a *side-loader*. That was fine for the Isle of Man, which was equipped with side-loading facilities, as opposed to the modern bow and stern links-pans in Portsmouth. But as cars drove off at high tide, their exhausts and fenders were crunching and ripping off on the quay. Pandemonium ensued and many complaints were made.

It was an old-fashioned, strange and rather camp ship. When I went to set up the small restaurant, it was situated on the open top deck. When it rained, no customers ventured up there. Truly old-fashioned. Ken, the purser, bought a box of Sealink silver. I was determined to make it as upmarket as possible. There was no galley attached. Food was supplied by the cafeteria galley on a lower deck. The orders and food were sent up and down using a hand-operated dumb waiter! We used a rope pulley.

In the bar I was amazed to see they sold kelp (seaweed) crisps as bar snacks. The Thomas Cook Money exchange was on the open promenade deck, outside a cabin on a trestle table – can you believe? Lolly, second steward by this time, was in a passenger cabin also on the prom deck. The showers were along the outside deck and one day he went for a shower, in just a towel, with his soap on a rope. Forgetting the cabin door was self-locking, Lolly found on his return that he was locked out. As he walked to the purser's office to get a key, embarkation had started. He had to make his way through throngs of startled passengers, in just a towel, clutching his soap on a rope!

It was a good-looking ship, extremely fast, often arriving in Cherbourg early. The crew accommodation was strange; the bathrooms, which I believe we shared with the stewardesses, were on the deck above our cabins. You had to mince up the stairs in a towel to get there. Charters could only be secured for limited periods; we ended up on and off many different ships that season.

After ten days we transferred to the Irish ferry *Saint Patrick*, 7,984 gt, though she seemed much larger. She was a beautiful ferry, with truly friendly Irish crew, who stayed aboard to complete the handover. (In a crowded crew lift someone actually felt my arse!) I was restaurant manager again. The second steward was Ken, Granny Smith. The restaurant was similar to the *Granville*. At the bow of the ship, it was magnificent, with fabulous views.

On one side was a spacious walk-in wine dispensary, with wine shelves, ice buckets and so on. Very professional and handy for me, Lolly and friends, to have a crafty slurp of wine or two.

One evening Granny Smith invited me to his cabin for his birthday drink. On arrival I found his cabin packed. I stood in the doorway while he fixed me a drink. There was a door on my right. Wondering what was in there, I opened it. To my horror the female controller was sat on the toilet, with her knickers round her ankles. She screamed and everyone looked. Dot said loudly, "Annie, we can see your growler" (a seaman's term for minge). She quickly cupped her hand over it, hastily closing the door. Everyone saw the funny side, even Annie when she eventually forgave me. Sadly the charter was only for one month. We paid off in Dover. Next ships were briefly *Earl Godwin*, *Saint Patrick*, and then back to *Earl Godwin* for a month. By the end of the season I didn't know if I was coming or going. I finally paid off the *Earl Godwin* December 1989 and went home for Christmas. Dominic had already paid off *Godwin* in November 1989. It was to be his final ship. He too went home for Christmas.

The following season, 1990, I found a waiter's job with P&O European ferries, on the *Pride of Cherbourg*, joining 6 April. I worked with an amusing Irish guy, Paddy. When I mentioned that the head waiter, Ken, seemed a great guy, he whispered, "He's a f—ing transvestite." I was shocked. Ken was plump and not terribly attractive. Apparently he had married a large lady on the opposite watch, so he could slip on the wife's frocks while she was working week on.

A young man, Simon, worked as one of my waiters. I'd met him in the Magnum gay club in Southampton. (Opened 1969, it was the oldest gay club in the country when it closed in 2004.) Simon asked me to be discreet regarding his sexuality. Even then, some young guys still felt the need to hide this. However an ex-Cunarder queen, Sean, was also onboard. He had a wicked tongue. He always seemed to have a pen plus clipboard. In front of the crew, he'd pick up the clipboard and start asking Simon, "When did you first realise you liked men, dear?" Poor Simon cringed with embarrassment. It was cruel but hilariously funny.

I met many delightful girls during my time working on and off the ferries. One of them, my mate Jackie Copping, is still a dear friend. There were many others too, like Long Tall Sally, Marlene Sylvia, and the two Carols, one known as Tannoy, due to her loud voice. They are all delightful ladies and still friends. Some of the parties aboard were truly outrageous, as were some of the girls. One lady, she'll know who if she ever reads this, finished up one night sleeping with one of the senior officers at the end of a party. Next day, as she sat at her cafe till, the daily inspection party passed through. The senior officer from the night before stopped and said to her, "Don't I know you?" "You should do," she said. "You f—ed me last night." He blushed to his roots and fled! That's how it was then: a lot of casual sex. And why not? But some sex meant more to women than to men.

On May 14th, Ken, our head waiter, was sacked for drinking. I was promoted to head waiter. It was preferable to waiter, though still hard work. My boss, the catering manager, was a rather fierce lady; I nicknamed her 'the Rottweiler'. At this time kids were being attacked by fierce dogs. The *Sun* newspaper published an article: "These dogs are dangerous" with photos of Rottweilers. I put the pictures on the crew notice board, with the words "Guess Who?" She sent for me, asking me to find out who was responsible for these pictures. "I'll leave no stone unturned," I told her, laughing to myself!

# 32

# The Vomit Comet

Later in the season we heard the news: Hoverspeed/Sea Containers were introducing a revolutionary car-carrying, high-speed catamaran for a Portsmouth to Cherbourg service. It sounded fantastic. Crew applications were being taken at the old Sealink office. I applied and secured a position as supervisor. Although they begged me not to go, I paid off the *Pride of Cherbourg* on June 5th, 1990, recommending lovely Simon for head waiter. He got the job and was most pleased. In May 1990, the new catamaran/vessel sailed from Tasmanian builders via New York to Portsmouth. She crossed the Atlantic in just over three days, winning the coveted Blue Ribbon.

Many of my ship mates from the West Coast/*Earl Granville* found jobs on the new high-speed catamaran, to be named *Hoverspeed Great Britain*. The crew was made up of many former airline cabin staff, mainly female. We signed company contracts, draconian airline-style documents, with many rules and regulations. Crew members were not permitted to sunbathe, give blood, or gain weight. Wages were compulsorily paid directly to our bank; there was to be no more cash. We also needed to live within a certain distance of our place of work. (No accommodation was available on the vessel.) Ladies were required to bring in a spare pair of tights. PSOs (passenger service officers) were in charge of the teams, assisted by supervisors like myself. The remainder of the team were known as cabin crew. Our uniforms were stunning and extremely professional. Men wore smart blazers, women smart airline-style uniforms, with hats, all trimmed with gold Hoverspeed badges. A staff meeting at the Portsmouth Holiday Inn was arranged between the entire crew and two Hoverspeed training officers. They were Gatwick Airport former PSOs well past their flying age. Probably they were not happy.

Onboard PSOs and supervisors like myself met them first. They wore name badges: Teresa and Siobhan. On introduction I mentioned I'd never seen the name Siobhan before, asking how to pronounce it. "How do you think?" she asked. "Siobang?" I answered. She fixed me a withering look, probably thinking, *What a peasant*, and explained the correct way was "Shivonne." I felt so embarrassed. I'd heard the name before of course, never realising it was spelt that way. During the meeting we were informed the *SeaCat*, as it was to be known, would be run airline-style: drinks, meals and duty-free were all served to the passengers' seats, using trolleys. Did anyone have any questions? I stood up, asking, "What happens when the ship rolls?" Teresa fixed me a pershing stare: making gestures like inverted commas with her index fingers, she asked, "I suppose you are an ex-seafarer?" I confirmed I was, and she then announced, "It is *not* a ship. It's a high-speed, *wave-piercing craft* and it *won't* roll!" *I can't wait to see this*, I thought. Even the stabilised, 65,000-ton *QE2* rolled! However, I kept my trap shut. I'd inadvertently annoyed them enough already.

The company scheduled the service to start July 1990. However, on *SeaCat*'s arrival in the UK, the MCA (Maritime and Coastguard Agency) weren't happy with quite a few safety aspects of the craft. The passenger cabin was situated above the car deck. The MCA felt if there was a fire on the car deck, the aluminium deck structure wasn't thick enough or insulated sufficiently to prevent it melting. Many safety recommendation were made. These needed to be actioned, which delayed the craft's entry into service by over a month. However, bookings had been made for the service; these were honoured when the re-floated, redundant, tatty *Earl Granville* was pressed into service in the *SeaCat*'s place! Many old hands joined the ship: I as restaurant manager and Dot as chef. It was like old times. Quite a few former airline cabin attendants joined the ship too. However, some passengers weren't happy. They'd thought they'd be whisked to France in two and a half hours on the gleaming new *SeaCat*. Instead they chugged across for five hours on a tatty old *SeaSlug*!

Fun and games abounded on board. Airline cabin crew had never previously worked on a ferry; they were new to alcohol secretly flowing and to encountering randy deckhands. One girl, Tracy, was given the crew nick name Dick Tracy (after the comic strip police detective). She was seeing a good-looking guy, Kevin. One evening while Kevin was on the front desk organising boarding, she was in his passenger cabin. After a few drinks, she went to reception to ask when he'd be finished. He told her to go to the cabin and he'd join her shortly. She tottered back to his cabin, took all her clothes off, laid on her back on the bed and fell asleep. Unfortunately, she failed to close the door properly and it swung open. Goodness knows how many embarking passengers walked past the cabin before he arrived and closed the door! It was a hilarious month aboard, until finally *SeaCat* was almost ready to sail.

During time off we performed training and safety drills aboard the *SeaCat*. Then, finally, it was time to make a practice run outside Portsmouth harbour, to test all the equipment. A morning practice took place. One full crew acted as passengers, the other crew served breakfast. At first all went well. The ovens, boilers and such all worked. Splendid airline-style breakfasts were produced and served at their seats to the crew acting as passengers. However, clearing the harbour entrance, we encountered deep rollers and waves. The famously infallible 'wave-piercing craft' began to heave, roll and lurch violently. Trolleys began rolling around. Food slid onto the deck. Cups of tea and coffee sloshed everywhere. Non-seafaring crew began vomiting violently into bins. To my delight, both Teresa and Siobhan were as sick as dogs. I struggled to conceal my mirth and say, "I'm sure I saw this thing roll."

The SeaCat was a beautiful-looking craft inside and out. It had a vast passenger lounge/cabin, with large windows all round, a bar at the aft end, and even a tiny mother and baby nursing room, with a bed and sink. We offered a very professional service. Before sailing to France we would muster in a portacabin in the ferry port for a briefing on weather, special passenger needs and the like. It was my job to check the uniform, hats and make-up were perfect. (Drag was good training!) I also checked they carried spare tights or stockings, in case of ladders. Then we'd all march together, through security and onto the craft. One day, clearing security, I heard a familiar voice say, "Hello, girl." When I looked round I was amazed to see it was Horseface Thelma, ex-*Northern Star*, working as a security officer. (I did this myself in later years when I retired.)

Fine weather greeted the first day of service, August 21st. We served breakfast, drinks and duty-frees with trolleys. The following day the weather was frightful. On sailing we quickly served breakfast. However, clearing Portsmouth harbour, the craft began to roll and pitch violently. Food flew off the tables, coffee even leapt out of cups. The voyage rapidly descended into complete chaos. Most of the non-seafaring crew and passengers were violently sick. Some actually made it to the toilets. The lavatories had storm steps to prevent water leaking in and out; the steps did the same for runny sick. I christened the toilet area Lake Vomit. It became necessary for trolleys to be lashed down. Everyone was confined to seats. It was utterly terrifying. I myself manned the aft bar, as all the crew were sick or seated. Even the bar was hideously badly designed. No locks or bolts on the fridge doors or shutters. Fridges flew open. Bottles, luckily plastic, flew out. Metal shutters crashed up and down like a ghost train. One man actually made it to the bar, clutching his duty-frees in a bag. He asked for a beer, telling me, "I never gets sick." A little while later he turned a shade of green, vomiting copiously into his bag of duty-frees. Yuk!

On a calm day work was pleasant and fun. Crew played amusing tricks on each other. One day a cabin crew member handed me a note to broadcast, saying, "Will a Mr Richard Head please make himself known to the cabin services officer." Hearing gales of laughter, I realised they'd *got me*: Richard Head = Dickhead! The cabin crew served duty-free perfume, and one lad, Chalky, made me chuckle. A lady passenger had asked him did he have something nice she could put behind her ears to attract men. He said he felt like saying, "Have you tried your ankles!"

One morning I was making preparations in the pantry, when Craig (a tall, good-looking boy) walked in. He seemed to be in some discomfort, so I asked him what on earth was the matter? "Have a butchers at this," he said, unzipping his trousers, and flopped out a massive cock with a large blister on the end! "Good grief," I said. "Put it away before one of the girls see it." (*Or worse*, I thought. There was only a curtain covering the door to the passenger cabin.) He explained he'd been to what he called "Grab a granny night" at his local dance hall, and had far too much to drink. Next day in his dressing gown, boiling some potatoes for roasting, he fell asleep. He awoke to find the pot boiled dry. As he went to place the pot in the kitchen sink, his knob was hanging out and the bellend made contact with the red-hot pan. Ouch! He asked for advice. I told him not to touch it. Burns usually blister and heal in three to seven days. If the skin bursts, you cover it with a sterile dry dressing. If infected, you see your GP. In the meantime, you *only* use it for peeing. Poor boy. I couldn't help laughing about it.

Our work routine was a week of days, and a week off. Then a week on nights, and a week off. Nights were the worst, bouncing around all night in the dark. I hated them. Teresa and Siobhan were not pleasant to work for. They made no allowance for the smallest mistake. They even gave me, as supervisor, a list of crew they wanted to sack. Any excuse would do. Some of those people on the list, like Lulu and Chalky, were my mates. I though these two women were evil witches. The movie *Witches of Eastwick* was currently a big hit, so I gave them a nickname, The Witches of Gatwick. The crew loved it. Somehow Teresa and Siobhan heard about it, asking me to find out who'd given them that name. I chuckled to myself. If only they knew.

In the weeks leading up to Christmas, the company offered staff a free bottle of spirit, to be collected on a free return trip to Cherbourg. We could take friends and family. I took my trip with Dominic, plus a good mate, Tony, and his girlfriend Mandy. A passenger comfort rule had been introduced, which meant we usually would not sail in anything over a Force 6 gale. When I checked the weather forecast it was Force 7 to 8. I warned my party we probably wouldn't be sailing. To my surprise, we did. I told them what to expect. As we sailed, cabin crew hurriedly served breakfast. Then, as we cleared the breakwater, the craft began pitching and rolling alarmingly. Breakfasts slid onto the deck. Coffee shot out of the cups as the vessel made violent descents.

People were rushing to the toilets. Others made use of seasick bags. It was a terrifying crossing, full of creaking and groaning. An outer door was ripped off, sliding past the windows. We were so grateful to reach Cherbourg and spend a few hours ashore for lunch. We even pondered the idea of getting a regular car ferry home to the UK. However, by departure time the forecast was much improved. The return crossing to England was reasonably comfortable.

Ultimately, the service was unsuccessful on the Portsmouth to Cherbourg run. The management had no idea how rough the sea can be in the English Channel. Sea Containers/Hoverspeed Ferries decided to cancel it at the end of the year, repositioning it to Dover. The last trip, as usual, I checked the weather forecast before leaving home. It was stormy: Force 8 to 9. I thought, *Good, we probably won't sail.* To my surprise, the captain said, "We have people to collect in Cherbourg. We're sailing." It was still dark when we left Portsmouth. On departure the *SeaCat* began rolling and pitching terrifyingly. There was no service of food or drink. Nearly everyone was seasick. Some of the crew were concerned, asking are we're going to make it to France. I went to the bridge to relay their, and my, fears to the captain. I made it to the bridge with some difficulty, grasping hand rails. The Old Man was belted in his seat and handed me some night vision binoculars. I saw a terrifying wall of monster waves, screaming, "Oh, my God. We're all gonna die." He laughed, thankfully saying, "We're turning round. It's too dangerous."

When the Portsmouth service finished, *SeaCat* was repositioned to Dover, to begin services to Calais and Boulogne. It would be replacing fuel-thirsty, costly and aging hovercraft. Southampton crew sailed it round there, thankfully with good weather, to perform 'berthing trials'. We were accommodated in a Dover hotel. They planned to sail to both Calais and Boulogne for the trials, also to show the vessel off to the Dover Hoverspeed team. It would be a demonstration of how we worked and so on, as the Dover people would be taking over the service from the Southampton crew. On the day of the trial crossing to Calais, a splendid buffet lunch was laid on, with cases of champagne and wine. The works! A whole pig's head with an apple in its mouth adorned the buffet. Just before lunch, the Hoverspeed crew boarded. On this maiden crossing, champagne flowed. Chef carved the meat joints, and it was all hugely convivial. Unfortunately, the weather wasn't. As we cleared the harbour, once again the craft started to pitch and roll alarmingly. Most passengers fast became extremely ill. The trestle tables fell over. Food shot all over the deck and the chef passed out, rolling round the deck. Amusingly, the pig's head was rolling around the cabin too.

On arrival at Calais the Dover Hoverspeed crew had had enough of this and disembarked. They travelled home on the hovercraft, leaving many leftover bottles of champagne, which strangely found their way to our hotel that evening, where we enjoyed quite a party. After copious champagne, along with one of the girls I even encouraged and assisted one of the officers to drag up, much to everyone's amusement. The next day the trip was repeated, with trials to Boulogne. This time they organised things a little better. However, the weather was rough again. On arrival at Boulogne, Hoverspeed crew again had had enough. They disembarked to take the next hovercraft back to Dover. On the return journey my crew tidied up, most feeling slightly hungover. I felt so ill I laid down in the mother's nursing room. One of the girls woke me just before Dover, saying I looked like a Mutant Ninja Turtle. She had a point. My skin was green and my eyes were red with bloodshot. On arrival in Dover, we were returned to Southampton by coach.

Hooray! Farewell forever, Vomit Comet.

## 33

# End of an Era

While working aboard *SeaCat*, due to the lack of British ships, it was decided to close the Shipping Federations (Pools). UK seafarers, including myself, were all made redundant and we got small amounts of redundancy money. This was another extremely sad day indeed. The shipping Pools had existed since 1890. Now there would be no more visiting the Establishment in order to ship out. With cheap foreign labour replacing nearly all British seafarers, this point was the final demise of most UK seafaring ratings and, sadly, the death of the British Merchant Navy. Dominic had suffered from a hideously painful bad back for a long time, the result of many years of hard work and standing around on bridges for hours. He'd been made medically unfit for deep-sea service and already left. The change had given him time to pursue his dream of owning and running our own bus company.

In 1991 the Swedish Stena Line made a hostile takeover of Sealink. It purchased all Sealink vessels and, more importantly, *all the routes*! The new company was renamed the Sealink Stena Line. (The Sealink bit didn't last long.) Later in 1991 an announcement was made of their intention to start a Sealink

Stena service from Southampton to Cherbourg, using their fine vessel the *Stena Normandy*. Being right on my doorstep, naturally I applied. My mate Bernie/Mommie kept in touch. He'd left *QE2* because of the poorly paid contracts, and was living in Plymouth, unemployed. I told him about the job opportunities on the *Stena Normandy* and he told me another friend, the delightful Geoff, also ex-RFA, was looking for a job too. They both applied.

Around this time, Dom and I had moved into an elegant, spacious Edwardian four-bedroom house in Upper Shirley, Southampton. This time we weren't adopted by a cat. Eventually we adopted one ourselves: Trish, the oldest, ugliest cat in the cat rescue centre. We loved her. The day before the interviews, Mommie and Geoff stayed the night. After a jolly evening in Southampton, next day we attended interviews at Sealink Stena. They both accepted jobs as stewards and I accepted the position of supervisor/restaurant manager.

About this time, Pearl fell out with us big time. We'd called round to see him and he didn't answer the door. We must have mentioned it to a mutual friend. They told Pearl and he got the right hump. We arrived home to find the keys to our house inside our front door with a rude, crumpled, scrawled note, saying, "Stick your keys up your arse and find some other c—t to look after your gaff." Dominic and I found this highly amusing, thinking she'd probably calm down eventually. Then we received a long, astonishing letter explaining why he hadn't opened the door. He said he'd called round to explain next day, but we were out. In the pub, dear? The letter also said he was suffering from severe depression and having a nervous breakdown. It went on to say that we "couldn't cope with someone who was genuinely ill." I'd been upsetting him for years and he'd been biting his tongue. Perhaps we'd better return the keys. This we did, and I wrote a letter explaining matters. Later we received a Christmas card from him saying,

"Friendship is like a set of good tyres. Eventually they wear thin and all you have left is a lot of air!"

I tried to make it up with Pearl over the years. The last time I tried, he never replied. He changed his telephone number. Our split was extremely sad, as we were both genuinely fond of him. He was a dear old friend we and would miss him dearly. But *c'est la vie*! It was an end of another happy era, as I'd known Pearl for so many years. He could be extremely kind, and funny. We'd had so much fun together.

In early June 1991, crew travelled by coach from Southampton to Harwich to join *Stena Normandy*. After cleaning, preparing cabins and such, we sailed to Southampton to launch a service to Cherbourg. She was a large ferry, 25,772 gt, built 1983, with an abundance of passenger cabins for overnight crossings. The restaurant was along one side of the ship, with wonderful sea views, and a large self-service restaurant aft. She was an excellent sea ship too; she hardly moved in rough seas. As usual, it was hard work and long hours. A no-alcohol policy was strictly enforced, which made life difficult. I found a wee dram before bed always helped me sleep. Without it, I lay tossing and turning all night, feeling wretched, to face an early start, plus a long day's work. The money was excellent, so I stuck it out. It wasn't my happiest time at sea, despite many mates being on board, including Trish from *Oriana*, Mommie, and Geoff, plus friends from Sealink, the West Coast and *SeaCat*.

The routine was one week in the restaurant, a week off, one week in self-service, and a week off. I loved the dining room, but not the self-service. It was extremely hectic. One day a commotion occurred at a cashier's station. As I approached, a man was shouting loudly at the cashier, Lucille. I asked what seemed to be the problem. He shouted, "This stupid woman will not accept anything less than a franc coin." I confirmed. "This is according to our instructions, sir." He told me he'd used them upstairs in the bar. I told him I doubted it. At that he became worse, shouting at me. I asked did he need to be so rude and aggressive. At this point he became truly nasty, shouting, "What's your name?" I pointed at my name badge, saying, "My name is Michael Rudder and why don't you piss off." Shocked, he said, "What?" I said, "You heard me. PISS OFF!" He stormed off. By this time Lucille was in floods of tears. I shut her till down and took her to the hotel manager to explain what happened. "Oh dear," he said. "I hope you told him to piss off in a nice way." I told him if Lucille hadn't been present, I'd have told him to f—k off. "How unfortunate," he said. "He might be a shareholder." I said, "It don't care who he is. I will not allow him, or anyone else, to be aggressive and rude to myself or any of my staff or co-workers." We left his office and didn't hear another thing about it.

By December, with the absolutely appalling office groups making Christmas party trips, I'd had a gut full. We had large tables of guests who, by the time the main course was served, were so drunk they were unable to remember what they'd ordered. They treated staff, including me, like shit. They were so rude that there was no point even trying to reason with them. I tendered my resignation. Bosses on the ship tried to talk me out of it, saying I was catering officer material. However, I signed off 22nd December 1991.

Seafarers rarely manage to spend Christmas in the UK. So it was a delight to enjoy one at home with my Dominic. In March 1992 I received a call from Sealink Stena: would I call in the office, with regard to a catering officer's position? They were chartering a freight ship for a new service on the Southampton to Cherbourg run. I was offered the job as purser/catering officer aboard the *Stena Traveller*. She was an 18,000-gt ferry, carrying a mixture of 245 passengers, mainly truck drivers. My mate Trish was one of my stewards aboard and I enjoyed my new job. One small drawback: the ship lacked stabilisers. In rough weather she rolled extremely violently. At night I was frequently tossed out of bed. (It was so bad, eventually she had to be fitted with stabilisers.)

Sadly the service was not a success. In September 1992 it was terminated, along with my job. Closing the ship down was sad. However, carrying out a stock count and valuation opened my eyes to exactly how much profit ferry companies made from duty-free sales. The basic wholesale duty-free cost of a litre bottle of spirits was around £2 to £3. They were selling aboard for £10 to £12. In 1984 the Channel Tunnel had opened, taking passengers and profits from ferry operators. In 1999 the European Union decided to end duty-free sales between member European Union countries. This, I believe, also contributed to the death of the hovercraft services between Dover and France, which were not fuel-efficient, and depended on duty-free profits. Hovercraft services finished in October 2000.

Following the *Stena Traveller* I looked around for further seafaring work with agencies and was offered an interview as personnel officer (human resources) with a dredging company. I managed crewing arrangements. The company said they wanted a sort of 'mother hen' figure. (I thought, *I've heard it all now!*) During the interview they explained my responsibilities, pay, hours and such. It all sounded excellent. They seemed very keen, asking me to think about it and give them a call. I discussed the matter with Dominic. He'd achieved his Certificate of Professional Competency, in Passenger Transport Operations, with big plans to start our bus company. I gave him an ultimatum: either we get cracking and start the bus service (which terrified me) or I become a 'mother hen'. He wanted to start his big plan, and that's exactly what we did. I called the dredging company with my decision. They sounded rather sad. I was too. The thought of looking after a crowd of seafarers was appealing, but it was not to be. Thus my sea career effectively ended. It'd been a wonderful ride. I wouldn't have missed it for the world. An amazing time, now sadly consigned to history.

# 34

# Moving on

We quickly forged ahead establishing the bus business. We'd used an excellent local accountant, Peter Carney. He registered the business as a partnership and the company name invented by Dominic: Air Lynx. To my surprise, Dominic told me operating 12-plus seat vehicles we could claim back all VAT. Strangely, local customs and VAT officers knew nothing of this, until they checked it out. It was a great help with our fledgling company. We claimed VAT back on everything – vehicles, fuel and spare parts. I urged and helped Dominic to get all we needed to run the business, renting an office, paperwork, advertising and so on. But he was absolutely marvellous at the finer points. He insisted we adopt a corporate image, smart comfortable vehicles, clean-shaven drivers in smart uniforms, vehicles spotlessly clean inside and out at all times. He even called the first minibus 'number 11' to make it appear we had more vehicles; it worked! I was good at paperwork, which I sorted out, whereas Dominic was not. He struggled with spelling and so on, sometimes appearing slightly dyslexic. This is why he is so clever. It's a fact that many successful businessmen (Richard Branson, Apple's Steve Jobs) and artists (John Lennon, Steven Spielberg and Orlando Bloom) are dyslexic. They see the 'bigger picture' in their endeavours; it really pays off.

We'd many dramas running the bus company, with plenty of fun and games… It was a time of massive change. Mobile phones had recently been invented. We embraced them in our business: they would change the world forever. Computers too became available to individuals and businesses. Now they were in manageable sizes. We embraced them too. Dominic even had a computer program written especially for us. It took bookings, printed invoices and even churned out drivers' orders. Prior to this, I wrote them all *by hand*! I also did all the wages and VAT myself by hand. This changed too when we computerised.

Once the internet was discovered, Dominic insisted we utilise it with our own website. The internet was to change the way the world worked forever, especially with regard to mobile phones, advertising, banking, and in fact all aspects of daily life. At that time we were paying a fortune to advertise in the now-defunct Yellow Pages trade directory, a thick paper volume. Now nearly all businesses have websites.

When my dear mum passed away in 2001, Dad called, understandably saying how totally heartbroken and lonely he felt. They'd been married for over sixty years. We invited him to stay with us. It really cheered him up. He disapproved of our barbecue in the garden, maintaining that in his day people ate indoors and s—t down the garden. "Now they s—t indoors and eat in the garden!" He'd mellowed a lot and eventually we became close, even going together on his first and only hilarious cruise to Amsterdam on the P&O *Aurora*. We even booked a chauffeur-driven Rolls Royce to take us to the docks. In Amsterdam, despite being in his eighties, he was highly amused that cannabis was legal. We took him to see the 'business girls' down the canal. He told me, "Some of the girls in the windows looked gorgeous, boy." I laughingly told him, "They're just window dressing, Dad. You may end up with some old boot!" We also took him for his first visit to a sex shop, where he gleefully bought a wind-up dancing willy to horrify the old boys in his pensioners' club. He really enjoyed himself and let his hair down.

Our relationship had changed for the better. I think he felt proud we'd both been seaman, and were also founding and operating our own excellent, successful business. Sadly, he would only ever accept we were 'business partners', despite sister Josie telling him otherwise. If he'd asked me outright, I'd have gladly told him the truth. The subject remained taboo and was never discussed. He often said to me that he thought Dominic was a good, kind man. (He was correct there.)

A great bonus of our sea careers was meeting so many wonderful people and friends, through whom we met many other interesting people, including a few celebrities. Our friend Brian/Vera lived in Hove, Brighton. With his larger-than-life, hilarious personality he became friends with many famous people. In the 1970s he was friendly with legendary Dorothy Squires. She'd been an international singing sensation in the fifties and sixties. She met and married Roger Moore in 1953, pushing his career while hers faltered. She could be very pugnacious and temperamental. When they parted, she had many problems trying to revive her career. No one would hire her. She hired the Palladium herself in 1970, making a spectacular comeback. Vera booked her to appear in Brighton, inviting us to the show, which was watched by a largely gay audience. (Dot looked like a drag queen anyway!) Her version of 'My Way' was amazing. And while singing 'Say It with Flowers', queens in the audience presented her with many bouquets. It was an extremely theatrical and memorable evening.

Vera was friendly with casts of various hit TV shows, including *The Bill* and *EastEnders*. We met quite a few of them at his parties in Hove. Every year he organised an outrageous *adult* Pantomime in Brighton after Christmas, starring wonderful talent like Phil Starr, Lee Tracey and Miss Jason. We'd organise bus trips from Southampton to the panto most years, with champagne served en route. It was a brilliant, hilarious night. Many celebs mentioned came to see the show too. Vera also became good friends with *EastEnders* stars Hilda Braid/Nana Moon and June Brown/Dot Cotton. Hilda visited us with Brian, and we dined with her occasionally. When civil partnerships were introduced in December 2005, she attended our ceremony, held the first magical day. When the registrar asked if anyone knew of any reason why we shouldn't be wed, Hilda said, "I think the flowers are lovely." Everyone tittered and the registrar confirmed that wasn't a valid reason. After the ceremony we hosted an open bar for everyone's drinks in the historic pub next door, the Duke of Wellington. It was run by my friend Ray Rose, ex-Special Boat Service. After drinks we hosted a meal. We paid a well-known local chef, Ennio, to lay on a hot buffet, with drinks/wine in a private room above the pub. It was a wonderful day, and one we will never forget. On the way home we stopped in our local pub, the Park Inn in Shirley. Everyone clapped and cheered. So delightful. The UK had come a long way, though it still has a way to go!

Vera brought June Brown to our home many times. She was one of the few people we actually allowed to smoke inside our home. She was extremely thoughtful, actually opening a window to let the smoke out. We sailed with her on a most enjoyable and hilarious mini cruise aboard the new 1995 P&O liner *Oriana*. Bobby Davro was aboard, and visited the cabin for drinks; he was an extremely delightful and amusing man. June also attended my sixtieth birthday party in the Novotel in August 2011, much to all my family and friends' delight. We laid on a free bar, a disco, a buffet, and hired Lee Tracy to entertain with his hilarious, saucy comedy drag act. It was a wonderful evening. June was an amusing, gracious lady and fine actor. It was a delight to know her.

Through Vera, we also became good friends with the late, great, unforgettable, Phil Starr, a delightful kind man and clever, brilliant, hilarious comedy drag artiste. A friend of ours and many others, Franco, ex-*Andes*, owned and ran Margarita's, a popular Italian restaurant in Southampton. One day he telephoned us to say he planned an 'evening of erotica' in the restaurant, with a male stripper and a drag comedian. He only knew how to find strippers. Could we help with the comedy drag? I recommended Phil Starr through Vera and it was all arranged. One Sunday Vera and Phil drove to us from Brighton, then to Margarita's for a late lunch, where Phil would later perform cabaret. A wedding was in full swing when we arrived. It was absolute chaos, with no sign of Franco. Phil asked the manager where he would be performing, to be told on a gantry high up in the roof of the restaurant! Phil's face-to-face comedy act needed to be in front of his live audience. He bluntly told the manager, "I'm a drag comedian, not a f—ing trapeze artist, dear. We're off!" With that, he departed with us in tow. We ended up in Oxford Street for a drink and a meal in Kutis restaurant. Poor Franco was furious and didn't speak to me for a long time. Eventually we made up and were friends until his later untimely death and extravagant funeral.

When we began communicating again, Franco called us one day to tell us he'd opened a new restaurant/nightclub, Ninety Degrees, in Bedford Place. The area was a popular night-time Southampton destination. He wished to invite us for Sunday lunch, with mutual friends Frank and Maria Parkinson. They too were seafarers. Maria was so Italian everyone referred to her as Maria Spaghetti. Franco collected us in his posh Jaguar car, drove into the car park beneath his beautiful apartment in

Ocean Village. We took the elevator up for champagne before he drove us to the Ninety Degrees to enjoy an unforgettable lunch.

In 2008, dear Franco was diagnosed with cancer. Dominic and I both prayed hard for him. However, despite this and putting up a good fight, cancer got the better of him. He passed away January 5th, 2009, aged just seventy-one. Maria Spaghetti was one of the people caring for Franco during his illness. She called us next day to ask if we wanted to say farewell to him. He was laid out in his apartment. On arrival, sure enough Franco was laid out in the Italian Catholic tradition in a beautiful open coffin. He'd been embalmed, dressed in one of his finest suits, and looked truly marvellous. There were magnificent flowers, with appropriate soft music playing. It was emotional and moving. His death was headline news in the local newspaper. He was so well known, and much loved, giving tirelessly to charity, especially children's charities.

Franco planned his own funeral, with no expense spared, making sure he went out with a bang! He was given a full Roman Catholic Requiem Mass in St Edmunds Catholic Church in The Avenue, Southampton. A team of white stallions, with fabulous pink plumes of feathers on their heads, took his glass carriage there. En route he passed his restaurant on Town Quay, then his previous original extremely famous restaurant next to the Mayflower Theatre. All the big acts playing there – including Shirley Bassey and Danny la Rue – dined at Francos. With his Italian charm, knew them all!

The church was packed, with standing room only. Many of Franco's seafaring friends attended the funeral. In Italian tradition, there was an open coffin to allow friends and family to say farewell to this wonderful man. One thing did amuse me: two of his and our old friends were mourners. Both were extremely ill and looked at death's door. One had advanced AIDS, the other was dying from excessive smoking. I had to chuckle when Dominic remarked quietly to me, "Franco looks better than both of them!" Following the ceremony, all family and friends were invited to Margarita's on Town Quay to celebrate Francos life with food and drink. Again, no expense was spared and we all enjoyed a wonderful afternoon eating, drinking, and reminiscing with much love about the incredible life of dear friend Franco.

In 2007, we sold our bus and coach business, becoming *rock dodgers*, working for Southampton's Red Funnel Ferries/'Red Jets'. Another new experience, with great workmates, many amusing moments and a few dramas.

Upon retirement, we worked in Southampton docks, as pier staff and in security when cruise ships are alongside. We met more wonderful friends working there, in particular one lady, Jo (Josephine) Mahoney. She was one of the most kind, interesting, educated, dignified, amusing and delightful women I have ever had the privilege of knowing. Even after she left working we continued to meet her and her husband, RN Commander John Mahoney (Retired), for luncheons. The most delightful, amusing company. I was terribly distressed when Jo sadly passed away in May 2023. Her family kindly asked me to say a few words at the funeral. It was impossible. I was a blubbering mess. I adored Jo and I still miss her so much.

We both have our wonderful families, at home and overseas, plus many wonderful friends. Some we've met ashore, plus we have many seafaring friends like Jackie, Tannoy, Carol, Maria, Kiwi Liz, Mommie/Bernie, Michael & Martin, Barry, Billy, Lesley and many others too numerous to mention.

Dominic and I are now more or less retired, devoted and happy. When you're truly in love it's an amazing feeling to have a best friend who is also the love of your life. We've had a wonderful life so far. God has been good to us. We are both sure it was His Will that we met that fateful 1974 October day in Lisbon. The song 'Nature Boy' has an incredible backstory: it was written by a homeless man living under the actual Hollywood sign in Hollywood. He decided Nat King Cole was the only one to sing it, tracked him down and offered it to him; the rest is history. It was a huge hit. The song is quite enchanting, and I'd encourage you to listen carefully to the lyrics. I think of my beloved Dominic when I hear those lines, and thank God for all our blessings.

We are also incredibly grateful for our wonderful sea careers. I've no idea where else I could ever have felt happy and content in a work environment. I might never have met Dominic, if I hadn't gone to sea. It was a fluke I ended up in the Merchant Navy, the furthest thing from my mind when I left school in landlocked Guildford. The fact that we were on two different ships, which just happened to be docked the same day in Lisbon, was a chance in a million. That we crossed paths, a miracle. We are also both so truly grateful to have worked at sea during this period. It was a time when there was a marvellous gay-friendly culture aboard ships. It gave people the freedom to live as they wanted. They could be themselves and not have to hide their feelings. A wonderful period of seafaring history, which sadly will never be repeated.

Dominic and I hope you've enjoyed reading this short segment of history.

*Michael Rudder and Dominic, Southampton*
*2024*

# Acknowledgements

I wish to acknowledge people who helped me on the journey creating this book. I thank Dr Jo Stanley from the bottom of my heart, for all Her professional help, advice, time and patience. I am forever grateful to her. Professor Paul Baker, who helped me in the early stage of the book. Our friend Su Rand, who early on edited. I thank our dear Families, friends and seafaring friends for their love and support. Plus Riza Pacalioglu and Mike Wheatley of sarumbear.com creators of websites and online branding.

Finally, the love of my life Dominic, without whom this story may never have taken place, have no meaning or happy ending. He helped me along the way, correcting mistakes and parts I forgot. This story would never have taken place without this dear, kind man in my life, I thank him from the bottom of my heart.

Michael